Heaven
THE
MYSTERY
OF
ANGELS

D0057328

Heaven

THE MYSTERY OF ANGELS

GRANT R. JEFFREY

Whitaker House

HEAVEN: THE MYSTERY OF ANGELS

Grant Jeffrey
Frontier Research Publications
P.O. Box 129, Station "U"
Toronto, Ontario M8Z 5M4
CANADA

ISBN: 0-88368-536-1
Printed in the United States of America
Copyright © 1996 by Grant R. Jeffrey

Whitaker House
30 Hunt Valley Circle
New Kensington, PA 15068

2 3 4 5 6 7 8 9 10 11 / 06 05 04 03 02 01 00 99

TABLE OF CONTENTS

HEAVEN
The Mystery of Angels

Revised and Enlarged

ACKNOWLEDGMENT

I would like to dedicate this book to my loving wife, Kaye, who has so faithfully completed the manuscript revisions and proofs. She is a continual encouragement, partner and inspiration in our ministry.

Grant R. Jeffrey
Toronto, Ontario
July, 1996

The Search for Heaven

Is Heaven real? Will I live forever? Do I have an eternal destiny? Does my life have meaning? Can I be certain of going to Heaven when I die? Will I have a body in Eternity? Do angels really exist? Will life in Heaven be interesting? Thoughtful people in every age and culture have asked these questions about our eternal destiny. The Bible's answer to these questions is a resounding YES!

Fortunately, God has not left us in darkness regarding our spiritual future. God has revealed truths about His nature, His purpose, and our ultimate destiny—Heaven or Hell. God accomplished this through His marvelous revelation of truth—the Bible.

Christ's promise to His followers is that we shall join Him in Heaven and partake in an everlasting life of joy, love, fellowship and purposeful activity. In New Jerusalem we shall never again experience sin, fear, pain or death. A future finer than all our dreams awaits us the in the "city which has foundations, whose builder and maker is God." The Bible tells us that Heaven is the final goal of the Christian life where we shall live for eternity.

When I finished the writing of my book, *Armageddon – Appointment With Destiny* I began to consider other topics for a future book. One area which has always fascinated me is the subject of Heaven. However, I was sure that bookstores and libraries would be full of excellent books on Heaven. I was surprised to find that very few books are available which research the tremendous number of biblical promises about our eternal life. There is a strange vacuum in recent Christian literature about Heaven. The best books written on eternity were penned by men like Dwight L. Moody, R. A. Torrey and E. M. Bounds in the last generation. When I began to talk to people about the subject I discovered that few Christians could remember hearing a teaching sermon on Heaven. The more I discussed this with pastors and laymen, the more convinced I became there was a great need for an accessible book which would present the Bible's promises about Heaven to our generation.

I was surprised to discover that almost every pastor I met during the last few years has admitted that they received very little instruction about the reality of Heaven during their several years of seminary training. It is little wonder that few of our pulpits declare the Bible's glorious teachings about Heaven and the resurrection body when our pastors were not trained in this vital area of biblical instruction. Many Christian laymen have told me that they cannot remember a single teaching sermon on the reality of Heaven during a decade or more of attending church. As a result of this virtual famine of teaching about the glory of Heaven, we today live in the most materialistic and "Laodicean" church that has existed in the last two thousand years. Many new believers have accepted Christ because they were promised an "abundant lifestyle" where they would be free from sickness, guilt and poverty. However, numerous Christians have little understanding about their future in eternity due to the almost total absence of teaching in our modern churches about the nature of Heaven and Hell.

This is startling when you consider the fact that Christians over the last two Millennium have longed for the reality of Heaven. This heartfelt longing for the heavenly city found its expression in glowing descriptions of Heaven revealed in wonderful hymns, sermons and countless books in the past. In previous centuries, at a time when living conditions and persecution made life difficult for most Christians, the biblical promises of Heaven's glory at the end of a faithful life was the best news that anyone could offer. However, modern Christians in North America and Europe share a culture where most people are living lives of great comfort and wealth compared to the wretched living standards of most people throughout the Third World. Our present standards of shelter, food, sanitation and health care are vastly improved over the standards that existed worldwide in past centuries. When you consider this transformation and improvement in lifestyles, it is easy to understand why the subject of Heaven has been pushed aside to make way for conferences on abundant living, marriage counseling and other assorted interests of those sitting in comfortable pews.

A Hypothetical Test on Your Desire For Heaven

To illustrate this lack of awareness of the reality of Heaven's glories, I have often during the last few years challenged congregations to participate in an experiment. I ask my audience to imagine for a moment that there is a button on the back of the pew in front of their seat. Then I suggest that they imagine that, if they pushed that button, they and their loved ones would be instantaneously transferred to Heaven to live forever. Then I ask the question, "Would you press the button?" The response of the congregation is fascinating. Usually about one-half of the church audience smile in anticipation of what awaits them in Heaven if their button actually translated them to the presence of Jesus Christ. However, at least half of the audience reveal a perplexed expression on their faces that showing that they have little interest in pushing that hypothetical button. Ask yourself this question: Would I want to go to Heaven today with all my loved ones? If the answer is NO; why not?

Your Mental Image of Heaven

I have asked congregation members in private conversations their real reasons why they would either "push the button" or not. Their responses were quite revealing. Your personal mental image of Heaven will determine to a great degree your attitude and longing for the eternal city. Those Christians who would press this hypothetical button are usually mature believers who are strong in their faith due to many hours spent studying the promises of God. As a result of personal Bible study, reading a book, or attending a church where the pastor taught these great truths, the Christians who would choose to press the button have obtained a strong conviction of the reality of God's promise. They are not suicidal; nor do they lack plans for their future. They simply believe that Heaven is as real as this Earth and they are prepared to joyfully go home whenever Jesus Christ calls them. On the other hand, those Christians who would not choose to push the button almost invariably had received little teaching about the reality of Paradise. When I asked these believers to describe the mental image that went through their mind when they thought about Heaven their answers were very revealing about why they wanted to avoid this as long as possible. They didn't want to avoid Heaven forever; they just had no desire to go there now because of their mental image of it. They would prefer to wait until they were ninety-seven years old with one foot in the grave before they pushed that button and went to the heavenly city.

What was the mental image of Heaven held by those who didn't want to go there now? Many of them told me that they thought they would spend eternity sitting on a cloud playing a harp in an endless eternal church service that would never, ever, ever end. In other words, if they were honest, they thought of Heaven as being an incredibly boring place with nothing worth doing, nowhere to go and an eternity of passivity with no activity. Naturally their vision of the New Jerusalem was about as exciting as watching the grass grow on your back lawn. It is no wonder that such Christians have little interest or motivation regarding God's promises about our eternal home. Does their description resemble your own present view of Heaven? If it does, then you are in for a delightful journey of discovery as we examine the true reality of what the Bible teaches us about the glories of Heaven.

Doesn't Everyone Want To Go To Heaven?

Someone once wrote that "everyone wants to go to Heaven, but no one wants to die." However, there are numerous people who have such a profound hatred of God and of holiness that they would actually prefer to go to Hell than to endure the goodness of Heaven. Richard Baxter wrote a profound study of the reality of Heaven called *The Saints Everlasting Rest* in 1657. In discussing this topic of men's desires regarding Heaven, Baxter wrote the following statement. "There is a great deal of difference between the desires of heaven in a sanctified man and an unsanctified. The believer prizeth it above earth, and had rather be with God than here. But to the ungodly, there is nothing seemeth more desirable than this world; and therefore he only chooseth heaven before hell, but not before earth; and therefore shall not have it upon such a choice." While Baxter's language is quaint his insight into the motives that affect our eternal choices is quite sound.

Throughout the balance of this book we will explore the biblical truth about God's promises regarding our eternal destiny. We will discover that Heaven will truly be the greatest adventure we have ever experienced. Far from the boring vision that most of us have held about a passive Heaven we will explore the wonders of the heavenly city, the New Jerusalem, and the exciting adventures we will enjoy as we travel through a universe so vast that we can barely conceive of all that Jesus Christ has created. You will learn of the incredible destiny that awaits us when we receive our glorious resurrection bodies in fulfillment of what the Apostle Paul calls "the manifestation of the sons of God" (Romans 8:19). In addition to enjoying the awesome intellectual and physical abilities of our powerful resurrection bodies that can travel from Heaven to Earth at the speed of thought, we will enjoy the most wonderful friendships with both biblical saints and the hundreds of millions of departed believers from past centuries. Imagine what it will be like to use 100 percent of the incredibly powerful brain God gave you instead of the limited 3 percent to 10 percent that most of us utilize today. We will be able to study and learn throughout eternity. The Bible assures us that we will rule over the nations on Earth forever. Revelation 5:10

tells us that the Lord has "made us kings and priests to our God; and we shall reign on the earth."

Although the heavenly city, the New Jerusalem, will be our permanent home we will still be able to travel to the Earth enjoying the wonders of beauty and variety that Christ created on this planet. We will participate in the most glorious worship of our Savior Jesus Christ in the presence of hundreds of millions of angels. John wrote about his glorious vision of Heaven, "Then I looked, and I heard the voice of many angels around the throne, the living creatures, and the elders; and the number of them was ten thousand times ten thousand, and thousands of thousands, saying with a loud voice: 'Worthy is the Lamb who was slain to receive power and riches and wisdom, and strength and honor and glory and blessing!' " (Revelation 5:11,12).

The Apostle Paul tells us, "But as it is written: 'Eye has not seen, nor ear heard, nor have entered into the heart of man the things which God has prepared for those who love Him' " (1 Corinthians 2:9). While this verse correctly describes the inability of man to perceive the truth about Heaven using his intellect or imagination, Paul then told us that God will reveal these sublime truths about our eternal destiny through His Holy Spirit inspiring men such as the Apostle John in the Book of Revelation. "But God has revealed them to us through His Spirit. For the Spirit searches all things, yes, the deep things of God" (1 Corinthians 2:10). Thirty years after Paul wrote these words the Apostle John was inspired by God to write his incredible visions about the wonders of Heaven and the New Jerusalem.

For thousands of years since our first parents left the paradise of the Garden of Eden man has struggled and lost the battle against death, our relentless enemy. No matter how promising, beautiful or brilliant a human life might be, from the moment a child is born they begin to die. Our hopes and dreams, even life itself, are overshadowed by the certain knowledge that all that we create or love will someday crumble into dust. This dilemma that governs human existence was created by the fall from perfect obedience by our first parents, Adam and Eve. But this was not how God created mankind nor how He wanted us to live our lives. The incredible sacrifice on the Cross by Jesus Christ has purchased both our individual salvation as well as the redemption of the planet Earth when He will return to establish His righteous kingdom from the Throne of David in Jerusalem. In the Book of Revelation John described his vision of the life that awaits all believers in Christ on the other side of death. John was filled with wonder by his vision of the glorious heavenly city, the New Jerusalem, descending from Heaven to the new Earth after this planet is restored from the curse of sin and death. "And I heard a loud voice from heaven saying, 'Behold, the tabernacle of God is with men, and He will dwell with them, and they shall be His people, and God Himself will be with them and be their God. And God will wipe away every tear from their eyes; there shall be no more death, nor sorrow, nor crying; and there shall be no more pain, for the former things have passed away.' Then He who sat on the throne said, 'Behold, I make all things new.' And He said to me, 'Write, for these words are true and faithful' " (Revelation 21:3-5). The promise of the Holy Scriptures is not just that we will enjoy the wonders of Heaven throughout eternity but that Jesus Christ will also redeem the Earth from the curse of sin and death forever.

My years of Bible research convinced me that Heaven will prove to be the greatest adventure in human history. Unlike the traditional boring view of Heaven where saints "floated on clouds and played harps for thousands of years," my research in prophecy convinced me that God promised that our life in Heaven will be the most exciting, and challenging life we could ever hope for. I would like to share the results of my own study and journey of discovery with those who have found Jesus Christ in their spiritual journey and with those who are still seeking Him.

Man is a spiritual being who must seek meaning in his life. While some philosophers have suggested that man is merely an accident in a meaningless universe, the awesome complexity and design of creation denies the possibility that life has happened accidentally. All cultures in human history have believed in God and an afterlife in eternity. There is an interesting story told about the parents of a small child who had lost their faith in God. They had become resolute atheists. When the child was old enough they felt that it was time to share with him that they no longer believed in God. After listening quietly for thirty minutes to their explanations for their atheism he solemnly replied: "Does God know that you no longer believe in Him?" It is fascinating to observe that the Bible does not even try to prove the fact of God's reality. It simply asserts what all men know in their hearts, even if their heads temporarily deny the fact. God's comment in Psalm 14:1 dismisses atheism as foolishness: "The fool has said in his heart; there is no God."

Beginning with the Book of Genesis through sixty-six volumes ending with the Book of Revelation the Bible progressively unfolds the revelation of God's purpose for man and describes our ultimate destiny. The collection of books we call the Holy Bible were written down in three languages, by more than forty men—including shepherds, tax collectors, farmers, fishermen, and kings—over sixteen hundred years, spanning the nomadic culture of Abraham to the sophistication of the Roman world in which the Apostle Paul lived. Yet, despite this incredible diversity of experience, times and culture, the Bible contains a consistent revelation regarding God's unfolding purpose in His dealings with mankind. It is the only valid source that brings light to our spiritual darkness and answers our questions regarding the future of our soul.

The Bible is God's wonderful gift to man because as the Apostle Paul states: "the Holy Scriptures are able to make you wise for salvation through faith which is in Christ Jesus. All Scripture is given by inspiration of God, and is profitable for doctrine, for reproof, for correction, for instruction in righteousness, that the man of God may be complete, thoroughly equipped for every good work" (2 Timothy 3:15,16).

The evidence presented by creation, the archeological and historical verification of the Scriptures, the precision of fulfilled prophecy, the revelation of the life of Jesus Christ and the quiet transformation of men's spiritual lives together are proof that the Bible is the inspired Word of God. In our search for the answers to the questions in our minds about eternity we can turn to the revelation inspired by God, the only one who really knows the answers.

In a vain attempt to avoid facing the God of the Bible, the world continues to turn to channelers, psychic mediums, contradictory visions, and selected positive "near death experiences" for comfort regarding our life after death. Several Eastern religions have imagined a nirvana of tranquil meditation, a descent into a pool of forgetfulness. Isn't it far better to examine what the Creator of the universe has to say about our ultimate future in the only reliable source of information on the subject? In the end we can only fully understand the Bible's revelations about Heaven through faith. The Book of Hebrews (11:1) tells us, "Now faith is the substance of things hoped for, the evidence of things not seen." We cannot know Heaven except for what God chooses to reveal about Himself and His eternal plan. The fact that God created the Universe and has shown Himself through the Bible is the premise upon which this book rests.

In my earlier book, *Armageddon – Appointment With Destiny*, I analyzed a great number of biblical prophecies which have been fulfilled precisely to the letter in history and in the life of Jesus Christ. When you logically examine these fulfilled prophecies, I believe you will realize that the odds against their coming true by accident are simply astronomical.

These fulfilled prophecies prove that a sovereign God is in control of human history and has chosen to reveal His purpose through His Word—the Bible. No other religious literature utilizes specific prophecy as part of their writings. The simple reason is that man, unaided by God, cannot prophesy the precise result of tomorrow's football game, let alone the exact destiny and events of nations thousands of years before they come into existence.

In Isaiah 46:9-11, God declares: "I am God, and there is no other; I am God, and there is none like Me, declaring the end from the beginning, and from ancient times things that are not yet done, saying, 'My counsel shall stand, and I will do all My pleasure,'. . . Indeed I have spoken it; I will also bring it to pass. I have purposed it; I will also do it."

In another verse God hurls forth the challenge to all false religions and false prophets: " 'Bring forth your strong reasons', says the King of Jacob. 'Let them bring forth and show us what will happen; let them show the former things, what they were, that we may consider them, and know the latter end of them; or declare to us things to come. Show the things that are to come hereafter, that we may know that you are gods; yes, do good or do evil, that we may be dismayed and see it together. Indeed you are nothing, and your work is nothing; he who chooses you is an abomination' " (Isaiah 41:22-24).

No man or spirit, not even Satan, can precisely predict future events. No other religious writing outside the Bible dares to make thousands of detailed predictions centuries before their fulfillment. Only God, through His written, "God-breathed" Word, dares to do that. The phenomenon of hundreds of fulfilled prophecies conclusively proves that God has revealed Himself through the Holy Scriptures.

Principles of Biblical Interpretation

In this study I will follow the literal method of interpretation, the method that gives to each word the same basic meaning it has or had in customary speech, thought or writing. The meaning of words in the Bible must be interpreted in relation to their historical and grammatical context. Bernard Ramm, in his Protestant Biblical Interpretation, states that "(a) the literal meaning of sentences is the normal approach in all languages; (b) all-secondary meanings of documents, parables, types, allegories, and symbols, depend for their existence on the previous literal meaning of the terms; (c) the greater part of the Bible makes adequate sense when interpreted literally; (d) the literal approach does not blindly rule out figures of speech, symbols, allegories, or types; but if the nature of the sentence so demands, it readily yields to the second sense; (e) this method is the only sane and safe check on the imaginations of man; (f) this method is the only one consonant with the nature of inspiration. The absolute inspiration of the Bible teaches that the Holy Spirit guided men into truth and away from error. In this process God used language, and the units of language are words and thought. The thought is the thread that strings the words together. Therefore, our very exegesis must commence with a study of words and grammar, the two fundamentals of all-meaningful speech."

With our understanding of the literal way in which Christ fulfilled the prophecies about His first coming, we can be confident that each biblical prophecy yet to be fulfilled will also come to pass literally. Therefore, when we discuss Heaven, the New Jerusalem and the Second Coming of Christ, we are not discussing imaginary myths and symbols. We are exploring biblical truths about the future reality of the greatest adventure in human history. My goal is to act as a commentary and guide in our joint exploration of the Word of God. I trust this volume will introduce to you a small portion of the inexhaustible mine of truth which God has revealed to man about our next appointment with destiny.

In the continually shifting marketplace of ideas, religious concepts and speculations about our spiritual destiny, there is one book which stands apart from all other volumes ever written. That book is the Bible. It dares to do what no other religious book could do. The Bible claims not just to contain the Word of God but to be the Word of God. The religious fashions of men today often espouse a man-pleasing philosophy which claims that no one religion or faith has an exclusive right to claim to be "the truth." The desire of many religious people is to join in a great ecumenical world church in which each participant sheds his distinctive doctrine in the interests of religious harmony for the whole community of faiths. This process produces exactly what the participants desire: a lowest common denominator of accepted generalities.

It is not surprising that in such an atmosphere there has been a shrinking away by many religious teachers from specific doctrinal teachings and a re-focusing of efforts to commonly accepted social goals. Yet in the midst of this ecumenical movement and its "lowest common denominator" abandonment of the basic doctrines of Christianity; a great vacuum has been created in the minds of this whole generation of believers. For the first time in nearly two thousand years of Church history, we have a situation in which many pastors and laymen have no firm idea of what the Bible teaches about Death, Heaven, Hell and the future Kingdom of God. This abandoning of clear biblical teaching about these important subjects began a hundred years ago in the mainline denominations, but it has now spread into the rest of the Church.

This lack of clear biblical teaching about Heaven and "the last days" has produced a vacuum concerning eternity in the minds of many. If you were to ask most Christians today to tell you specifically about their expectations for their life in Heaven, you would frequently get a blank stare. They might suggest there would be "streets of gold" and "angels." Often that is the full extent of their knowledge of where they hope to spend the next trillion or so years. While most of us hear the word Heaven in a hymn or message every Sunday, very seldom have we had the opportunity to study the tremendous promises of the Word of God about the wonderful eternal life that Christ has prepared for us. In conversations I have been amazed to find that many have no clear understanding about the reality of Heaven. Many Christians have expressed the opinion that the Bible must not say anything very specific about Heaven and that must be the reason no one talks about it anymore. Nothing could be further from the truth. The Bible contains thousands of verses which refer to the very real life we shall enjoy and discuss the details of our future destiny. It is interesting to see that many older Christians who have enjoyed the privilege of sitting under the teaching of some great Bible teachers of the past generation often have a greater appreciation for the promises about Heaven.

There are tragic consequences of this current famine of teaching about Heaven and our future life. One problem is that New Age teaching and occult groups are now trying to fill this void by offering their spurious and Satanic doctrines to our youth. God created a natural desire in the heart of men and women to know the future and to explore the reality of eternity. When the Church abandoned the subject of genuine teaching about Heaven, Satan was quite willing to supply a counterfeit substitute. Many modern heresies were born in the vacuum created by the failure of today's church leadership to hold forth the great doctrines of Heaven, Hell and Eternity. Few today realize that for almost two thousand years, until this last generation, the Church has consistently taught these great truths about Heaven. The historically taught creeds contained explicit teaching about the Second Coming of Christ, Heaven and Hell. These creeds formed the basis of the teaching curriculum for new converts and mature Christians.

We live in the first generation in the history of the Church which has lost sight of our long-term goal—going home to our Father to realize our highest joy and purpose forever in Heaven. The problems we face today in this area are twofold. One, many pastors who are entering pulpits today have managed to get through three years of theology in modern seminaries without encountering any detailed studies to prepare them to teach about these subjects. Secondly, in the past many Christians studied these biblical truths at great length in their own private devotions and Bible studies. We now live in a culture with so frantic a pace that few Christians spend any significant time each day in deep Bible study. Tragically, with all the competition for our time and attention, many Christians are studying the Bible less. Often they do not have access to good translations, concordances and other Biblical research tools. You can search the shelves of many excellent Christian bookstores and find hundreds of devotional, table books and impressive theological textbooks on every conceivable topic. But where are the books on Heaven?

In my own desire to know the reality of our life with Christ in Heaven, I searched through many wonderful old commentaries and spent countless hours studying the prophecies which unfolded these scriptural truths about Heaven. I believe there may be many other Christians who would love to find a source which would explore in one book all the promises of God regarding Heaven.

Our pioneer forefathers came to this continent to build a rich new life and discovered a frontier which inspired their generation. A frontier challenges man to explore, to reach out beyond the limits of our previous experience. I have called this book, *Heaven – The Mystery of Angels* because the Bible promises us experiences and challenges beyond anything we have ever dreamed. As Christians we stand poised to embark on a great journey of discovery to the frontiers of the Messianic Kingdom, the New Heaven and the New Earth. It is my hope that this book will act as a guide and commentary to help you explore the tremendous future frontier which Jesus Christ has promised to all those who will accept Him as their Lord.

CHAPTER 1

The Promise of Heaven

The ancient creeds of the Church tell us "That the chief end of man is to glorify God and enjoy Him forever." While these words may seem strange and foreign to our ears, they are the standard which the Bible itself sets for us. "Whether you eat or drink, or whatever you do; do all to the glory of God." Our goal as Christians is to know God as He knows us.

The promises of God almost stagger us in their tremendous richness and variety. Possibly this overwhelming list of promises about Heaven has caused men to withdraw in unbelief in our generation from either the teaching or contemplation of Heaven. Yet the promises in the Word of God are unmovable despite the changing tides of religious fashion and doctrinal emphasis. While we may not be able to grasp all the truths about our eternal destiny, we must if we will be faithful to Lord and His Word, try to understand and believe His promises about Heaven. Christ's invitation is: "Come, you blessed of My Father, inherit the kingdom prepared for you from the foundation of the world" (Matthew 25:34). In the midst of all our worldly pursuits and interests it is sometimes almost impossible to remember that this life is simply a testing ground, a place of training for the wonders of our eternal life with Christ.

We cannot at this stage in our journey see the reality of Heaven. Although we cannot fully understand the richness of His promises; we must in faith accept and believe His words. For the Word tells us that "without faith it is impossible to please God." To be a follower of Christ we must believe by faith, live by faith and walk by faith. Today most people believe only those things which they can see with their own eyes. Many of us in this cynical world are 'from Missouri:' "I'll believe it when I see it." Yet the paradox of the Christian life is that we are commanded to "Believe and then you will see it." The disciple Thomas did not initially believe the prophecies of Jesus about His death and resurrection. In mercy, Christ appeared to Thomas face to face and let him put his hand into His wounds to prove to him that He had truly risen from the dead. However, Jesus said, "Thomas, because you have seen Me, you have believed: blessed are those who have not seen, and yet have believed" (John 20:29).

The disciple John tells us why God gave us the Bible: "But these are written that you may believe that Jesus is the Christ, the Son of God, and that believing you may have life in His name" (John 20:31). After the wonderful miracle of the loaves and fishes the people anxiously followed Christ and asked, "What shall we do, that we may work the works of God?" Jesus answered and said to them, "This is the work of God, that you believe in Him whom He sent" (John 6:28,29). Jesus continued, "For I have come down from Heaven, not to do My own will, but the will of Him who sent Me. And this is the will of Him who sent Me, that everyone who sees the Son and believes in Him may have everlasting life; and I will raise him up at the last day" (John 6:38,40).

The coming of Jesus Christ into the visible universe not only changed the map of the world regarding those things which pertain to eternity and Heaven, but He also effected a revolution in the standards by which we judge the things of earth. He introduced a completely different standard of morality into the cruel pagan world of the first century. The teaching and example of Christ provided the philosophical foundation for the spiritual liberation of man.

Life on earth, with its unresolved complexities, never seems just or fair. If "three score and ten" years are all there is in which—as the writer of the ancient Book of Job states—"the wicked often prosper and the good often suffer evil," our futures truly look very bleak. However, both vision and intuition have convinced man there must be something beyond "dust to dust and ashes to ashes." We all hope for a day in which justice will be finally be realized.

An interesting discovery by sociologists shows that every known society has a belief in "god" and an afterlife where man will finally find justice. Whether they are native North American tribes or the most primitive stone-age tribes in New Guinea, all societies without exception reveal a profoundly deep belief in God and an eternal life which is affected by their behavior now. Obviously, this does not prove there is a Heaven, but the fact that such a universal belief exists adds to the burden of proof.

If our souls are eternal, as intuition, reason, and the Bible assure us, then the subject of where we will spend eternity should be of paramount importance to us. Christians, those who are "sons of God through faith in Christ Jesus" (Galatians 3:26), are promised an eternal life where "we shall always be with the Lord" (1 Thessalonians 4:17). Surely, it is essential that we study what God's Word has to tell us about the "many mansions" which Jesus said are waiting for those of us who accept Christ as our personal Savior (John 14:2).

Imagine that you would be leaving your country soon and would spend the next thirty years of your life in a remote new country you knew nothing about. Imagine that a book was supplied to you with reliable information about your new home. It contained a great deal of specific information about life in that new place, including precise details on how to get there. Would you read the book? Most of us would answer yes. However, though most people hope to spend eternity in a place called "Heaven," very few have ever studied or read the exciting details in the only reliable travel guide to Heaven there is—the Bible.

Why do you suppose we are reluctant to want to spend the time finding for ourselves what God has waiting for us on "the other side?" I think there are three reasons.

Everyone Wants to Go to Heaven,
but Nobody Wants to Die

The subject of death and eternity is the last real taboo in conversation in our modern culture, even for Christians. If you doubt that statement, try a small experiment. At the next party you attend, in the middle of a conversation, mention the death of someone you are all familiar with and then ask if anyone has spent much time thinking about death personally. Watch their reaction. Usually, a deathly quiet will take over the robust conversation. While the subject of sex was the great conversational taboo for our Victorian ancestors, today, in our modern, "liberated" society, the one subject we studiously avoid is the fact that each of us will someday die and be faced with an eternity of Heaven or Hell.

We have more euphemisms and verbal evasions for death than our grandparents ever did to avoid openly discussing sex. A well-trained insurance man can spend two hours selling life insurance to you and never once use the words "death" or "die." We say that someone has passed on, expired, breathed his last, departed, gone to his eternal rest, to name just a few. We hate to say the word death.

Those Who Know the Truth About Heaven
are Reluctant to Share

The second reason we do not know much about Heaven is that those whose job it is to prepare us for death—ministers, parents, even doctors—have as deep an aversion to the word death as we do. Christians who attend church Sunday after Sunday seldom hear a sermon of any depth about Heaven or Hell. We sing about it from our hymnbooks, but we do not hear any in-depth details from the pulpit. When was the last time you heard a serious Bible study on Heaven? Have you ever heard one?

Some Find the Bible Difficult to Study on their Own

A third reason people do not spend more time in trying to find out about their eternal home is that many Christians, both new Christians and those who accepted the Lord years ago, find the Bible hard to study on their own. Unlike a modern text which is arranged in sections and chapters, with all the facts on a given subject set out in outline form, a topical study in the Bible, such as the study of Heaven, will require you to study the entire sixty-six books. Unless you are willing to spend considerable amounts of time to learn how to study the Bible and how to use excellent Bible study helps such as commentaries and concordances, it would be difficult for you to find out all the facts the Bible reveals about Heaven or any subject.

It is this perceived need for a single book that would draw together all the different verses and commentary on Heaven that has prompted my own years of study on the subject.

In the following chapters I will attempt to organize the great scriptural truths about salvation, resurrection, rewards and our life in Heaven into a form which can be easily studied by anyone who has an interest in their eternal future. Beginning with the First Resurrection and the Rapture of the Church we will study the great promises which Christ has given to His followers. The Bible's prophecies will be examined about the Great Tribulation, our Resurrected Body and our life in the New Jerusalem, the home of the Church. Fascinating new research on Israel's historical search for their Messiah and their startling discovery of the Book of Ezekiel on stone tablets should prove interesting to those who love biblical research. In later chapters you will read exciting material on Israel's plans to rebuild the Third Temple and the prophecies of the coming Millennial Kingdom. Following a study on the rewards in Heaven we will turn to the wonderful truths about Angels, the Messengers of God. The concluding chapters cover the topic of the New Heaven and Earth which God will create after the Millennium and an overview of Questions You Always Wanted To Ask About Heaven. While it would take an encyclopedia to cover the vast subject of Heaven and the Messianic Kingdom, I trust that this book will act as a guide to your own continuing study of the tremendous promises which God has prepared for all who choose eternal life.

CHAPTER 2

The Firstfruits of Resurrection

"But now Christ is risen from the dead, and has become the firstfruits of those who have fallen asleep. For since by man came death, by Man also came the resurrection of the dead. For as in Adam all die, even so in Christ all shall be made alive. But each one in his own order: Christ the firstfruits, afterward those who are Christ's at His coming" (1 Corinthians 15:20-23).

The historical truth about the resurrection of Jesus Christ is the essential bedrock upon which the Christian faith stands. The Apostle Paul declares, "If Christ is not risen, then our preaching is empty . . ." (1 Corinthians 15:14). Even liberal scholars now admit that the accounts of the life, death and resurrection of Jesus were written and distributed within thirty-five years of the events recorded in the Gospels. Thousands of people who saw Jesus were alive to read these widely distributed documents about His Resurrection. These eyewitnesses did not dispute the facts of His Resurrection. The Roman historian Tacitus records the supernatural eclipse which occurred when the heavens were darkened at the crucifixion of Jesus. There is more historically verifiable evidence that Jesus Christ lived, died and rose from the dead than exists to prove that Julius Caesar ever lived. While God calls for us to walk in faith, He has supplied ample proof to any honest inquirer who truly wants to know if Jesus rose from the dead.

Some people in our world, having rejected God, seek a false comfort in believing that they will never have to face God as their Judge. They hope that when we die, all life ceases. Therefore, why not "eat, drink and be merry for tomorrow we die?" This worldly philosophy is not one the Bible teaches. The Bible teaches there is life after death. Our bodies will undergo a transformation and a transition to prepare us for eternity. The body dies, yes, but the soul and spirit live on.

The German philosopher and poet, Goethe, was walking on the road to Weimar at sunset one beautiful summer evening with the writer Johann Peter Eckermann. As they stood gazing at the majestic setting sun, Goethe exclaimed: "Setting, nevertheless the sun is always the same sun. I am fully convinced that our spirit is a being of a nature quite indestructible, and its activity continues from eternity to eternity." He showed his realization that, though to our natural eyes the soul of a man may set, yet it still exists and always retains its identity and consciousness.

The Early Christians' Hope

To the amazement of the pagan Romans, the early Christians often faced death and martyrdom with joy and hope in Christ. They considered the grave as a mere resting place for their bodies until they should be transformed by Christ at His coming. They regarded their departed spirits as now being free to rejoice in the presence of God, enjoying a glorious and exciting life in Heaven. Early texts remind us of the courageous death of these martyrs who loved Jesus Christ more than their lives. It was their transforming belief in personal resurrection and Heaven which motivated these saints to go bravely to their deaths with hymns of praise upon their lips.

The catacombs were tunnels beneath the city of Rome that Christians met secretly in and used to bury their dead between the second and fourth centuries. Inscriptions found on tombs in these tunnels reveal the beliefs of the persecuted Christians buried there. These epitaphs show that the early Church clearly taught the consciousness of the spirit after death and that one day our bodies would be resurrected at the Rapture.

"She departed, desiring to ascend to the ethereal light of Heaven," A.D. 383.

"Eutuchius, wise, pious and kind, believing in Christ, entered the portals of death, and has the reward of the light of Heaven," A.D. 393.

"Here sleeps in the sleep of peace the sweet and innocent Severianus, whose spirit is received into the light of God."

"He sleeps but lives."

"He reposes in the Lord Jesus."

"The soul lives, unknowing of death, and consciously rejoices in the vision of Christ."

"Here rests my flesh; but at the last day, through Christ, I believe it will be raised from the dead."

"I believe, because my Redeemer lives, and in the last day shall raise me from the earth that in my flesh I shall see the Lord."

"Non mortua sed data somno," was written on the resting place of the young woman Prudentius. "She is not dead, but sleeps."

Chrysotom, in his Homily in Matthew, says of Christians who have died: "They say not of the departed, 'He is dead,' but he is perfected."

To the early Christians, the very idea of death as finality was rejected. Death to them was a mere transformation, a rebirth into our new eternal life with Christ in Heaven. The grave was only a "place of sleeping" or "resting." The Christians called the catacomb tombs the cæmeterium (cemetery), the resting place. The very word cemetery is a Christian concept unknown to the pagans for whom the grave either meant annihilation or the horrors of the damned.

Rev. H. W. Beecher once said: "I avow again, as I have before, may God give me a sudden death: I would rather have it instantaneous as lightning . . . but I would rather die with the harness on, in the midst of the battle. But as to the time, manner and place, that's God's will, not mine. Dying to me is not humiliation, but exaltation—emerging from that which is nothing but an egg, into the plenitude of power, into hope, into waves of affection and soul-loving that shall satisfy the amplitude of yearning in that direction. . . . I shall not die downward toward Hell, but upward toward Heaven. So let us shake the tree of life that the leaves of it will drop down for the healing of the nations."

The death of Dr. David Livingstone is one example of the transformation of lives effected by the truth of the resurrection. Dr. Livingstone, the great missionary explorer, had made many arduous and historical journeys throughout the mysterious continent of Africa. His life of heroism and service to humanity has seldom been exceeded. He won thousands of Africans to salvation through faith in the Lord. By his efforts many were liberated from the scourge of a life of slavery. When he knew that his life was ending he asked his native friends to bury his heart under a large tree in the soil of the land that he had given his life to liberate from slavery and spiritual darkness. On my last trip to England I visited the great cathedral of Westminster Abbey and stood by this tomb of one of Scotland's finest sons.

A newspaper in Scotland reported the details of Livingstone's last days on earth. "During the last days of April, 1873, he was very ill. He had plaintively said to his men: 'Build me a hut to die in. I am going home.' In that hut at Ilala, on the night of the 30th of April, in great pain and weakness, he had been tenderly laid upon the couch by his faithful followers. About four in the morning, a Negro, who was watching beside him called out to Susi, who with five more of his men, hastened into the hut. A candle, stuck by its own wax on the top of a box, gave light enough to see that Dr. Livingstone was not in the bed, but kneeling by the side of it, his body stretched forward, and his head buried in his hands upon the pillow. For a minute they watched him. He did not stir. There was no sign of breathing. Then one of them, Matthew, went softly to him and laid his hands upon his cheek. Life had been gone some time. The body was almost cold. Dr. Livingstone was dead. On his knees, at the throne of grace, that noble spirit had ended his pilgrimage and entered in through the gates into the city. His poor, shrivelled body, preserved in salt, was carried to the coast, a distance of more than a thousand miles, by his humble but affectionate body-guard of black men, everyone of whom was a liberated slave. This funeral march was a grander and more touching memorial than any tomb that can be raised to his honour in Westminster Abbey."

The Two Resurrections

All men and women, saved and unsaved, will rise again after death but there is a great difference between the destiny of these two groups. The Bible describes two different resurrections: the First to life and the Second to spiritual death. The First Resurrection of Life involves all those who repent of their sin and accept the pardon of God. They participate in a resurrection to spiritual life. This First Resurrection has several different stages within it as the Bible describes the "firstfruits" who rose two thousand years ago and describes the future "rapture" of the Christian believers in our future. After the Rapture a group of Jewish and Gentile tribulation saints will also be resurrected when Christ returns at Armageddon according to Matthew 24:40, "one will be taken and the other left." All who participate in this First Resurrection to Life are saved and will enjoy life in Heaven forever.

The Second Resurrection involves those who reject God's pardon and die in their sin. They too will rise at the last day, after the Millennium, to stand in their resurrected body before the Great White Throne Judgment of God. Revelation 20:14 says, "This is the second death." All those who participate in this tragic Second Resurrection will experience spiritual death for eternity.

The Firstfruits of Resurrection

The Bible uses the word "firstfruits" to describe this First Resurrection which leads to eternal life in Heaven. In Israel the Feast of Firstfruits happened in the spring of the year to celebrate the first fruits of the harvest. As the Jews brought these tokens of the bounty of the coming harvest to the Temple they were acknowledging that God was the provider of the harvest. This word "firstfruits" became a proper symbol of this first group of resurrected saints, a token of the great harvest when Jesus, the Lord of the Harvest, will come to gather the saints to meet Him in the air.

The writer of the Book of Hebrews, after recounting the many acts of faith of Old Testament saints, told his readers about their life in Heaven. He declares "we are surrounded by so great a cloud of witnesses" (Hebrews 12:1). They still live! They have been transformed and are now in Paradise, watching our walk of faith. Many of those Old Testament saints participated in this first stage of the First Resurrection, when Jesus rose from the grave.

Matthew 27:52,53 describes the amazing and exciting events that happened after Jesus rose from the dead, during the Feast of the Firstfruits: "And the graves were opened; and many bodies of the saints who had fallen asleep were raised; and coming out of the graves after His Resurrection, they went into the holy city and appeared to many."

The various writers who observed this miraculous resurrection recounted it in their histories of the day. Jesus Christ had risen from the dead and won victory over death, not only for Himself as the Son of God, but also for those saints who had died centuries before and for all who would believe in Him as their Lord and Savior for centuries to follow.

Writings by Christians of that time have been collected in the *Ante-Nicene Library*. They describe that more than twelve thousand of these Old Testament saints walked through Galilee for forty days, appeared in Jerusalem before many, and later ascended into Heaven when Jesus Christ ascended to His Father.

This undeniable fact of Christ's Resurrection and the resurrection of Old Testament saints who identified themselves to many Jews created a ground swell of belief in the claims of Christ that He was the Messiah and the true Son of God. The Lord proved forever that His power of resurrection and eternal life was available to all who would receive His offer of salvation. God will not force you to accept eternal life, nor will He force you to live in Heaven if you choose not to claim this "indescribable gift" (2 Corinthians 9:15) as Lord and Savior.

These saints who rose from the dead when Christ arose were the "firstfruits" of the first resurrection to eternal life in Heaven. It is no coincidence that this seventeenth day of Nisan in A.D. 32 was the Feast of the Firstfruits. Other notable events connected with resurrection also happened on this anniversary.

On this day the ark of Noah rested on Mount Ararat and the human race was resurrected following the flood. Almost a thousand years later, on this anniversary, Moses led the people of Israel through the Red Sea to be resurrected as a nation from the bondage of Egypt. Forty years later, Israel crossed the Jordan on the seventeenth day of Nisan, and the people enjoyed the firstfruits of the Promised Land. In the sovereignty of God, He caused Jesus Christ to rise from the dead and to bring these saints with Him into new life on this same day, during the Feast of Firstfruits.

These resurrected saints had bodies that were real. Several documents from this era claim that among those raised by Jesus were the Temple priest, Simeon, who had once waited in the Temple to see the baby Jesus, and his two sons who lived in Arimathea. The records state their resurrection was specifically investigated since they were well-known to the Sanhedrin because of their Temple service as priests. After so many centuries, it is impossible to ascertain the documentary accuracy of these ancient texts, but it is interesting to note that they confirm the details of the event which Matthew recorded in his Gospel.

These records in the *Ante-Nicene Library* claim that during the investigation each of the sons of Simeon was separately and simultaneously interrogated. They both told the same story, namely that Christ had appeared to them in Hades, preached to all, and that those who had earlier responded to God were miraculously given new bodies and resurrected when Christ rose from the grave.

Matthew's record of this event is tantalizing in both what it reveals and what it conceals. He states that these Old Testament saints "went into the holy city and appeared to many." Remember that all the events involved with the death and resurrection of Jesus happened in Jerusalem during the busiest season of the year, the Feast of Passover. Every Israelite male who was capable made an effort to come to Jerusalem for the Passover festival. Deuteronomy 16:2 records this as a command of God. Each home in the holy city had upper rooms which were supplied without cost to fellow Israelites who came on these pilgrimages. Therefore, during this Feast of Passover, the population of Jerusalem had swollen to five times the normal number. Flavius Josephus, the Jewish historian, says in his *Jewish Wars* that, according to Roman records, the number of sheep sacrificed during the Passover was 256,500. Since one sheep would serve as a sacrifice for five people, the conclusion is that during the time of Christ up to 1,250,000 people would come to the city during Passover instead of the usual 250,000 city dwellers.

Both the New Testament and letters of first century Christians record that these resurrected saints identified themselves to the people as historical, biblical characters. With 1,000,000 visitors already in the city, obviously these resurrected saints must have appeared different in some way from other men, or they would simply have been lost in the crowd. Possibly their faces were transfigured with God's reflected glory as the faces of Moses and Elijah were on the Mount of Transfiguration.

Those saints who rose with Christ did not die again, according to the writings of the first century. They were raptured to Heaven when Christ was raptured. These saints are now enjoying a "better that is, a heavenly country . . . for He has prepared a city for them" (Hebrews 11:16). These raptured believers are the firstfruits of the first resurrection, which is "the resurrection of life" John 5:29).

Paul described this resurrection in his first epistle to the church at Thessalonica: "If we believe that Jesus died and rose again, even so God will bring with Him those who sleep in Jesus" and if we are still alive on earth, "we who are alive and remain shall be caught up together with them in the clouds to meet the Lord in the air. And thus we shall always be with the Lord" (4:14,17) in eternal life in the New Jerusalem forever. The rapture of the saints will be discussed in greater detail in the next chapter. Those who miss the first resurrection will also rise again, but they will partake of the dreaded second resurrection, which is a spiritual, eternal death in the Lake of Fire (Revelation 20:15).

The Old Testament Believers

The entire company of Old Testament believers went to "the bosom of Abraham." It is recorded by God that when each of the great Patriarchs died he was "gathered to his people" (Genesis 25:8; 35:29; 49:29). Some have suggested that this often repeated phrase does not prove that the patriarchs believed in a personal resurrection from the dead but merely refers to their expectation of being buried with their ancestors.

Upon close examination of the passages, however, it appears that these Old Testament saints did believe in a personal resurrection in which they would be reunited in Heaven with those who had died earlier in the faith. As one example, consider the passage in Genesis 49:29 and 33, which records the death scene of Jacob addressing his twelve sons: "I am to be gathered to my people; bury me with my fathers in the cave that is in the field of Ephron the Hittite. . . . And when Jacob had finished commanding his sons, he drew his feet up into the bed and breathed his last, and was gathered to his people." Jacob was not buried in that cave immediately. First there was a period of seventy days required for embalming and mourning in Egypt. Then, "Joseph, all the servants of Pharaoh, the elders of his house, and all the elders of the land of Egypt . . . the house of Joseph, his brothers, and his father's house" made the long journey north to Canaan to reach the burial cave. But notice that the passage says he "breathed his last, and was gathered to his people," with no indication of waiting until he reached the grave site. When he died his spirit was in the presence of his people who had gone to Heaven before him.

The firstfruits of the first resurrection—Jesus first and then those Old Testament saints who walked the streets of Jerusalem—is but a sample of what will happen in the next stage of the first resurrection, the Rapture of the Church. Jesus and these resurrected saints had resurrected bodies. He proved to His disciples that He was flesh, "Handle me and see, for a spirit does not have flesh and bones as you see I have" (Luke 24:39), and He ate, "They gave Him a piece of broiled fish and some honeycomb. And He took it and ate in their presence" (vv. 42,43). He even fixed breakfast for His disciples (John 21:9,12,13). Yet He could walk through a closed door (John 20:26) and defy gravity when He was "carried up into Heaven" (Luke 24:51). And that is where He is now, waiting for us; for He promised that "in My Father's house are many mansions; if it were not so, I would have told you. I go to prepare a place for you" (John 14:2).

Resurrection of the Saints

The resurrection of these Old Testament saints is an important passage because it provides an illustration of Christ's power over death and sin to resurrect, not only Himself, but a whole class of believers in Him. We can learn several important things from examining this passage. Those who died before the resurrection of Christ experienced the same benefit of salvation from His atonement for our sins by His death on the cross as well as those who lived since. As the author of Hebrews 13:8 affirmed the vital principle of God's unchanging nature, "Jesus Christ the same yesterday, and to-day, and for ever." Perhaps the most important lesson from this incident in the Gospels is that Jesus Christ conquered and disabled death through His triumphant death and resurrection. The saints that rose from the dead with Christ were the crowns of His victory over the power of death. When Jesus defeated the power of sin and death, He led "captivity captive," by fulfilling the Scripture, "Wherefore he saith, When he ascended up on high, he led captivity captive, and gave gifts unto men" (Ephesians 4:8).

In the years since I wrote the first edition of *Heaven* several individuals have commented on this portion of my book dealing with the supernatural resurrection of the saints when Christ arose from the dead as recorded in Matthew 27:52,53. Some critics have rejected my literal interpretation of this passage that accepts the actuality of their physical resurrection and that they likely ascended to Heaven with Christ. Several challenged my statements that there were numerous references to this passage as an actual event that appeared in the early writings of the Church. In response to their challenge and to provide you with the evidence for your own examination, I will include several of these fascinating references in this revised edition of *Heaven – The Mystery of Angels.*

The Resurrection of the Saints in the Writings of the Church Fathers

Several early Christian manuscripts recorded in the *Ante-Nicene Library* describe early Church histories and traditions that numerous saints rose from the dead with Jesus Christ (one manuscript claimed 12,000) and that they appeared to many witnesses in Jerusalem. Some of these sources also mentioned that these resurrected saints later ascended to Heaven. The *Ante-Nicene Library* is a collection of manuscripts by important Christian writers from the time of Christ until the Church council known as the Council of Nicea in A.D. 325. These valuable writings were translated into English and edited into a ten volume set of books in 1890. Reprints of these books can be ordered from Christian bookstores. While these early Christian sources outside the Bible should never be used to establish doctrine; they certainly are valuable evidence to help us understand how the early Church writers, who lived shortly after these events occurred, interpreted the facts about the resurrection of our Lord. I realize that many of my readers do not have access to these writings so I am recording some excerpts from these fascinating records of the early Church about the resurrection of these saints at the same time as Jesus Christ rose from the dead. However, we must always keep in mind that only the Scriptures of the Old and New Testament are truly inspired by God and are free of error.

Clement of Alexandria—The Stromata, or Miscellanies

(Chap. 6, page 491, *Ante-Nicene Library*, Volume 2) "They went down with them therefore into the water, and again ascended. But these descended alive, and again ascended alive. But those who had fallen asleep, descended dead, but ascended alive." Further, the Gospel says, "that many bodies of those that slept arose,"—plainly as having been translated to a better state. There took place, then, a universal movement and translation through the economy of the Saviour."

Ignatius – Epistle of Ignatius to the Magnesians

(Chap. 9, page 62, *Ante-Nicene Library*, Volume 1)
"How shall we be able to live apart from Him, whose disciples the prophets themselves in the Spirit did wait for Him as their Teacher? And therefore He whom they rightly waited for, being come, raised them from the dead."

Irenaeus – Fragments from the Lost Writings of Irenaeus

(Chap. 28, pages 572-573, *Ante-Nicene Library*, Volume 1)
"This event was also an indication of the fact, that when the holy soul of Christ descended [to Hades], many souls ascended and were seen in their bodies . . . so, when the Word of God became one with flesh, by a physical and hypostatic union, the heavy and terrestrial [part], having been rendered immortal, was borne up into heaven, by the divine nature, after the resurrection."

The Story Concerning the King of Edessa

(Page 653, *Ante-Nicene Library*, Volume 8)
"He humbled and emptied and abased Himself, and was crucified, and descended to Hades and broke through the enclosure which had never been broken through before, and raised up the dead, and descended alone, and ascended with a great multitude to His Father."

The Gospel of Nicodemus

(Latin Version [Page 454] *Ante-Nicene Library*, Volume 8)
Chap. I (17) .— Then Rabbi Addas, and Rabbi Finees, and Rabbi Egias, the three men who had come from Galilee, testifying that they had seen Jesus taken up into heaven, rose up in the midst of the multitude of the chiefs of the Jews, and said before the priests and the Levites, who had been called together to the council of the Lord: When we were coming from Galilee, *we met at the Jordan a very great multitude of men, fathers who had been some time dead. . . .* And they went, and walked round all the region of Jordan and of the mountains, and they were coming back without finding them. . . . And, behold, suddenly there appeared coming down from Mount Amalech *a very great number, as it were, twelve*

thousand men, who had risen with the Lord. And though they recognized very many there, they were not able to say anything to them for fear and the angelic vision; and they stood at a distance gazing and hearing them, how they walked along singing praises, and saying: The Lord has risen again from the dead, as He had said; let us all exult and be glad, since He reigns for ever. Then those who had been sent were astonished, and fell to the ground for fear, and received the answer from them, that they should see Karinus and Leucius in their own houses. And they rose up and went to their houses, and found them spending their time in prayer."

Commentary References to
The Resurrection of the Saints

Several commentaries from the last century provide interesting insights into this small passage of the Gospels that is seldom taught today. These great students of the Word had some interesting insights into the resurrection of these saints.

New Testament Commentary—David Brown—1872

David Brown included these statements in his commentary on this passage. "These sleeping saints (see on 1 Thess. 4. 14) were Old Testament believers, who—according to the usual punctuation in our version—were quickened into resurrection-life at the moment of their Lord's death, but lay in their graves till His resurrection when they came forth. . . . But this was a resurrection once for all, to life everlasting; and so there is no room to doubt that they went to glory with their Lord, as bright trophies of His victory over death."

New Testament Commentary—Joseph Benson—1854

Joseph Benson wrote that "their resurrection was a most extraordinary event, and doubtless was much spoken of in Jerusalem among those to whom they appeared, and other well-disposed persons to whom they mentioned it. It is not improbable that Christ's prophecy, recorded in John 5:25, referred to this event, and thereby received its accomplishment, being distinguished from the general resurrection predicted in verses 28, 29 of that chapter. As it is only said, these saints appeared to many in Jerusalem, but not that they continued with them, it is probable that as they were undoubtedly raised to immortality, they attended their risen Saviour, during his abode on earth, and afterward accompanied him in his ascension, to grace his triumph over death and the grave."

CHAPTER 3

The Rapture

Christians today often speak about the "Rapture" the miraculous moment when Christ will cause all living Christians to "rise to meet Him in the air." Although the word, as such, does not appear in the English translations of the Bible, the concept is clearly taught in several different verses. It is worth remembering that the word Trinity also does not appear in the Bible but the concept of a triune God is declared in many passages.

The word Rapture comes from the Latin word "rapere" which means to "snatch away" or be "caught up." It is an excellent word to describe what the Bible declares will happen to all living saints who are alive at the moment when the "last trump" is blown and Christ calls His Church home to Heaven.

When we talk about the "Rapture" we refer to the rapture or "taking home" of the Church. Paul talks about this event in his first letter to the church at Thessalonica: "For the Lord Himself will descend from Heaven with a shout, with the voice of an archangel, and with the trumpet of God. . . . Then we who are alive . . . shall be caught up [raptured] . . . to meet the Lord in the air. And thus we shall always be with the Lord" (1 Thessalonians 4:16,17).

Although we eagerly await walking on "streets of gold" in the presence of the Lord Jesus Christ, few of us want to undergo the experience of the "valley of the shadow of death." Perhaps that is why Christians, from the time of Paul, have looked for Christ's coming during their lifetime so that they could go to Heaven without having to die. We naturally fear the experience of death. And, although the Bible says that normally "it is appointed for men to die once" (Hebrews 9:27), there will be a generation of Christians who will not see physical death before entering Heaven—they will be raptured. They will pass from "Life unto Life" rather than from "Death unto Life." This will be the first generation in history who will escape the curse of death.

The First "Rapture" in History

The first mention of a "rapture-like event" was recorded by Moses who declared that "Enoch walked with God; and he was not, for God took [raptured] him" (Genesis 5:24). Enoch lived in the seventh generation from Adam. When Enoch was sixty-five years old, before his son Methuselah was born, he evidently had a very special spiritual experience. Genesis 5 says that from that time "Enoch walked with God three hundred years" (v. 2) until his rapture to Heaven.

The Book of Jude, in the New Testament, says that during those years, "Enoch, the seventh from Adam, prophesied . . . saying, 'Behold, the Lord comes with ten thousands of His saints, to execute judgment on all, to convict all who are ungodly among them of all their ungodly deeds which they have committed in: an ungodly way, and of all the harsh things which ungodly sinners have spoken against Him'" (Jude 14,15). This prophecy of God through Enoch not only told about the final judgment of God but also prophesied the judgment that was to come, not in his lifetime, but after his son Methuselah died.

In Hebrew, "Methuselah," the name of Enoch's firstborn son, means "After he goes, then it happens"—"it" being the flood. God gave Enoch a revelation of His coming judgment upon the wickedness which was developing in the generations before the flood. Genesis 6:5-7 declares, "Then the Lord saw that the wickedness of man was great in the earth, and that every intent of the thoughts of his heart was only evil continually. And the Lord was sorry that He had made man on the earth, and He was grieved in His heart. So the Lord said, 'I will destroy man whom I have created from the face of the earth, both man and beast, creeping thing and birds of the air, for I am sorry that I have made them.' "

God blessed Enoch's faithfulness by giving him this prophecy. Then God blessed his son Methuselah by giving him a very long life—969 years, the longest life of any person recorded in the Bible. Methuselah died the day of the Flood. It was as though God was giving mankind a chance to repent of his continual evil, because, "after he goes, then it happens." When Enoch was 365 years old, as the Jerusalem Bible puts it, he "vanished because God took him" (v. 24). Enoch was "raptured" before God's judgment fell on the evil people of that day. This is an example of how God first delivers a prophetic warning, then removes the righteous and finally delivers the judgment. Later, the Bible tells us that the prophet Elijah was also raptured to Heaven by the "chariot of God."

The Teachings of Jesus and Paul about the Rapture

The first teaching about the Rapture in the New Testament comes from the words of Jesus to the grieving Martha after the death of her brother, Jesus' close friend, Lazarus. Martha said, "Lord, if You had been here, my brother would not have died." Then Jesus told her about the Rapture: "Your brother will rise again." Martha then said: "I know that he will rise again in the resurrection at the last day." But Jesus was talking about more than the resurrection of the physically dead in Christ: "I am the resurrection and the life. He who believes in Me, though he may die, he shall live." He continued to say, *"And whoever lives and believes in Me shall never die"* (John 11:21, 23-25) [italics added].

For many years, when I read this passage in the gospel of John, I believed that Christ was simply repeating himself in this last sentence. However, upon closer examination, I believe that this passage contains the first clear teaching in the New Testament about the Rapture of the Church—the Body of Christ—in the generation when Christ returns. Notice that Jesus is talking about two distinct groups of believers.

The first group is made up of those believers who have died, and will continue to die, during the period between the birth of the Church and the coming of Christ: "He who believes in Me, though he may die, he shall live."

The second group is covered in His second statement. This was an entirely new revelation: "And whoever lives and believes in Me shall never die." There will be a generation of believers who will not have to pass through death to reach eternal life, but who will be "caught up together . . . to meet the Lord in the air" as Paul says in 1 Thessalonians. These believers who are alive on the day when Jesus Christ comes will be caught up physically, and their bodies will be transformed so that they are fit to live in Heaven forever with Christ.

This great promise to the Church is affirmed by the Apostle Paul: "Behold, I tell you a mystery: We shall not all sleep, but we shall all be changed—in a moment, in the twinkling of an eye, at the last trumpet. For the trumpet will sound, and the dead will be raised incorruptible, and we shall be changed. For this corruptible must put on incorruption and this mortal must put on immortality. So when this corruptible has put on incorruption, and this mortal has put on immortality, then shall be brought to pass the saying that is written: 'Death is swallowed up in victory' " (1 Corinthians 15:51-54).

In this passage, Paul provides a new revelation which the church had not previously known about the coming of the Lord and the rapture of the saints. (1) Not all Christians will die; many will be alive in the final generation when Christ returns. They will pass from this earthly life to life eternal without dying first. (2) Before those who are alive are raptured, Christ will, "in the twinkling of an eye," resurrect the bodies of those believers who have died in the faith up to this time. (3) It will be an instantaneous event. (4) The Rapture will be accompanied by the blowing of the last trumpet. (5) All believers—both dead and alive—will be changed. Their mortal, corruptible earthly bodies will be transformed into incorruptible, immortal, heavenly bodies fit for eternity.

Paul wrote this letter to the church at Corinth during his third missionary journey, probably during the winter of A.D. 55, twenty-three years after Jesus Christ taught His disciples about the events of the last days as recorded in Matthew 24. By this time, Jesus' disciples were going about the world as Jesus had commanded them, telling all the things they had heard Jesus teach as they lived with Him during His years of ministry. Although the Gospel accounts were not yet written down as we know them, they were passed faithfully and without error from church to church, kept fresh by the power of the Holy Spirit.

Belief in the Second Coming
During the Middle Ages

The Second Coming, including the translation or "catching up" of the Church, was widely taught in the early Church. The early Apostolic Church taught the prophetic truths about the Pre-Millennial Return of Christ for hundreds of years. In my book, *Armageddon*, I quote from twelve early Church writers who clearly reveal the almost universal belief in the Apostolic Church that Christ would return in glory before the Millennium. Although they naturally did not use the English word Rapture to describe the fact that Paul declared the Christians would be "caught up to meet Him in the air," they constantly warned their readers to be watchful for the soon return of Christ. I have not found one theologian in the early church before A.D. 250 who denied the truth of the Rapture which was taught by Paul in 1 Thessalonians 4:13-18.

During the years leading to A.D. 300, several teachers began to teach a method of biblical interpretation that "spiritualized" many truths of the Bible. Led by Origen of Alexandria, Egypt, this party gradually grew within the Church. They began to spiritualize and "allegorize" many biblical teachings, among them the prophecies about the return of Christ and the Millennium. They denied the literal return of Jesus. They also denied that He was the Son of God.

As the Church became involved with emperors like Constantine (288-337), who supported Christianity, it began to take on political status. The belief in the actual return of Christ quickly withered away. Naturally, a Roman Emperor like Constantine did not look with favor on the biblical prophecy that all Gentile world empires would be overthrown by the Second Coming of Christ. Augustine (354-430), the most influential theologian since Paul, began to teach that the Return of Christ, the Battle of Armageddon, and the Millennium were allegories to be understood only symbolically. In his book, *The City of God*, he denied a future Millennium with Christ's return and reign. Tragically, this denial of the Scriptures set the tone for the majority of Catholic and Protestant theologians for centuries to come.

As the Catholic Church grew in political power, people accepted the belief that the Millennial Kingdom existed here and now, instead of something that called for the miraculous return of Christ. With few, brief exceptions, the study of prophecy was, for the most part, ignored by church leaders during the Middle Ages until the time of the Reformation by Martin Luther in 1520. In the theological battles waged between Protestant reformers and the Catholic Church, prophecy was seldom dealt with—aside from one great exception.

Most of the reformers lost family and friends to religious persecution by the Church and the Inquisition. Therefore, when they read in their Bibles the prophecies about the great Whore of Babylon, the Antichrist and the "blood of martyrs," spoken of in Revelation 17, they naturally concluded that the Papacy and the Church of Rome were the primary elements referred to by these predictions.

In most of their writings about prophecy, the reformers focused solely on these conclusions and usually misinterpreted the 1,260 days of the books of Daniel and the

Revelation to be a period of 1,260 years. They tried to fit this conclusion of a 1,260-year reign of Antichrist into the history of the papacy. In my library are several hundred books written following the Reformation that tried to pick a date for the starting year of the papacy (i.e., 606), and by adding this assumed period of 1,260 years, tried to predict the final destruction of their religious enemy, the Church of Rome. At one time, I had counted fifty-two different authors who arrived at separate concluding years.

This method, known as the "historical" method of interpreting prophecy, has generally been abandoned by modern students because every possible combination was tried without success. Few of the reformers studied any other detailed area in prophecy. Thus it is not surprising that the doctrine of "the translation of the saints," the Rapture, should remain largely undeveloped until 1825. Then, the Plymouth Brethren began to systematically study the scriptures on this topic. John Calvin, the great reformer, wrote a commentary on every single book of the Bible except the prophetic Book of Revelation which he stated he did not understand. If you examine the history of theology it is apparent that God continues to reveal His truth to men in deeper ways as the centuries pass. Apparently the Holy Spirit was causing men's minds to concentrate on different progressive revelations of God's truth in different epochs of the history of the Church. For instance, the liberating truth of justification by faith was lost for centuries until the reformers recovered this rich truth which had been in the Bible, though ignored for a thousand years.

The reformers rejected the allegorical method of interpreting the Bible and laid the basis for a return to the eschatology of the early Church. However, they did not recover the teachings of the Pre-Millennial return of Christ at the beginning of the Reformation. The first Calvinist reformer to begin to see the truth about what would later be termed the Rapture was a French clergyman in Rotterdam. In 1687, Peter Jurieu, known as the "Goliath of the Protestants," wrote a book on *The Accomplishment of the Scriptural Prophecies or*

The Approaching Deliverance of the Church. In this wonderful book, which I found on my last trip to Wales, Peter Jurieu brilliantly recovers and defends the biblical teaching on Pre-Millennialism.

While tentatively teaching the emerging truth about the coming rapture of the Church, he wrote against the prevailing anti-millennial views of both Catholic and Protestant writers. He says, "There is a first coming of Christ, and it may be a first resurrection. . . . Who can be certain that this coming of Christ, to establish His Kingdom upon Earth, shall not be in that manner, with the voice of an arch-angel, and in great magnificence and Glory? Who can prove that at that first coming of Christ He shall not raise some of the dead, as St. John seems expressly to have fore-told? . . . Our Lord should for a short space come down from Heaven to establish a Kingdom for a thousand years, and to give His seal to the Conversion of all the nations, by some glorious Apparition, returning back to Heaven immediately after."

Peter Jurieu continues his argument against those who deny the possibility of the "clandestine coming of Christ" for His Church. He says that their denial is based on "a false supposition; viz., that there shall be no other coming of Christ, but for the last and final judgment, which is not true: the Coming of Christ here spoken of, is to settle the Peace, and Glory, and Kingdom of His Church; and we may be certain that this meant in almost all the Passages, where the coming of Christ is spoken of." Following Jurieu, many other reformers came to believe in the Pre-Millennial return of Christ. Then, in 1825, John Nelson Darby, a Plymouth Brethren preacher in Scotland, began to develop in detail the teaching about the translation of the saints. This was when the word Rapture was coined.

It may seem incredible to you that it took so long for the legitimate teachings of the end times to take hold in the hearts of God's people. However, remember that throughout the history of the Middle Ages most Christians did not even have the Bible in their own hands or in their own language to read what God had revealed in the Scriptures. For almost eight hundred years, only the priests were allowed legal access to the Bible and many of them could not read. For instance, until 1870, it was illegal for a Catholic in Italy to have his own Bible. In light of these factors, it is understandable why there was little detailed teaching about the Rapture until 1825. This is no reason to reject the doctrine. The question which must be determined is this: Does the Bible teach it?

Some have suggested that the timing of the Rapture is unimportant to us. While others are Pre-Tribulation, Mid-Tribulation or Post-Tribulation in their view; these Christians say they are "Pan-Tribulation;" they feel that "whenever the Rapture happens, it will all pan out in the end." However, we are commanded to search the Scriptures to examine these things. The Tribulation will be a time of unparalleled horror in which all must either take the Antichrist's "mark of the beast" or reject it with their martyrdom or fleeing to the wilderness. Whether we in the Church will have to experience mass martyrdom must be a matter of serious study and concern. I cannot agree that the timing of the Rapture is unimportant.

The Timing of the Rapture

What is the chronology of these events of the Second Coming of Christ? Will the Church be raptured before the Great Tribulation begins? Many readers believe that the Rapture will precede the Great Tribulation. Others believe that while there will be a Rapture, it may not happen until the return of Christ in glory at the Battle of Armageddon. Some doubt that the Rapture is taught by the Bible. Why should the Church be raptured, or to use the New Testament words, "be caught up together" to meet Christ in the air? Surely the first answer is: The Bible says so. But, why should God Rapture the Church?

Jesus Christ repeatedly promised the Church throughout the Gospels that the fact of His own bodily resurrection is the absolute proof that we will be resurrected with a new body at His Second Coming. He has promised that our new bodies will be like His resurrected body, incorruptible and immortal. When He comes for His Bride, the Church will consist of two distinct groups: those who have died in the faith and those who are still alive. We cannot go into an incorruptible Heaven with a corruptible body which is subject to decay and death. Paul said it best in 1 Corinthians 15 "For this corruptible (our natural body) must put on incorruption, and this mortal must put on immortality" (v. 53).

If there was no Rapture in our future, then we would have to spend eternity without a body. We must receive a new spiritual body to enjoy all that Christ has prepared for us in Heaven. Therefore, at the moment of His coming, He will transform the bodies of the living simultaneously as He transforms the bodies of those who died as believers. Those Christians who have died in the faith are now in Heaven, the Paradise which Christ promised to the thief on the Cross, "Today you will be with Me in Paradise." However, they do not yet have the resurrection body which they will receive on the day of the Rapture. "The dead in Christ will rise first" indicates that the spirits of the Christians in Heaven will then receive their new transformed bodies which rises to meet their spirits descending in the air with Christ. During the Rapture at the moment their spirits join their new spiritual bodies, then "we who are alive and remain will be caught up together with them . . . in the air. And thus we shall always be with the Lord" (1 Thessalonians 4:17).

The Apostolic Church Looked for the Imminent Return of Christ

When we examine the writings of the early Apostolic church we find two different, and seemingly contradictory, themes. The first taught that Christ would return to set up His Kingdom six thousand years from the time of Adam. The second theme taught that Christians must be watchful because the resurrection of the believer could happen at any moment.

This "six thousand year" belief lay in their understanding that the week of creation in Genesis was a microcosm of the great week of human history. The six days related to six thousand years. The sabbath day of rest would correspond to the thousand years of Christ's kingdom as described in the Book of Revelation. Hippolytus, Cyprian, Justin Martyr, Lactantius and many other Christian writers supported this Apostolic interpretation of 2 Peter 3:8: "But, beloved, do not forget this one thing, that with the Lord one day is as a thousand years, and a thousand years as one day."

There were differing opinions as to where they stood in this time scale (their estimates ranged from four thousand to five and a half thousand years from Adam). These Bible scholars clearly expected that Christ would not immediately return to set up His Millennial Kingdom.

But, the command to "be watchful" for the Return of Christ was taught by all the church fathers. One example is a letter known as the *"Teachings of the Twelve Apostles,"* apparently written around the year A.D. 120. Although it certainly is not canonical, it gives us an indication of how Christians in the early Church viewed the timing of Christ's coming to resurrect our bodies. In Chapter XVI it states, "Watch for your life's sake. Let not your lamps be quenched, nor your loins unloosed; but be ye ready, for ye know not the hour in which our Lord cometh. . . . And then shall appear the signs of the truth; first, the sign of an outspreading in Heaven; then the sign of the sound of the trumpet; and the third, the resurrection of the dead; yet not of all, but as it is said: The Lord shall come and all His saints with Him. Then shall the world see the Lord's coming upon the clouds of Heaven."

Although they did not use the word "Rapture" to describe this imminent resurrection of the believers, they understood and awaited the translation of the saints' bodies as a different event than His later coming "with ten thousands of His saints" to judge the world at Armageddon.

Why Didn't the Bible tell us
When the Rapture Would Happen?

The New Testament tells us in many places to be watchful for the coming of the Son of Man. The net result of these passages is that Christians have been forced to live in a spiritually dynamic tension of not knowing just when the Lord will come to resurrect us. If Christ had clearly stated that His return would not be for more than nineteen hundred years, the Church might have lost its sense of urgency and mission. There might have been fewer missionaries who felt compelled to "Go therefore and make disciples of all the nations, baptizing them in the name of the Father and of the Son and of the Holy Spirit, teaching them to observe all things that I have commanded you; and lo, I am with you always, even to the end of the age" (Matthew 28:19,20).

The great outpouring of missionary and evangelistic efforts since A.D. 1800 came primarily from denominations that believe strongly in the literal Second Coming of Christ, and hope fervently that it will happen in their lifetime. Far from hindering the urgency of the Gospel, the belief in the Pre-Millennial and imminent Return of Christ has been the great motivation for Christians to fulfill the command of Christ to "go into all the world and preach the Gospel."

The Holy Spirit has, in a sense, kept us on our toes spiritually for two thousand years by refraining from telling us exactly when Christ would return. Obviously, God did not want us to know the exact hour when Jesus would return. Jesus said we would not know. (See Matthew 24:36,42,44,50; 25:13; Mark 13:32; Luke 12:40,46.) If the Bible had included one simple statement regarding the exact sequence of events regarding the Rapture and the coming of Christ in glory to set up His Kingdom, all confusion in this matter would have been removed forever. Since there is no such clear statement, it must have been the intention of the Holy Spirit to leave a certain degree of ambiguity about the timing of the Rapture. As a result, many excellent and sincere Bible teachers arrive at differing conclusions regarding whether the Rapture will happen before the Great Tribulation or after, when Christ returns at the Battle of Armageddon.

Those who take part in the Rapture will receive transformed resurrected bodies; then the believers in Christ will appear before Him at the Judgment Seat of Christ "that each one may receive the things done in the body, according to what he has done, whether good or bad" (2 Corinthians 5:10). In the next few chapters the timing of the Rapture, the Great Tribulation, and the nature of our Resurrected Body will be explored in greater detail.

The Early Church Teaches the Pre-Tribulation Rapture

A previously unknown A.D. 373 manuscript by Ephraem on the Pre-Tribulation Rapture

Many of those who hate the doctrine of the Pre-Tribulation Rapture have dogmatically asserted that this doctrine was never taught before A.D. 1830. Obviously, the truth or error of the Pre-Tribulation Rapture can only be determined by an appeal to the authority of Scripture. However, the enemies of the Pre-Tribulation Rapture have confused many Christians with their false assertion that "the Rapture can't be true because no one ever taught this doctrine in the first 1800 years of the Church." As an example, George E. Ladd wrote in his book *The Blessed Hope*, "We can find no trace of pretribulationism in the early church; and no modern pretribulationist has successfully proved that this particular doctrine was held by any of the church fathers or students of the Word before the nineteenth century." Dave MacPherson claimed in his book *The Incredible Cover-Up*, that no one ever taught the Pre-Tribulation Rapture until a woman named Margaret Macdonald proclaimed it during a trance vision in A.D. 1830. He claimed that this was the origin of the theory of the Rapture as widely taught by John Darby and the Plymouth Brethren. However, this argument is false! John Darby claimed that he derived this doctrine from the clear teaching of the New Testament and no one has ever proven his statement to be false. But more importantly, my research has proven that the doctrine of the Pre-Tribulation Rapture as derived from the Scriptures was taught by a number of people in the centuries before 1830. In my book *Final Warning*, I prove that numerous Bible scholars saw this doctrine in the New Testament passages and wrote about it in their commentaries including Peter Jurieu (1697), Dr. John Gill (1748) and James MacKnight (1763). Most significantly, new evidence proves that the Pre-Tribulation Rapture was taught by a prominent theologian in the early days of the Church over sixteen centuries ago.

After ten years of careful searching, I discovered a fascinating manuscript that proves that the doctrine of the Pre-Tribulation Rapture was taught in the early church. Ephraem the Syrian (A.D. 306 to 373) was a major theologian of the early Church living in Asia (Turkey). His hymns are still used in the liturgy of the Eastern Church and appear in the *Post-Nicene Library* (a collection of writings after the A.D. 325 Council of Nicea) but most of his commentaries were never translated from the original Latin. Ephraem's fascinating teaching on the Rapture was never published before in English until I quoted it in my book *Final Warning*. This important manuscript reveals that he taught a literal principle of biblical interpretation and he believed in the Pre-Millennial return of Christ. However, Ephraem's most important statement clearly describes the Pre-Tribulational return of Christ to take His Elect saints to Heaven to escape the coming tribulation. In addition, Ephraem describes a Jewish Antichrist who will rule a revived Roman Empire and a literal great tribulation of 1,260 days with a rebuilt Temple and the Two Witnesses. Ephraem's text was called *On the Last Times, the Antichrist, and the End of the World*. Ephraem's ten section manuscript described the last days in chronological sequence beginning with the Rapture, the seven-year tribulation, the three-and-a-half-year Great Tribulation as the last part of the seven-year tribulation period and the tyranny of the Antichrist followed by Christ's return at Armageddon. Significantly, in Section 2, Ephraem wrote about the Rapture as an "imminent" event that will occur without warning. *"We ought to understand thoroughly therefore, my brothers what is imminent or overhanging"*

Ephraem then described the Pre-Tribulation Rapture as follows: *"For all saints and the Elect of the Lord are gathered together before the tribulation which is about to come and are taken to the Lord in order that they may not see at any time the confusion which overwhelm the world because of our sins."* Ephraem reminded his Christian readers that we need not fear the coming tribulation, *"we neither become very much afraid of the report nor of the appearance . . ."* because the Rapture will occur prior to the tribulation that is coming. Further, Ephraem calls on Christians to *"prepare ourselves for the meeting of the Lord Christ, so that He may draw us from the confusion, which overwhelms the world."*

Ephraem described the "great tribulation" as lasting "three and a half years," precisely "1,260 days." He summarized: *"there will be a great tribulation, as there has not been since people began to be upon the earth."* In Section 10 he wrote: *"And when the three and a half years have been completed, the time of the Antichrist, through which he will have seduced the world, after the resurrection of the two prophets . . . will come the sign of the Son of Man, and coming forward the Lord shall appear with great power and much majesty."* In another of his manuscripts, *The Book of the Cave of Treasures*, Ephraem revealed that the whole tribulation period encompassed "that sore affliction" lasting "one week" of seven years. He wrote that the 69th week of Daniel 9:24-27 ended with the crucifixion of Jesus. Although there are curious elements in Ephraem's manuscript, he clearly taught that the 70th week of Daniel's 70 Weeks will be fulfilled in the final seven years of this age. *"At the end of the world and at the final consummation. . . . After one week of that sore affliction* (Tribulation), *they will all be destroyed in the plain of Joppa. . . . Then will the son of perdition appear, of the seed and of the tribe of Dan."*

This discovery of the 1600-year-old Ephraem manuscript reveals that the doctrine of the blessed hope and deliverance of the saints was clearly held by some of the faithful at the beginning of the Church age. The full text of this vital manuscript from the early Church can be read in my book *Final Warning*. The promise of God remains our hope today. "For the Lord himself shall descend from heaven with a shout, with the voice of the archangel, and with the trump of God: and the dead in Christ shall rise first: Then we which are alive and remain shall be caught up together with them in the clouds, to meet the Lord in the air: and so shall we ever be with the Lord. Wherefore comfort one another with these words." (1 Thessalonians 4:16-18).

CHAPTER 4

The Resurrected Body

"Behold, I tell you a mystery; We shall not all sleep, but we shall all be changed—in a moment, in the twinkling of an eye, at the last trumpet. For the trumpet will sound, and the dead will be raised incorruptible, and we shall be changed. For this corruptible must put on incorruption, and this mortal must put on immortality." (1 Corinthians 15:51-53).

The Bible clearly tells us that once we have gained Heaven, we will have a spiritual but "real" body, like the body Christ displayed to His disciples after His resurrection. This spiritual body will have the recognizable human characteristics of identification which we have in our present "earthly" body. Our present bodies are "corruptible" but we are promised a new body which is "incorruptible." It will not be subject to death, disease or decay. Our present mortal body will be transformed into an immortal spiritual body which will never die. For two thousand years Christians have confidently expected that they would see their departed loved ones in Heaven.

In the Book of Revelation, John sees "a great number that no man could number" surrounding the throne of God in Heaven who "came out of the great tribulation." He immediately identifies them as resurrected men and knows that they are not angels. This shows that these future saints have the distinct appearance of men, not angels or nebulous spirits. Our very nature as men and women demands a personal spiritual and physical identity which transcends the finite limits of this short life on Earth.

"But someone will say, 'How are the dead raised up? And with what body do they come?' " (1 Corinthians 15:35).

"There is a natural body, and there is a spiritual body. And so it is written, 'The first man Adam became a living being.' The last Adam became a life-giving spirit. . . . The first man is of the Earth, made of dust; the second Man is the Lord from Heaven" (1 Corinthians 15:44-47).

The Lord contrasts the natural and spiritual bodies. The natural body is the normal human one which Adam and all men have. The spiritual body is our future resurrected one which will be identical to the body which Jesus Christ displayed following His resurrection.

The Bible tells us that we are individual human beings, now and forever. We shall stand in the last day as individuals to meet Jesus Christ, our Creator, as either our Judge or our Savior. Our new spiritual bodies will be transformed and made glorious by Christ in the Rapture. They will still retain in their nature the unique imprint which our Creator has endowed for each one of us. Scientists now tell us that even our fingerprints and eye retina patterns are so unique that they will serve in a court of law as absolute identification factors. We are each created as unique individuals right down to the last cell of our fingernails. Our individual DNA cellular structure is uniquely different from the other six billion people alive today. The same awesome, intelligent God who designed our natural body with such particular care for diversity and identity has also designed a heavenly body for us to live in foreveL When our bodies are transformed at the glorious rapture and made fit for the New Jerusalem, we will arise as unique individuals, not as some small indistinguishable drop in some vast pool of spiritual consciousness.

We Will Not be Angels

When many people think about life in Heaven they see themselves in a white robe, with wings, sitting on a fluffy cloud playing a harp, as they imagine angels do. However, when we get to Heaven we will not be angels. We will talk about angels in another chapter; they are a distinct creation. Both Psalm 8:5 and Hebrews 2:7 show that man is "a little lower than the angels," a unique creation. Jesus remarked that those who rise from the dead will be "like angels in Heaven" (Mark 12:25), but He wasn't saying we are identical to angels. The context of the passage shows that He was speaking of the fact that death, Leverite marriage and laws of inheritance would not affect men or angels in Heaven. This is discussed in detail in the chapter on Angels. The fact that we will not be angels in Heaven is emphasized in 1 Corinthians 6:3 where we are told that "we shall judge angels" after the Millennium. John, in the Book of Revelation, saw "a great multitude which no one could number, of all nations, tribes, peoples, and tongues, standing before the throne" that had "come out of the great tribulation." John recognized them as resurrected human beings, not angels.

If we will not be angels, what will our resurrected bodies be like? Will we know one another? Will we get hungry, cold, lonely? Will we feel? Do we have to do without food? Will love continue in Heaven? Will we remember things that happened on Earth?

We Will Have Bodies like Christ's Resurrected Body

"For our citizenship is in Heaven, from which we also eagerly wait for the Savior, the Lord Jesus Christ, who will transform our lowly body that it may be conformed to . . . the working by which He is able even to subdue all things to Himself" (Philippians 3:20,21).

The clearest indication we have of our future body was shown in the resurrection of Jesus Christ. He appeared to His disciples and His followers on many occasions during the forty days after He rose from the grave. He specifically promised us that, in the resurrection, our body would be like His body. He knew the tendency of humans to assume the life after death would be some eerie ghost-like existence. He taught us the reality of our future heavenly body.

"Jesus Himself stood in the midst of them, and said to them, 'Peace to you.' But they were terrified and frightened, and supposed they had seen a spirit. And He said to them, 'Why are you troubled? And why do doubts arise in your hearts? Behold My hands and My feet, that it is I Myself. Handle me and see, for a spirit does not have flesh and bones as you see I have.' . . . He said to them, 'Have you any food here?' So they gave Him a piece of a broiled fish and some honeycomb. And He took it and ate it in their presence" (Luke 24:36-43).

On the first day of the week when Jesus rose from the dead and appeared to His disciples His resurrected body was similar to, yet different from, His mortal body before His death on the cross. His body was tangible, you could touch it. He invited Thomas to put his finger on the scars in His hands, and his hand on the scar on His side. His hands and feet were still scarred from the cross. Jesus showed that He still had "flesh and bones" (Luke 24:39). Some have concluded from this verse that Christ taught that He did not have any blood in His resurrected body. However, the verse simply describes His reality as "flesh and bones"; it does not state He had no blood. He ate and drank showing that He still experienced sensations including taste. Yet there was an indefinable quality about Christ's resurrected appearance which caused Mary and His disciples to initially fail to recognize Him. After being with Him for a little while, He was recognized by those who had known Him. Mary did not know Him when He first appeared to her outside the tomb. Neither did the two believers on the road to Emmaus. This could partly be because they had not really expected that He would rise from the dead. But recognition came to them when He did or said something characteristic of Him.

His body was and is incorruptible. It will never again experience pain; it will never wear out, decay, or die. Yet He declared that His body had "flesh and bone." Therefore, since our body will be like His, we shall have a body with flesh and bone. As His body still had the appearance of a man, we too will have the appearance we had on Earth, either male or female. That is, we shall have a real, though spiritual body which occupies time and space. However, space and matter did not hinder Him. He walked through closed doors and disappeared from one place only to reappear in another. In Heaven we too will have this supernatural control over matter.

Once we gain Heaven we will have a spiritual body such as Jesus Christ had after His resurrection. "For our citizenship is in Heaven, from which we also eagerly wait for the Savior, the Lord Jesus Christ, who will transform our lowly body that it may be conformed to His glorious body, according to the working by which He is able even to subdue all things to Himself" (Philippians 3:20,21).

We Will be Recognizable to our Family and Friends

Although our bodies will be transformed, we will still retain our human characteristics that will make us recognizable to those who have known us on Earth. We will also be recognized by that great "cloud of witnesses," those who never knew us on Earth. The disciples recognized Elijah and Moses on the Mount of Transfiguration although they had never met them. Jesus said that the rich man recognized Abraham and the beggar, in Hades. Our recognizable personalities and physical uniqueness will transcend the finite limits of this short life on Earth.

There may be some choice in our appearance. Those who die after eighty or ninety years of life may choose to have a new body issued to them in the appearance of a mature adult. A child who dies at the age of three may choose a more mature body in Heaven. Some may choose to have their body express the same physical appearance as the day they died. Whatever the outward expression, our intellectual and spiritual nature in Heaven will be that of a mature saint having the complete faculties of an adult so that we may enjoy all that Christ has prepared for us. Our aged parents who may have lost much of their physical vigor in their last years will meet us in Heaven with a rejuvenated and spiritual body, now able to enjoy everything which can be experienced there. When a parent arrives in Heaven, their child who died so suddenly in the springtime of life, may then wear the outward clothing of a mature form. Yet that spiritual essence of unique personality which manifests itself to a mother even in the first days of her baby's life will, I believe, enable a parent to recognize their departed child who now awaits them in Heaven.

What a glorious prospect! On that wonderful future day in which believers will rise to meet Christ in the air, our joy will be multiplied by the greatest family reunion in history. All the tears we have shed for departed believers will be wiped away in one moment of indescribable, pure joy when we shall find our loved ones again. How exciting it will be to see and recognize Abraham, Moses, David, Esther, Peter, and other believers who have gone to Heaven before us.

We Will Still Have our Emotions and Feelings

Jesus ate with His followers after His resurrection. We do not know if He felt the pangs of hunger, or if He just felt like eating with His friends. We will be able to enjoy food and drink just as Christ did. The Bible describes the great feast in Heaven at the Marriage Supper of the Lamb. We will still feel the same love for our parents, spouses, children and friends. God gave us our emotions. We will still have a rich emotional life described in the Bible as joy, peace, love and thanksgiving.

We will no longer be subject to physical death, disease or decay, nor will we ever suffer pain. We will have "perfect" bodies. Jesus still retained His glorious scars. Martyrs may choose to still bear the visible evidence of their suffering as a badge of honor. Jesus will resurrect the bodies of those who have been burned to ashes, devoured by wild animals and turned to dust in the grave. He will restore all that we have lost. If we never had normal limbs, sight, hearing, intelligence in our earthly lives, the Creator will recreate our resurrected bodies in total perfection there.

If we were married on Earth, there is no reason to assume this special spiritual relationship and love will end in Heaven. God gave Adam and Eve the gift of marriage before the Fall. The Lord uses the image of marriage to symbolize the eternal relationship of Christ to both Israel and His Church. In the beautiful Song of Songs, written by King Solomon, the Bible compared his beautiful married love which he expressed for his new bride, the Queen of Sheba, with the wonderful love God has for His chosen Bride, the Church.

The Scriptures do not indicate that Christians will have new children in Heaven; therefore, theologians conclude that resurrected Christians will not experience married physical love relationships. The Church, the Bride of Christ, will be complete in its final number when the Rapture occurs. Since none of the Church will die after the Resurrection there will be no need for reproduction in Heaven. However, the spiritual essence of a pure, holy love must find its highest expression in an eternal cherishing of our loved ones. "For now we see in a mirror, dimly, but then face to face. Now I know in part, but then I shall know just as I also am known. And now abide faith, hope, love, these three; but the greatest of these is love" (1 Corinthians 13:12,13). In Heaven we shall experience far greater joy, knowledge and relationships in the presence of the Lamb than we have ever known on Earth.

We Will Have Greater Knowledge and Awareness

Some Christians express fear that once they are in Heaven they will not be able to enjoy the activities they enjoy on Earth. They are afraid they will lose all knowledge and awareness of earthly relationships and interests. Why should we? Heaven is a place we will enjoy. World travel will be unlimited. Our creative talents will flourish and we will be able to study the vast knowledge which will be available about the universe.

We will be able to satisfy our curiosity about creation, history, science, and we will finally understand why certain things happened in history as they did. Just as we can see far more from a mountain peak or a plane than we can from a valley; we will have greater vision and awareness when we are not limited by physical barriers or lack of knowledge. Scientists believe that even a genius like Einstein utilized only 10 percent of his mental potential. In Heaven we shall use all the faculties and gifts which our Creator has given to us.

Not only will our interests continue, they will be intensified when we can see the interrelated events in the world and witness how the sovereign hand of God continually moves in the lives of individuals and nations. From the vantage point of eternity we will understand clearly the reality of Christ's words when He said, "We do not wrestle against flesh and blood, but against principalities, against powers, against the rulers of the darkness of this age, against spiritual hosts of wickedness in the heavenly places" (Ephesians 6:12).

We will be aware of these things even before we receive our resurrected bodies if we are among "those who have fallen asleep" and go to be with Jesus before the Resurrection. The members of the Church who are now in Heaven are already witnessing what happens down here on Earth. They are looking at events from the perspective of eternity; they are not limited only to what we can see here and now. That is why there are no tears in Heaven, why there is no worry or pain, because the saints in Heaven can see and understand God's sovereign will and purpose. This "cloud of witnesses" spoken of in Hebrews 12 are aware of those still left on Earth who are struggling against principalities, powers and rulers of darkness.

Heaven will not cause a diminishment of our knowledge and interests, rather we will find these things are expanded and increased.

In Heaven Our Personalities and Character Will Continue

Every day of our lives we are building the house of character and the essence of the final person we shall be for eternity. With every decision we make, every step we take, we form the identity we will live with forever. While character can be easily influenced in the very young, once a character has formed, by the age of thirty or forty, it is usually set for life — except for the transformation that happens when we are spiritually reborn. The Bible tells us that salvation through Christ frees us from captivity to sin and from being what we do not want to be. Yet, we still have to choose to change. Each act we perform, each thought we allow to linger in our minds, adds another brick to the house of character we shall live with throughout eternity. Within your house of character is room for only two: yourself and one other. That companion will be your greatest friend, Jesus, or the worst enemy of your soul, Satan. We can change jobs, houses, friends, countries but we never lose the two persons within our character. If we choose Christ as our companion, we will still have to contend with old nature which struggles to reassert itself. Jesus promises that He will strengthen us in this process of transformation called sanctification through His Holy Spirit.

Many assume once we enter Heaven we will automatically become a bland, neutral saint without distinctive features. Not so! In eternity we shall manifest the perfected form of the character we are building today. Christ will remove the sin in our lives, but we will still have those characteristics which make us unique as individuals. This diversity of personality will provide one of the great joys of our future life. That is probably one way we will be recognized by others.

One example of this is seen in the character of Elijah. All his life he fought against evil and idolatry. The prophet

Malachi identifies Elijah as one of two witnesses who will appear to fight against the Antichrist and his army during the Tribulation before Christ returns at the Battle of Armageddon (see Malachi 4:5). The resurrected Elijah will manifest the same character he did when he was fighting against King Ahab, Queen Jezebel, and the prophets of Baal.

Do you like the character you are building for eternity? In our Christian life, our daily devotions, prayers, worship and fellowship with other Christians prepare us to be citizens of the heavenly city. The Bible has many suggestions on how you can build a better character so that you will like the person you will live with throughout all eternity. "Put on tender mercies, kindness, humility, meekness, long-suffering; bearing with one another, and forgiving one another. . . . But above all these things put on love . . . and let the peace of God rule in your hearts, to which also you were called in one body; and be thankful. Let the word of Christ dwell in you richly in all wisdom, teaching and admonishing one another in psalms and hymns and spiritual songs, singing with grace in your hearts to the Lord. And whatever you do in word or deed, do all in the name of the Lord Jesus, giving thanks to God the Father through Him" (Colossians 3:12-17).

Unfortunately, if your choice of a companion is Satan, he also will be with you throughout eternity. If you choose to continue to rebel against God and reject the salvation that is provided through Jesus Christ, you will remain rebellious and sinful in Hell. Once you die, there is no hope for you to change your decision, your character or your situation. You will live for uncountable trillions of years in the same prison you lived in during your lifetime—with the devil as your cell mate. You will have plenty of company—every evil tyrant, dictator and torturer in history will be there. They will also be the same in Hell as they were on Earth. Even earthly prisoners suffer at the hands of fellow prisoners. How much worse will it be in Hell where you continue to feel pain and terror but will never experience the escape of death?

We should remember that it was the terrible truth about the reality of Hell that motivated Jesus Christ to volunteer to die on the Cross to save all men—all who would accept His pardon—from the horrors of an eternity in Hell. In the most incredible display of love ever known, He endured the punishment of Hell for you and me so that we might escape eternal separation from God. "But God demonstrates His own love toward us, in that while we were still sinners, Christ died for us. Much more then, having now been justified by His blood, we shall be saved from wrath through Him. For if when we were enemies we were reconciled to God through the death of His Son, much more, having been reconciled, we shall be saved by His life" (Romans 5:8-10).

CHAPTER 5

The Great Tribulation

When will the Great Tribulation happen? Does the Bible give a definite time when we can expect this terrible event so that we can prepare for it? As you probably know, this is an area where sincere, godly scholars differ. But it is supremely important—if we are the generation that will experience these end-time events—that we understand God's unfolding plan.

The Holy Spirit inspired biblical writers to write the things that God knew were essential for our spiritual health. Therefore, we must do as the Bereans did with Paul and Silas: "They received the word with all readiness, and searched the Scriptures daily to find out whether these things were so" (Acts 17:11).

Although the Bible talks about the Great Tribulation, many people would rather not discuss it. But we know that "the last days" are approaching, and part of that end-time is the Great Tribulation. We therefore should search the Scriptures to see what they reveal to us about this terrible period. Only those who understand the prophecies will be able to fulfill Paul's command to the Church, "Comfort one another with these words" about Christ's Second Coming (1 Thessalonians 4:18). How can we "comfort one another" if we have the Great Tribulation to look forward to?

After twenty-five years of biblical research on prophecy and history I have concluded that the burden of evidence clearly shows that the Rapture will precede the time known in the Bible as the Great Tribulation. Therefore, I am among those Pre-Tribulationists who believe that (1) we are now living in the end times and (2) the Church will be raptured before the time of the Great Tribulation. Now that I have made that statement, let me tell you why I believe as I do. It is not a conclusion lightly arrived at or one which comes merely out of wishful thinking that I would escape this coming persecution. To the reader who is interested in seeking an indepth discussion of all the scriptural passages which bear on these issues, I refer you to the excellent book *Things to Come* by Dr. J. Dwight Pentecost.

The Church Will Not Endure the Great Tribulation

Before I give you reasons I believe the Bible teaches that the Church will not endure the Great Tribulation, I need to explain that Christians have been and always will be persecuted until Jesus comes. Christ did not promise the Church that we would never be persecuted or in tribulation. First-century believers were persecuted before they ever got out of Jerusalem! Just read the Book of Acts. From the time Jesus began His ministry until today, the Church has been in tribulation somewhere in the world. We all know that millions of believers behind the iron and bamboo curtains have given their lives because of their faith in Christ. But this is not the Great Tribulation.

This failure to differentiate between the specific period called the "Great Tribulation" and the many tribulations and persecutions the Church has suffered has led to two opposite errors in belief. First, many Christians who believe in the biblical promise of the Rapture are totally unprepared for any persecution they might undergo because of their faith, even here in North America. Second, many Christians, realizing that the Church was warned that we will have tribulations, have confused this fact with the specific prophetic period of the wrath of God known as the Great Tribulation. They therefore reject the many scriptural promises about the Rapture because it conflicts with what they believe about reality of persecution for the Church.

If you ask the question: "Is the Church promised escape from tribulation and persecution?" the answer is clearly NO!

However, if you ask, "Is the Church promised escape from the wrath of God which will be poured out on all mankind during the period of 'the great tribulation' [Christ's words, not mine]?" then the answer is YES!

There is another factor to keep in mind about whether the Church must experience the Tribulation. The vast majority of the Church have already died and their spirits are now in Heaven with Christ, awaiting their resurrected bodies at the Rapture. They have obviously escaped the Great Tribulation, although many underwent tremendous persecutions in their lives as Christians. They are part of the "Church, without spot or wrinkle" without enduring the Great Tribulation under the Antichrist. We are purified by the blood of Christ; not by the Great Tribulation. Let us search the Scriptures, as the Bereans did, and see why the Church will not endure the Great Tribulation.

The Church Will Not be Subject to the Wrath of God

The time of the Great Tribulation is described as "the great day of His [God's] wrath" (see Revelation 6:17). It involves the judgment of God upon a sinful world for a defined period of three and one-half years (1,260 days). God promises in His Word that the Church will not be subject to the wrath of God. The penalty for our sin has been paid by the blood of Jesus Christ on the Cross. Paul tells us that we are "to wait for His Son from Heaven whom He raised from the dead, even Jesus who delivers us from the wrath to come" (1 Thessalonians 1:10).

Paul continues by informing the Church that God has set two opposite appointments with destiny for two different groups of people: unbelievers and believers. Of the unbelievers he says: "When they say, 'Peace and safety!' then sudden destruction comes upon them, as labor pains upon a pregnant woman. And they shall not escape." But to the believers, Paul says: "But you, brethren, are not in darkness, so that this Day should overtake you as a thief. You are all sons of light and sons of the day. . . . For God did not appoint us to wrath, but to obtain salvation through our Lord Jesus Christ, who died for us, that whether we wake or sleep, we should live together with Him. Therefore comfort each other and edify one another, just as you also are doing" (1 Thessalonians 5:3-5,9-11).

Mankind has an appointment to meet Christ in judgment at the Battle of Armageddon. But those who trust in Jesus are promised that they have an appointment to salvation—to meet Christ as their Savior in the air at the Rapture. Although God, in His mercy, sometimes chastens his children, He reserves His wrath for those who remain rebels to Christ.

If we examine the lives of Enoch, Methuselah, Noah, and Lot at Sodom, the pattern of God's judgment throughout human history is unchanging. First, the prophet warns of the coming doom. Next the righteous believers are removed by God from danger. Then, the prophesied judgment falls upon those who continue in their sin without repenting. Jesus told His disciples that the time of the end would be "as it was in the days of Noah" (Luke 17:26) and that they were to remember the lesson of Lot's wife (v. 32). God protected Noah and his family by sealing them in the Ark before the judgment. The angels warned Lot that, despite the terrible sin of Sodom, God would not destroy the city until Lot and his family were safely away. There is no example in the Bible when God allowed the righteous to be destroyed by His judgment of the unrighteous.

As one more example, one day when Jesus and His disciples were on the Temple Mount in Jerusalem, someone commented on the beauty of the Temple buildings. Jesus then prophesied that "when you see Jerusalem surrounded by armies, then know that its desolation is near. Then let those who are in Judea flee to the mountains, let those who are in the midst of her depart" (Luke 21:20,21). At first glance this advice seemed impractical. It was as though He had said, "When you are surrounded flee to the hills." How can you flee if your city is surrounded by enemy soldiers?

Jerusalem was under the rule of the Roman Empire. Just a few years later (in A.D. 66), the Jews did attempt to rebel from Rome. The battle lasted for four years. At one point the Roman General Vespasian ordered his son, General Titus, to withdraw his armies from Jerusalem. He was to hold them ready, if needed, to bring them back to Rome to support his father's claim as emperor following the death of Nero. During this withdrawal, all the Christians in Jerusalem fled to the city of Petra and other places. When the siege was resumed, and the city fell, the entire population of Jerusalem that remained in the city was either killed or sold into slavery. The Romans recaptured most of Palestine, Jerusalem fell, and Herod's Temple was burned to the ground (A.D. 70). But those Christians who heeded Jesus' prophetic words were saved.

In keeping with this established pattern of God's judgment and deliverance, it is consistent to believe that the Church will be removed to safety before this pouring out of the wrath of God upon the Earth.

The Prophecies About the Great Tribulation do not Focus on the Church

The Bible describes the judgment of the Great Tribulation on Israel and Gentile nations, not on the Church. In the unfolding pattern of God's dealings with mankind, the existence of the Church, the Bride of Christ, was hidden as a "mystery" which was not revealed to the disciples until after Israel rejected her Messiah. Only then did Christ call out "a people to His name" (Acts 15:14) from the Gentiles. Earlier He had told His disciples, "Do not go into the way of the Gentiles, and do not enter a city of the Samaritans. But go rather to the lost sheep of the house of Israel" (Matthew 10:5). When Jesus was talking about the timing of the end of the age, He was talking to His Jewish disciples about the events leading to the Second Coming of their Messiah to Israel, (see Matthew 24), During the time of these conversations, the Church did not yet exist. The birth of the Church did not occur until after Israel rejected the Messiah and Christ was raised from the dead. Then, fifty days after Christ arose, the Holy Spirit endowed the Church with power, and the mystery of the Church began to unfold.

Twenty years later, the Apostles, under the inspiration of the Holy Spirit, began to write down the great truths of God's plan to turn to the Gentiles—including the Jewish remnant who would accept Christ—and make of them a "chosen generation, a royal priesthood, a holy nation, His own special people" (1 Peter 2:9) who were to become the Bride of Christ.

Those who teach that the Church will be present during this terrible time neglect to distinguish between God's plan for Israel, which this passage in Matthew 24 talks about, and God's plan for the Church, which would not be revealed until Pentecost. Although these teachers acknowledge the many strong promises in the Bible of a Pre-Tribulation Rapture, they inevitably come back to their interpretation of Matthew 24, which, in their minds, overrides the other Scripture passages.

In the conversation recorded in Matthew 24, Christ explained to His Jewish disciples on the Mount of Olives about those events which will occur in Israel and other nations that will lead up the return of Christ as the acknowledged Messiah of the Jews. He was not talking about the Church, because the Church was not yet revealed. We cannot arbitrarily insert the Church into the passages about Israel's future Tribulation. The disciples' question involves the coming of Israel's long-promised Messiah—in this case, the Second Coming, since the people as a nation have not yet acknowledged Jesus as their Messiah. Read this passage in this light and you will see more clearly what Jesus was telling His Jewish followers.

We find that Israel is the primary subject in this prophecy in Matthew 24. At verse 15, Jesus says that the future Antichrist will set up the "abomination of desolation" (a miraculous statue of the Antichrist) to be worshiped in the rebuilt Temple in Jerusalem. After describing the events of the Tribulation and the Battle of Armageddon, then in verses 40 and 41, Jesus says: "Then two men will be in the field: one will be taken and the other left. Two women will be grinding at the mill: one will be taken and the other left." This occurs at the end of the Great Tribulation. God will send His angels and "they will gather together His elect from the four winds, from one end of Heaven to the other" (v. 31). Is this "gathering" the Rapture?

Who are these "elect" ones? When you examine the context of the passage you will see that they are the Jews and Gentiles who will become believers during the Great Tribulation of three and one-half years. This "gathering together" is not the Rapture, though it has several similarities. This gathering of tribulation believers happens after the Great Tribulation, whereas the Rapture of the Church must happen sometime before the beginning of the Great Tribulation and before Antichrist reveals himself in the Temple as "god." Notice the difference in these two events: in the Rapture of the Church, "The Lord Himself will descend from Heaven with a shout, with the voice of an archangel, and with the trumpet of God. And the dead in Christ will rise first" (1 Thessalonians 4:17): In the second gathering the angels "will gather together His elect" (Matthew 24:31) before the Battle of Armageddon.

The Rapture includes the resurrection of the dead in Christ first, then those who are living. There is no mention of the dead being raised when this second gathering of Matthew 24 happens. In the Rapture we instantly rise to meet Christ in the air; in the second gathering—ending the Tribulation—the angels will gather the elect Jewish and Gentile believers from the four corners of the Earth. This second gathering which involves the elect Tribulation saints will happen at the conclusion of three and one-half years of the most detailed prophetic events ever predicted. Therefore, this gathering of the elect Tribulation saints cannot happen imminently or immediately. The Bible describes many Tribulation events which must happen before the gathering of the Tribulation saints; therefore this second gathering cannot be described as "imminent."

As I described in my book *Armageddon – Appointment With Destiny*, there are many indications about the approximate time of the Battle of Armageddon, but the coming of Christ for His Church has no warnings, no signals. The Rapture can happen at any time. It has always been imminent. The Church was told to be watchful for the imminent coming of our Lord.

The Tribulation Chapters of Revelation 4 to 19 do not Mention the Church

The first three chapters in the Book of Revelation are filled with instructions to the seven churches of Asia Minor. The messages while directed at specific historical churches, also contain a message which applies spiritually to all churches for the next two thousand years. However, when we examine the detailed prophecies of the Great Tribulation in chapters 4 through 19 we find that the Church is not mentioned once as being on Earth during this time of Tribulation. In these chapters the Bible describes the Church participating in the Marriage Supper of the Lamb in a joyous reunion in Heaven with Christ and with all those who died in the faith in earlier generations. In fact, before describing the terrible judgments which God says will be poured out upon the Earth, John says that a voice called out, " 'Come up here, and I will show you things which must take place after this.' Immediately I was in the Spirit; and behold, a throne set in Heaven, and One sat on the throne. . . . Around the throne were twenty-four thrones, and on the thrones I saw twenty-four elders sitting, clothed in white robes; and they had crowns of gold on their heads" (Revelation 4:1,2,4).

The first thing John saw in Heaven was the throne of God surrounded by twenty-four elders with golden crowns. These elders represent both Israel and the Church. Their crowns show that they have participated in the Bema Judgment in which Christ grants crowns to believers as rewards for soul-winning, martyrdom and for "all those who love His appearing," (see chapter 13, The Judgments).

These crowns are not granted on the day believers die, but are reserved until the Bema Judgment when "we shall all stand before the Judgment Seat of Christ. . . . So then each of us shall give account of himself to God" (Romans 14:10,12). Again, in his Epistle to Timothy, Paul confirms that these crowns will not be granted until the Rapture, when all believers stand before Christ: "Finally, there is laid up for me the crown of righteousness, which the Lord, the righteous Judge, will give to me on that Day, and not to me only but also to all who have loved His appearing" (2 Timothy 4:8).

John, in describing the twenty-four elders with their crowns, is witnessing events in Heaven that follow the Rapture and the Judgment Seat of Christ when such crowns are distributed. After he finishes this description of the raptured saints, John then describes the visions of the beginning of the Great Tribulation on Earth with the Four Horsemen of the Apocalypse.

Those who believe in a Post-Tribulation Rapture, have a problem in explaining the timing of this event in connection with other events which the Bible describes. They are forced to imagine a scenario in which living and dead Christians rise to meet Christ in the air and immediately, "in the twinkling of an eye" return with Christ at Armageddon. During this "twinkling" these people must participate in an instantaneous Judgment Seat of Christ and Marriage Supper of the Lamb in Heaven. They then do an about-face and return to Earth with Christ in a victorious army at the Battle of Armageddon. All this must happen in a fraction of a second known as the "twinkling of an eye."

The Bible does not seem to indicate that the Judgment Seat of Christ and the Marriage Supper of the Lamb happen instantly. The Church will be taken to Heaven in their resurrected bodies to stand before the Judgment Seat of Christ and receive their rewards. After participating in the glorious Marriage Supper of the Lamb, the Church will enjoy Heaven until we join the heavenly army of Christ at Armageddon. After that battle the Church will live with Christ in the New Jerusalem in Heaven until that time when the New Jerusalem descends to a New Earth after the Millennium. Although we will rule the Earth with Christ; our permanent home will be the New Jerusalem.

Israel is Preparing to Rebuild the Third Temple

Israel's growing interest in rebuilding the Temple in Jerusalem is an exciting indication that we are living in the last days. The Book of Revelation declares that before the Tribulation, before the return of the Messiah, the Temple will be rebuilt on the Temple Mount.

In a store in Hebron sits a box on a counter with a sign requesting donations for the Temple rebuilding fund. On the side of the box is an artist's picture of the rebuilt Temple on the Temple Mount. While I was writing this chapter, a news bulletin announced that members of the Faithful of the Temple in Israel had tried to bring a three-ton cornerstone up onto the Temple Mount. They did this to awaken interest within their fellow Israelis of the need to prepare for the rebuilding of the Temple and their coming Messiah.

Rabbis in synagogue services often refer to prophetic passages that tell about God sending "a son of David" in the last days to restore the crown of Israel and lead Israel into the "age of redemption." While visiting some shops in the Old City of Jerusalem I was surprised to see a poster depicting the Temple Mount. Superimposed on the photo was a picture of a model of the second Temple, which was burned in A.D. 70. Above this retouched photo was the title "Project 2001."

During the Six Day War of June, 1967, Israel reconquered the old city of Jerusalem and the Temple Mount. For the first time in almost two thousand years the Temple Mount was guarded by Jewish soldiers. Israeli troops stormed the area, even while Jordanian snipers continued to rain bullets on them. Paratroopers from the famous Fifth Brigade, with Chief Rabbi Goren ran to the Western Wall. As Rabbi Goren, with tears in his eyes, blew on the Shofar, the ram's horn, the soldiers touched the sacred stones of the Wailing Wall which had known the tears of more than seventy-five generations of Jews.

This was the holy place over which the great King Solomon, on the Feast of Tabernacles, the day the Temple was dedicated, had prayed: "Your servant is praying before You today: that Your eyes may be open toward this temple night and day, toward the place of which You said, 'My name shall be there.' That You may hear the prayer which Your servant makes toward this place. And may You hear the supplication of Your servant and of Your people Israel when they pray toward this place. Then hear in Heaven Your dwelling place; and when You hear, forgive" (1 Kings 8:29,30).

"Stones with Human Hearts"

The Lord had promised that His Divine Presence would dwell in a special way in the holy Temple. Even today, thousands of Jews from around the world come daily to this ancient wall to pray to the Lord and insert their written prayers in the cracks between the stones of the Western Wall. A former Chief Rabbi of Israel wrote of the sacred Western Wall: "There are men with hearts of stone and there are stones with human hearts." This wall became the "wall of tears" for the Jews of the Diaspora over the thousands of years of captivity after the destruction of the Temple.

The subject of the rebuilding of the Temple is the most sensitive religious and political problem in Israel today. Many Orthodox Jews long to see the Temple rebuilt; but after all, the Moslem Dome of the Rock sits on the Temple site. If anything would start the great war, some say, it would be the tearing down of the Dome of the Rock to build a Jewish Temple. Yet the Temple will be built on the Temple Mount. David, as psalmist, explains why Israel cannot choose a less controversial site to rebuild its Temple: "Let us go into His tabernacle; let us worship at His footstool. Arise, O Lord, to Your resting place, You and the ark of Your strength. Let Your priests be clothed in righteousness, and let Your saints shout for joy. For Your servant David's sake, do not turn away the face of Your Anointed [Messiah]. The Lord has sworn in truth to David; He will not turn from it: 'I will set upon your throne the fruit of your body'. . . . For the Lord has chosen Zion; He has desired it for His dwelling place: 'This is My resting place forever; here I will dwell, for I have desired it' " (Psalm 132:7-11,13,14).

God has chosen Jerusalem and the Temple Mount as the precise location for His Temple. How will Israel fulfill the ancient prophecies? Some have speculated that Israel will transform the beautiful Great Synagogue, which is outside the Old City of Jerusalem, into the rebuilt Temple. But they ignore the direct words of the Bible regarding where the Temple must be placed. Israel must rebuild the Temple on the exact spot chosen by God and shown to King David and his son Solomon.

A fascinating passage in the Mishneh Torah by Rambam quotes Jewish Talmudic writings from the time before the burning of the Temple in A.D. 70. These eyewitness sources declare that the Temple was not built dead centre on the Temple Mount, the location now occupied by the Muslim Dome of the Rock. Rambam states that "the Temple Courtyard was not situated directly in the centre of the Temple Mount. Rather, it was set off farther from the southern [wall] of the Temple Mount than from [the wall of] any other direction." The reason is that worshipers usually entered and exited through the southern Hulda gates. They needed adequate room to congregate in that area. Rambam continued to quote sources that declare that the Temple itself was situated directly opposite the Eastern Gate in the northern part of the Temple Mount. These "five gates were placed in a straight line" from the Eastern Gate into the entrance hall of the Holy of Holies. These gates were "the

Eastern Gate [now sealed], the gate of the Chayl, the gate to the Women's Courtyard, the gate of Nicanor, and the gate of the entrance hall. Thus, had the Temple been built on flat ground, one would have been able to see through all the gates at once" (Mishneh Torah, Commentary Halachah 5 and 6).

The Levites in their Temple model in the Old City of Jerusalem show these five gates in a straight line in their detailed lucite model that clearly illustrates that the original Temple stood in the open area north of the Dome of the Rock. A person standing on the Mount of Olives can see directly above the sealed Eastern Gate a huge open area north of the Dome. A surveyor's laser beam through the center of the Eastern Gate would cut right through the center of the small Arab cupola known as the Dome of the Tablets. This small structure sits over an open area of the bedrock of Mount Moriah, described in Talmudic literature as the Even Shetiyeh, the Foundation Stone. Rambam, in chapter 4 of the Mishneh Torah volume on the Temple, states: "The Ark was placed on a stone in the western portion of the Holy of Holies." Halachah 1 records: "Yoma 53b refers to that stone as the foundation stone, and explains that it was given that name because it was the foundation upon which God fashioned the world."

As I discussed in my earlier book, *Armageddon – Appointment with Destiny*, recent archeological discoveries by Dr. Asher Kaufman, and these biblical and Talmudic documentary sources, have convinced many Jewish and evangelical scholars that King Solomon built the ancient Temple in the area north of the Dome of the Rock. In an article several years ago in the authoritative Biblical Archeological Review, Dr. Kaufman reported on his extensive research of the ruins of the Temple structures on the Temple Mount. Although several of these structures were removed by Muslim authorities who now control the Mount, photographs and eyewitnesses confirm this strong evidence for the location of the Temple in the northern area.

The Western Wall "Rabbinical Tunnel" excavation

During one of our trips to Israel, my wife, Kaye, and I entered a very secretive archeological dig known as the Western Wall Excavation. Since the Six Day War, Israeli archeologists have been digging a tunnel north from Wilson's Arch along the sacred Western Wall. While a few writers have been allowed into the entrance room, we were allowed to explore the complete 900 foot long tunnel complex for several hours with a group of Jewish scientists. We were led by an archeologist who has worked on the dig for many years. As we explored along those ancient walls we photographed the enormous Herodian foundation stones, each of which measures over 46 by 10 by 10 feet. Scientists estimate that the largest cut stone weighed over 458 tons. To put this in perspective, the largest stone in the Great Pyramid weighs only 20 tons. The accuracy of the stonemasons was such that I could not insert a slip of paper between these stones. There are no cranes in the world capable of moving such an enormous stone today.

Farther along the tunnel we came to an old painting of a Menorah, the Golden Candlestick, hanging on a spike upon the Western Wall. When I asked Ariel Barnea, the Israeli archeologist, why this valuable painting hung in a working archeological dig, he replied that they had calculated that the ancient Menorah in the Second Temple had once stood behind this portion of the wall. The painting reminded them of the sanctity of their work.

Several hundred feet along the tunnel we came to the underground Western Gate dating from the time of King Herod and Christ. Archeologists discovered this secret Herodian Gate following the Six Day War. It opened into a huge underground complex of passages underneath the entire Temple Mount. Before exploring this tunnel, they sought permission of the Chief Rabbi because of the special restrictions governing digs on the Temple Mount. Before the permission was granted, Muslim authorities learned of the discovery of this gate and a terrible riot broke out as Arab youths stormed into the long tunnel. To quell the riot and tension, Israeli authorities ordered this one tunnel sealed as shown in my photos. A table in front of the sealed entrance holds sacred Torah scrolls. Senior Israeli rabbis come here to pray at this holy place because it is the closest they can come to the ancient Holy of Holies until the Temple is rebuilt.

Ashes from the Burning of the Temple in A.D. 70

Ariel pointed to a dark spot on the Western Wall several yards away. "These are actual ashes from the burning of the Temple on the night of Av in A.D. 70." For twenty centuries these ashes have hung undisturbed in a large crack in the foundations of the Temple until their discovery several months ago. Hundreds of feet below the accumulated rubble of the ruins of the Temple the archeologists have uncovered a link with that tragic day when the beautiful Temple was burned by the Roman army two thousand years ago. I felt that in this sacred spot I could almost reach back and experience those awesome events that forever changed the course of human history.

The importance of this archeological research cannot be overestimated. If Israel can prove conclusively that the original Temples stood in this open area north of the Dome of the Rock, then it is conceivable that they could rebuild the Temple here without disturbing the Muslim Dome. The prophet John in his Revelation seems to prophesy about this when he states: "The angel stood, saying, 'Rise and measure the temple of God, the altar, and those who worship there. But leave out the court which is outside the temple, and do not measure it, for it has been given to the Gentiles. And they will tread the holy city under foot for forty-two months'" (Revelation 11:1,2). It is fascinating to see that "the court which is outside the temple" would correspond to the Court of the Gentiles of the ancient Temple. If this research on the Temple's location is correct, then the Dome of the Rock is in the Court of the Gentiles, exactly as described by the prophet John two thousand years ago.

The tremendous interest in Israel today about rebuilding the Temple gives ample proof that we are rapidly approaching the final days of this era. First the Temple must be rebuilt; then, the daily sacrifice must begin. Then, the Antichrist can enter the Holy of Holies. These preparations for the Temple show how close we are to the Rapture of the Church, the Great Tribulation and the coming of the Messiah.

CHAPTER 6

The New Jerusalem

The earthly city of Jerusalem has a special place in the heart of God. Beginning with the binding of Isaac by his father Abraham in "the land of Moriah" and continuing till Jesus as Messiah-King makes His entrance through the Eastern Gate, God has met with men on this sacred site. Yet, special as this place has been, the heavenly New Jerusalem surpasses the earthly Jerusalem as the sun surpasses the moon in glory. Even now, God is preparing the heavenly city to receive the saved of all generations. There we will live eternally.

The Apostle John tells us about the New Jerusalem. He was probably the only one of Jesus' original twelve to live to be an old man. According to Scripture and other church writings, ten were martyred because of their faith in Christ, and Judas committed suicide. John did not escape persecution however. He was one of the many whom the Roman Emperor Domitian exiled in an attempt to stop the growth of Christianity. John's place of banishment was Patmos, an island off the coast of Turkey.

There on the island prison of Patmos, John recorded the prophecies of the end-times which God revealed to him. The word "Revelation," also called the Apocalypse, means "to break through" or reveal. One part of this extraordinary vision of things to come was a description of the New Jerusalem: "And I saw a new Heaven and a new earth, for the first Heaven and the first earth had passed away. Also there was no more sea. Then I, John, saw the holy city, New Jerusalem, coming down out of Heaven from God, prepared as a bride adorned for her husband" (Revelation 21:1,2).

Heaven is the home of God and the great hosts of angels. The Bible does not reveal the exact location of Heaven. Many believe that it must exist in another dimension. However, the Scriptures always describe the location of Heaven as being "up" and "in the north." Some Christian astronomers believe that Heaven may exist in our dimension enormous light years away from the Earth in a northern direction. The city of New Jerusalem is located in Heaven now. After the Millennium the New Jerusalem will descend to the New Earth where it will take its place among many new cities on the New Earth; but it will not be like the other cities. It will be a very special place, the home of the Bride of Christ.

The New Heaven and the New Earth

The day will come when the New Jerusalem will descend from Heaven and be positioned somewhere on Earth. But before that can happen, both Heaven and the Earth must be purified of all sin's pollution, purified with fire. "Purify the Heavens?" you may ask. Yes, remember, a part of the Heavens is still open to Satan who stands before God to accuse us "day and night" (Revelation 12:10). Job's Accuser appeared before the throne of God to accuse him (see Job 1). After the Millennium this Accuser, Satan himself, will be "cast into the lake of fire and brimstone where the Beast and the False Prophet are. And they will be tormented day and night forever and ever" (Revelation 20:10). Sin will not exist in the eternal New Heaven and New Earth or the New Jerusalem.

Thousands of years ago, in the days of Noah, God cleansed the Earth by the purifying effects of water because "the earth also was corrupt before God, and the earth was filled with violence" (Genesis 6:11). He will cleanse the earth again after the Millennium, this time by divine fire because of the great sin of Satan's final rebellion. "The world that then existed perished, being flooded with water. But the heavens and the earth which are now preserved by the same word, are reserved for fire until the day of judgment and perdition of ungodly men . . . the heavens will pass away with a great noise, and the elements will melt with fervent heat; both the earth and the works that are in it will be burned up" (2 Peter 3:6,7,10). Then, the New Jerusalem will descend from Heaven to Earth.

The Heavenly City

This great city has the glory of God filling her with His divine Presence. This causes the whole city to glow with an internal light like a beautiful "jasper stone, clear as crystal" (Revelation 21:11).

It is a real city, having dimensions, gates, mansions, streets and inhabitants. John described this glorious city in the best language and terms he had available. John used the only language at his command to describe the wonderful city that God is preparing for His people. He said the city: "is laid out as a square, and its length is as great as its breadth. And he measured the city with the reed; twelve thousand furlongs. Its length, breadth, and height are equal. Then he measured its wall; one hundred and forty-four cubits, according to the measure of a man that is, of an angel" (Revelation 21:16,17). The size of the New Jerusalem is tremendous: 1,500 miles by 1,500 miles by 1,500 miles (12,000 furlongs). "Its wall: one hundred and forty-four cubits (216 feet). . . . And the construction of its wall was of jasper" (vv. 17,18).

Can you visualize such a city? There are two possible three-dimensional shapes that correspond to this description. One is a cube and the other is a pyramid shape. The pyramid shape is probable since the city wall, with twelve gates, is 216 feet high. It is hard to visualize a cube-shaped object of that size having a wall 216 feet high around it. However, a pyramid shaped city of that size could have a base 216 feet high with twelve gates through which the people would enter. Architects have calculated that the enormous size of the New Jerusalem would easily provide a mansion of over a half mile in length and breadth to every believer from Adam to the present.

Supporting the jasper wall are twelve layers of stone foundation; on each layer "were the names of the twelve apostles of the Lamb" (v. 14). The walls have "three gates on the east, three gates on the north, three gates on the south, and three gates on the west . . . each individual gate was of one pearl" (vv. 13,21). "The foundations of the wall of the city were adorned with all kinds of precious stones: the first foundation was jasper, the second sapphire, the third chalcedony, the fourth emerald, the fifth sardonyx, the sixth sardius, the seventh chrysolite, the eighth beryl, the ninth topaz, the tenth chrysoprase, the eleventh jacinth, and the twelfth amethyst" (vv. 19,20).

John then says that "the street of the city was pure gold, like transparent glass" (v. 21). Years ago it was almost impossible to conceive of the reality of this description. Yet in nearly every major city, great skyscrapers are built today with walls of glass that transform the building into pure gold in the sunset. One modern construction device is to apply a very thin sheet of gold to the outside glass and metal of these gigantic towers. When the sun hits it, the whole building appears to glow with gold. Yet when you look directly through the golden windows from the inside, you can see that they are transparent glass. This technique not only gives a beautiful golden appearance to the building; it also provides excellent heat control and conservation. If man can create earthly buildings like this to reflect the glory of the earthly sun, think how magnificent the New Jerusalem will be when it reflects the glory of the Son of God. Earth's most sought after mineral, gold, will be so plentiful in the New Jerusalem that John described the streets and city as "transparent gold." The Light of God will illuminate the city of the saints for eternity.

John "saw no temple in it, for the Lord God Almighty and the Lamb are its temple" (v. 22). While the Bible does describe a Temple in Heaven, the New Jerusalem will not have a Temple because God Himself will dwell with us. This reminds us of what Jesus said to the woman at the well when she challenged Him about the proper place to worship God.

"Woman, believe Me, the hour is coming when you will neither on this mountain, nor in Jerusalem, worship the Father. . . . But the hour is coming, and now is, when the true worshipers will worship the Father in spirit and truth; for the Father is seeking such to worship Him. God is Spirit, and those who worship Him must worship in spirit and truth" (John 4:21-23). In this vision, John could see what Jesus talked about. The very Spirit of God will pervade the entire New Jerusalem so there will be no need for a special building such as a Temple where men normally communicate with Him.

The glowing golden light of the city was "the glory of God . . . and the Lamb. And the nations of those who are saved shall walk in its light, and the kings of the earth bring their glory and honor into it" (Revelation 21:23,24). Although the Bible describes the continuation of the sun and a moon in the New Earth, there will be no need of sun or moon to provide light in the New Jerusalem, because "there shall be no night there" (v. 25). The presence of God internally lights the whole city. Since there is no night and no danger of an enemy besieging the city, the "gates shall not be shut" (v. 25).

We will no longer be subject to the curse which God put on the Earth after Adam's sin. There will be no rust or decay because the very process of entropy, the running down of the universe, will have ceased. When the curse of sin is removed, decay, germs and decomposition will also be eliminated. Nothing "that defiles, or causes an abomination or a lie" (v. 27) will ever enter there, though the gates are left open. The angels of God will guard the city forever.

The New Jerusalem is an eternal city, built by God, one which the faithful, beginning with Abel, have been waiting for (see Hebrews 11). It will be a holy city because sin will be eliminated. Only those who are "white as snow" (Isaiah 1:18) because of the blood of Jesus Christ, whose names "are written in the Lamb's Book of Life" (Revelation 21:27) will inhabit the New Jerusalem.

The Inhabitants of the City of God

The New Jerusalem in Heaven is now inhabited by the angels, the spirits of those who died in Christ, and those Old Testament saints who were raised from the dead as part of the firstfruits of the first resurrection, "and the graves were opened; and many bodies of the saints who had fallen asleep were raised; and coming out of the graves after His resurrection, they went into the holy city and appeared to many" (Matthew 27:52,53). These resurrected saints ascended into Heaven with Jesus.

At the Rapture, the spirits of those departed saints already in the New Jerusalem will receive their resurrected bodies as the "dead in Christ" rise first. Immediately after that, we "who are alive and remain" will be transformed into our new bodies. Jesus told the Church that He was going away "to prepare a place for you . . . that where I am, there you may be also" (John 14:2,3). That place is the New Jerusalem in Heaven. Also included will be the Old Testament saints who were not part of the firstfruits of the resurrection when Christ arose. Paul says that these saints "all died in faith, not having received the promises, but having seen them afar off. . . . But now they desire a better, that is, a heavenly country. Therefore God is not ashamed to be called their God, for He has prepared a city for them" (Hebrews 11:13,16).

Abraham, one of those saints, had left a great city, Ur of the Chaldees, to travel through desert lands, living in tents. He eagerly awaited the city which God had promised him that had "foundations," the New Jerusalem and the Promised Land of Israel. His son Isaac and grandson Jacob, "heirs with him of the same promise . . . all died in faith, not having received the promises, but having seen them afar off were assured of them, embraced them and confessed that they were strangers and pilgrims on the earth. For those who say such things declare plainly that they seek a homeland." Abraham never again lived in a city with houses and walls, nor did Isaac or Jacob. "All these, having obtained a good testimony through faith, did not receive the promise," but they will—not just the Promised Land of Israel, but also the New Jerusalem (Hebrews 11:9,13,14,39).

The Book of Hebrews reassures the Church, the Bride of Christ, that we too will come to "the city of the living God, the heavenly Jerusalem, to an innumerable company of angels, to the general assembly and church of the firstborn who are registered in Heaven, to God the Judge of all, to the spirits of just men made perfect, to Jesus the Mediator of the new covenant" (Hebrews 12:22-24).

Paul in Philippians 4:3 speaks of the day when we will be reunited with those "whose names are in the Book of Life." John, speaking of the city that has "no need of the sun or the moon," says that "there shall by no means enter it [the New Jerusalem] anything that defiles, or causes an abomination or a lie, but only those who are written in the Lamb's Book of Life" (Revelation 21:23,27). The sole qualification to be named in the Book of Life is our acceptance of the pardon of sin offered by the Father to all who will accept His Son as their Lord and Savior.

Life in the New Jerusalem

Although the New Jerusalem will be the final home of all the righteous sons of God, from Adam to the last member of the Church, the members of the Bride of Christ will not be restricted to the heavenly city. We will go in and out of the gates, exploring the New Earth and the New Heaven, ruling and reigning with Christ. We shall have access to the "pure river of water of life, clear as crystal, proceeding from the throne of God and of the Lamb" (Revelation 22:1). The Tree of Life, which was removed from Earth after Adam sinned, will stand near the river and will bear "twelve fruits, each tree yielding its fruit every month" (v. 2). We will have fruit to eat in season in the New Jerusalem. The mention of months and seasons shows that we will undoubtedly have a variety of climate conditions. We will be able to approach "the throne of

God and the Lamb" and will serve Him. We "shall see His face, and His name shall be on [our] foreheads" (vv. 3,4).

John must have thrilled as he heard a loud voice from Heaven saying, "Behold, the tabernacle of God is with men, and He will dwell with them, and they shall be His people, and God Himself will be with them and be their God. And God will wipe away every tear from their eyes; there shall be no more death, nor sorrow, nor crying. There shall be no more pain, for the former things have passed away" (Revelation 21:3,4).

God declared from His throne the glorious words: "It is done! I am the Alpha and the Omega, the Beginning and the End. I will give of the fountain of the water of life freely to him who thirsts. He who overcomes shall inherit all things, and I will be his God and he shall be my son" (Revelation 21:6,7).

Then in the midst of these glorious promises was a note of warning: "He who overcomes shall inherit all things, and I will be his God and he shall be My son. But the cowardly, unbelieving, abominable, murderers, sexually immoral, sorcerers, idolaters, and all liars shall have their part in the lake which burns with fire and brimstone, which is the second death" (vv. 7,8).

John ends the Book of Revelation with, "And the Spirit and the bride say, 'Come!' And let him who hears say, 'Come!' And let him who thirsts come. Whoever desires, let him take the water of life freely. . . . Surely I am coming quickly.' Amen. Even so, come, Lord Jesus!" (22:17,20).

CHAPTER 7

The Search
for the Messiah

While visiting Israel several months before writing this book, I talked to many Israelis who spoke of the need for Messiah to come to solve the terrible problems Israel and the world faces. Bumper stickers in Jerusalem stated, in Hebrew, "We want Moshiach Now." Even in New York City these stickers are now appearing: "We want Messiah now." Every few days a speaker in the Israeli parliament, known as the Knesset, will refer to the coming of the Messiah. *The Jerusalem Post* and other secular newspapers continually refer to the need for Messiah to come and lead Israel to "the peace of Jerusalem." A growing number of bookstores in Jerusalem contain books that refer to the Talmudic and biblical teachings about the Messiah.

Songs on the radio in Israel proclaim a longing for the coming of Messiah and the age of redemption. In one of these songs, which the young people sing, are these words: "O Moshiach, how we want you now. Hurry and open the gates. Please return us to our homeland Yisroel. Ad Mosai, how long must we wait?"

The Promise of the Messiah

While the term Messiah (Moshiach in Hebrew) was not a proper noun in the Old Testament, the concept of the "anointed one" was prophesied by all of Israel's prophets. The name "Moshiach" became the accepted term for the coming King who would sit on the throne of David.

Dr. Alfred Edersheim, a great Jewish Messianic scholar, wrote in 1863, *The Life and Times of Jesus the Messiah*. In the appendix he lists 456 Old Testament passages which were interpreted in ancient Jewish writings as applying to the coming Messiah. Seventy-five of these are from the five books of Moses (Genesis through Deuteronomy); 243 are from the writings of the prophets; 138 from the balance of the Old Testament. Also, Dr. Edersheim details 558 separate quotations from ancient rabbinical writings that apply these passages to the Messiah. The Jews of Christ's days understood these passages as applying to the Messiah.

In an old bookstore in Pennsylvania I discovered a wonderful book, *A History of Messianic Speculation in Israel*, signed by the author, Abba Hillel Silver, D.D. Dr. Silver spoke about the great expectation Israel had around the time Jesus was born that the Messiah would soon come. "Jesus appeared in the procuratorship of Pontius Pilate (26-36 C.E.). The first mention of the appearance of a Messiah in Josephus is in connection with the disturbances during the term of office of the procurator Cuspium Fadus (c. 44 C.E.). It seems likely, therefore that in the minds of the people the Millennium was to begin around the year 30 C.E. Be it remembered that it is not the Messiah who brings about the Millennium. It is the inevitable advent of the Millennium which carries along with it the Messiah and his appointed activities. The Messiah was expected around the second quarter of the first century C.E. because the Millennium was at hand. Prior to that time he was not expected, because according to the chronology of the day the Millennium was still considerably removed."

Talmudic sources contain many traditions and comments about the Messiah. Rabbi Elijah (not the prophet), who lived about two hundred years before Jesus, told his students: "The world will exist six thousand years. The first two thousand years were those of chaos [without the Torah]. The second two thousand years were those under the Torah. The last two thousand years are the Messianic years."

The Great Messianic Prophecy of Moses

One of the greatest Messianic prophecies was delivered to Israel by Moses, the great lawgiver. To Christians, Moses might appear to be just one of many wonderful godly men of the Bible. However, to the Jews, he occupies a place of supreme importance, even higher than Abraham, the father of the Jews. For over three thousand years Israel has looked back with reverence to their great prophet, Moses. He was a unique leader with outstanding qualities as a prophet, priest, teacher, savior, and lawgiver. None of the other prophets or leaders came close to duplicating this multiple role.

"A Prophet like unto Moses"

Yet, in one of his most specific predictions, Moses declared that God would raise up another Jewish prophet in the future whose life would closely resemble his. This prophecy of Moses that the Messiah would be like him is important to Israel in determining the credentials of the Messiah. Moses prophesied of "a Prophet like me from your midst, from your brethren. Him you shall hear. . . . And the Lord said to me: I will raise up for them a Prophet like you from among their brethren, and will put My words in His mouth, and He shall speak to them all that I command Him. And it shall be that whoever will not hear My words, which He speaks in My name, I will require it of him" (Deuteronomy 18:15;18,19).

These prophecies were fulfilled in detail in the life, death and resurrection of Jesus: "Then those men, when they had seen the sign that Jesus did, said, 'This is truly the Prophet who is to come into the world' " (John 6:14).

The Talmud declares "that the Messiah must be the greatest of future prophets, as being nearest in spirit to our master Moses." Throughout the Gospels and the Epistles we find the claim that certain Messianic prophecies were accomplished in the life of Jesus. For example, when the scribes sent people to question John the Baptist, they asked two questions. The first was, "Are you Elijah?" (John 1:21), referring to Malachi's prophecy that Elijah would come as a messenger before the appearance of the Messiah. Jews around the world still set out a cup of wine for Elijah at Passover— the prophesied forerunner of the Messiah. The smallest boy in the family is delegated to open a door to invite Elijah to join the Passover Seder.

Was Jesus the Prophet "Like unto Moses"?

The second question the people asked John was, "Are you the Prophet?" (John 1:21). This referred to Moses' prophecy that God would send "a Prophet like me." When Philip found Nathanael, he "said to him, 'We have found Him of whom Moses in the law, and also the prophets, wrote—Jesus of Nazareth, the son of Joseph' " (v. 45). After Jesus fed the five thousand, the men referred to the well-known prophecy of Moses, "This is truly the Prophet who is to come into the world" (John 6:14). In his defense speech, the martyr Stephen declared that Jesus was the promised Messiah: "This is that Moses who said to the children of Israel, 'The lord your God will raise up for you a Prophet like me from your brethren. Him you shall hear.' " (Acts 7:37,38).

Was Jesus' life a parallel to Moses? Yes, so much so that no other person in history came close to fulfilling this prophecy. In the last verses of Deuteronomy, writing after the death of Joshua, tells us that even Joshua missed the mark: "There has not arisen in Israel a prophet like Moses whom the Lord knew face to face" (34:10).

In a complete analysis of the life of Moses and Jesus of Nazareth, at least fifty elements and events are parallel in both lives. Many of these were beyond the ability of any human control. Consider the roles which Moses and Jesus both played: prophet, priest, lawgiver, teacher, leader of men. Both taught new truth from God and confirmed their teaching with miracles. Both spent their early years in Egypt, miraculously protected from those who sought their lives. Moses' family initially did not accept his role, but later his brother Aaron, and sister Miriam, helped him. Jesus' mother, brothers and sisters initially failed to follow Jesus, but later his brother James became the leader in the church in Jerusalem.

Each was considered the wisest man in his day. Both confronted demonic powers and successfully subdued them. As Moses appointed seventy rulers over Israel, Jesus anointed seventy disciples to teach the nations. Moses sent twelve spies to explore Canaan, Jesus sent twelve apostles to reach the world. The Bible does not state that either one experienced sickness. Neither of their bodies remained in a tomb. Both fasted for forty days and faced spiritual crises on mountain tops. As Moses stretched his hand over the Red Sea to command it, Jesus rebuked the Sea of Galilee and quieted the waves. Both of their faces shone with the glory of heaven—Moses on Mount Sinai and Jesus on the Mount of Transfiguration.

While Moses rescued Israel from the dead religion of pagan Egypt, Jesus rescued Israel from the dead letter of the law of tradition. Moses and Christ both cured lepers and proved their authority through the miracles they performed before many witnesses. As Moses conquered the great enemy of Israel, the Amalekites, with his upraised arms, Jesus conquered our great enemy sin and death by His upraised arms on the cross. Moses lifted up the brazen serpent in the wilderness to heal his people; Jesus was lifted up on the cross to heal all believers from their sin.

The people were ungrateful and rebelled against the leadership of both men. The generations that rebelled against them died in their lack of faith—one in the wilderness and one in the siege of Jerusalem in A.D. 70. Moses and Jesus both died on a hill. Moses promised that another Prophet would come; Jesus promised the Church that His Father would send them another "Comforter," the Holy Spirit.

In the month of Nisan, on the fourteenth day, which was the Feast of the Passover, both Moses and Jesus freed all who would trust them. On the seventeenth day, the Feast of Firstfruits, Moses brought about the resurrection of the children of Israel as they passed through the Red Sea; on the anniversary of that day Jesus became the Firstfruits of resurrection as He arose from the dead. Fifty days later, on the Feast of Pentecost, God delivered the great gift to Israel and the nations through the giving of the Torah, the Law. Fifty days after His resurrection, God gave the Church the great gift of the baptism of the Holy Spirit.

The evidence is quite compelling that Jesus was the prophesied Messiah, the prophet like Moses. Why, then, has Israel rejected her Messiah?

Why did Israel Reject Jesus as Their Messiah?

The Jews believed that the Messiah, the prophet which Moses spoke about, would come and deliver them from Roman bondage and set up a kingdom where they would be the rulers. Two of the disciples, James and John, even asked to sit at Jesus' right and left in His cabinet when He came into His glory. The people of Jerusalem also thought He would deliver them. They shouted praises to God for the mighty works they had seen Jesus do, and called out "Hosanna, save us" when he rode into Jerusalem on a donkey. They treated Him like a conquering king. Then when He allowed Himself to be arrested, tried and crucified on a cursed cross, the people stopped believing that He was the promised prophet. They rejected their Messiah.

Therefore, the promised kingdom was postponed. But God is a covenant-keeping God and the kingdom promises are still in force for Israel. Paul told the Roman Church, "I do not desire, brethren that you should be ignorant of this mystery, lest you should be wise in your own opinion that blindness in part has happened to Israel until the fullness of the Gentiles has come in. And so all Israel will be saved, as it is written, The Deliverer will come out of Zion, and He will turn away ungodliness from Jacob; for this is My covenant with them, when I take away their sins. . . . For the gifts and the calling of God are irrevocable" (Romans 11:25-27,29).

Note that Paul tells the Church that the spiritual blindness of Israel is a "mystery" that had not previously been revealed. For thousands of years Israel had been the one nation that looked to God while the Gentile nations generally rejected the light and chose to live in spiritual darkness. Israel and her inspired prophets revealed monotheism—one God who was personally interested in mankind's destiny of heaven or hell, the path to salvation, the written Word with the Ten Commandments. Yet Israel rejected her prophesied Messiah, and the promises of the kingdom of heaven were postponed. A veil of spiritual blindness fell upon the eyes of the Jews who previously were the most spiritually discerning people. As Paul explained, this hardening in part of Israel led to the blessing of the Gentiles who would believe in Jesus and accept Him as Lord and Savior.

The Jews rejected Jesus because He failed, in their eyes, to do what they expected their Messiah to do—destroy evil and all their enemies, in this case the Romans, and establish an eternal kingdom with Israel as the pre-eminent nation in the world. The prophecies in Isaiah and Psalm 22 described a suffering Messiah who would be persecuted and killed, but they chose to focus on those prophecies that discussed His glorious victories, not His crucifixion.

The commentaries in the Talmud, written before the onset of Christianity, clearly discuss the Messianic prophecies of Isaiah 53 and Psalm 22 and puzzle over how these would be fulfilled with the glorious setting up of the Kingdom of the Messiah. After the Church used these prophecies to prove the claims of Christ, the Jews took the position that the prophecies did not refer to the Messiah, but to Israel or some other person.

During a recent research trip to Israel, I searched in several Jewish theological bookstores in the old city of

Jerusalem for some specific material on the Temple and the Messiah. Several times, rabbinical students engaged me in conversation regarding my research. First, they were curious about my genuine interest as a Christian in Israel and in Jewish commentaries on the Bible. Then invariably they turned the conversation to Jesus and His claims to be the Jewish Messiah. The words, "He could not have been the promised Messiah because he failed, he was killed," were spoken in each conversation. They could see that Jesus fulfilled many Old Testament Messianic prophecies – His birth in Bethlehem, coming out of Egypt, living in Nazareth, being preceded by a messenger, awesome miraculous powers and tremendous teaching. However, they still felt as their fathers did two thousand years before: Jesus had failed, he was killed: Therefore, he could not be the glorified Messiah.

During Jesus' ministry, the Jews continually asked His identity because they knew that, according to the prophet Daniel, the Messiah was supposed to come at that time. Jewish commentaries, even during the Middle Ages, admit that the Messiah was prophesied to appear before the destruction of Jerusalem in A.D. 70. They knew that the Book of Daniel declared that the Messiah would come sixty-nine weeks of years (483 biblical years of 360 days each) from the decree to rebuild the walls of Jerusalem. That well-known decree was given to Nehemiah on the first day of Nisan, March 14, 445 B.C. The final year was A.D. 32. (See *Armageddon – Appointment with Destiny*.) The growing expectations of the Messiah's coming is reflected in the scribes' explanation to King Herod that the Messiah was to be born in Bethlehem. It is noteworthy that, before Jesus, no one falsely claimed to be Messiah. First came the genuine, then the copies.

The Two Messiahs of Jewish Belief

The Jews are still looking for their Messiah to come. Although the Church has always taught that the Messiah would come twice, Jewish teachers have rejected the idea. However, recent Jewish commentaries of the Talmud proclaim two future Messiahs. One, they suggest, will appear before the War of Gog and Magog (the coming Russian-Arab invasion of Israel). He will lead the forces of Israel to victory, as described in Ezekiel 38,39. He is called Moshiach Ben Joseph—Messiah the son of Joseph. They claim he will be killed in the battle with Russia, thus fulfilling the suffering Messiah prophecies. Then, they suggest that the second Messiah, Moshiach Ben David—Messiah the son of David, will come forth. He will lead Israel into the promised Kingdom and the "age of redemption." This interesting interpretation is their way of dealing with the undeniable and difficult fact that the Scriptures do prophecy two separate comings of the Messiah: one to persecution and death, the second to glorious victory over the enemies of God and Israel. The curious factor here is that this interpretation of two comings of the Messiah is precisely the claim of the New Testament. However, Christians present the evidence that Jesus of Nazareth fulfilled the prophecies of the first coming during His First Coming, and that He will return to redeem both Israel and the Church in the near future, in the Second Coming.

A startling document came into my possession during my studies in Jerusalem that sheds additional light on the coming of the Messiah. Moses Maimonides, known affectionately as Rambam, was the greatest Jewish commentator and scholar of the Middle Ages. In Jewish tradition they refer to him as follows: "From Moses to Moses (Maimonides), there is no one like Moses." In Rambam's Mishneh Torah, a commentary of the first five books of the Bible, are some startling facts about the history and Messianic claims of Jesus Christ. This great Rabbi reveals his honest intellectual struggle to come to terms with apparent contradictions regarding the separate prophecies about the suffering Messiah and the glorified Messiah. The Mishneh Torah, composed of fourteen volumes, is the most authoritative Jewish commentary of their understanding of the Law of God as it related to Israel, the Messiah and the Temple. The final fourteenth volume, Hilchot Melachim U'Milchamoteihem (the Laws of Kings and Their Wars) is about the coming of the Messiah.

The Qualifications of the Messiah

Rambam believed that the coming of the Messiah was the key to the restoration of the Temple, the fulfillment of the Torah and the coming of the Messianic age of redemption. "He [the Messiah] will build the Temple, gather the dispersed of Israel. Then, in his days, all the statutes will return to their previous state. We will offer sacrifices and observe the Sabbatical and Jubilee years, according to all their particulars mentioned by the Torah" (Halachah 11:11).

Compare the qualifications of the Messiah, which Rambam enumerated from his study of the Old Testament prophets, with the history of Jesus Christ. "If a king will arise from the house of David who is learned in Torah and observant of the mitzvot (commandments), as prescribed by the written law and the oral law, as David, his ancestor was, and will compel all of Israel to walk in [their light] and reinforce the breaches; and fight the wars of God, we may, with assurance, consider Him the Messiah. If he succeeds in the above, builds the Temple in its place, and gathers the dispersed of Israel, he is definitely the Messiah. He will then improve the entire world [motivating] all the nations to serve God together as [Zephaniah 3:9] states: I will make the peoples pure of speech that they all will call upon the Name of God and serve Him with one purpose" (Halachah 11:4).

In this passage, Rambam has described in the first paragraph the first coming of the Messiah; in the second paragraph the second coming. Jesus fulfilled the prophecies as the Son of David and astonished His listeners as a teacher of the Torah Law. In His unfolding purpose to accomplish the salvation of all those who would believe in Him, Christ allowed Himself to be sacrificed on the cross after fulfilling this first group of prophecies. This ultimate sacrificial gift to mankind was anticipated by God's miraculous offering of the ram to replace Abraham's sacrifice of Isaac on Mount Moriah almost two thousand years earlier. When Christ returns as promised, He will completely fulfill the remaining prophecies. He will build the Millennial Temple as described in Ezekiel 40-48 and gather the dispersed of Israel into the Kingdom of heaven on Earth.

In one fascinating part of his commentary, Rambam deals with the puzzle about the historical Jesus, the problems associated with His partial fulfillment of the Messianic prophecies and the claims of Christianity. "If he [the Messiah] did not succeed to this degree or he was killed, he surely is not [the redeemer] promised by the Torah. [Rather] he should be considered as all the other proper and complete kings of the Davidic dynasty who died. God only caused him to arise in order to test the many, as [Daniel 11:35] states, and some of the wise men will stumble, to try them, to refine, and to clarify until the appointed time, because the set time is in the future" (Halachah 11:4).

This conclusion of Rambam that the death of Jesus proves that He was not the promised glorified Messiah has been repeated for hundreds of years. However, Rambam makes an astonishing admission: If the person legitimately fulfills part of the prophecies, but is killed before completing the restoration of the Temple, etc., he is to be considered as "all the other proper and complete kings of the Davidic dynasty who died," not as an impostor.

He then considers the historical evidence he had in his possession about Jesus Christ. As the greatest scholar of his day, he had access to rabbinical literature (which was available at that time) that dealt with the period before the burning of the Temple in Jerusalem in A.D. 70. It is important to remember that most Jews over the last two thousand years have assumed Jesus never lived, died or rose from the dead. Many Jews have thought that the Gospel records of Matthew, Mark, Luke and John were contrived documents composed long after the events in question. Even liberal scholars now admit that all the Gospels were written before the destruction of Jerusalem in A.D. 70. This is important because if the Gospel records about the teachings, miracles, prophecies, death and resurrection of Jesus existed within thirty-five years of their occurrence, it is tremendous proof that these events happened. The theories of the higher critical school of the last century, which categorically denied the early existence of the Gospels, have been overturned by recent scholarly research. It is almost impossible now to maintain the previous theory that the Gospels were mythical or imaginative material composed hundreds of years after all living witnesses had died. Why would the Gospels have been accepted as truth by people who were willing to die for their faith if living witnesses could stand up and deny their truthfulness?

Secret Material on Jesus of Nazareth

In studying the great work of Rambam, I found material in Israel that has not been previously available because it was censored for over six hundred years by the amazing joint decision of Jewish and Christian religious authorities during the Middle Ages. During fifteen years of study I kept finding mysterious references to the existence of censored passages of the Mishneh Torah that referred directly to the historical reality of Jesus Christ. In one recent example, the Jewish commentary on the Book of Daniel (page 310 in the ArtScroll Tanach Series) quotes only parts of these passages. Following these partial quotes from Rambam's Mishneh Torah, is an explanation that additional material was "censored out of our editions," and referred to special sources in Israel. Whenever I tried to discover these sources I was told they were unavailable or non-existent. It is very difficult to find any significant Jewish material related to the subject of the Messiah in new or rare bookstores in North America or the United Kingdom. However, my search was finally rewarded in a rabbinical bookstore in the Jewish Quarter of the Old City of Jerusalem in the spring of 1989.

Why was Jesus Censored from
the Talmud and Mishneh Torah?

The reasons for the censoring of this material from the Mishneh Torah are unusual and fascinating. Some material refers to Jesus in an unflattering light because of the Talmud's rejection of the Gospels' claims that Jesus was the Messiah. During the terrible centuries of persecution of the Jews by the Catholic Church, it was not uncommon for an ignorant, bigoted priest to quote some of these unflattering passages to his angry congregation. Then he would lead a furious rampage into Jewish ghettos to burn the "Christkillers." These priests forgot that the Romans were the actual physical killers of Jesus and that all Gentiles are also included by the Bible as the killers of Jesus. It was the sin of each one of us that caused the crucifixion of Jesus. Some of the enlightened leaders of the Church were appalled at this terrible misuse of the Jewish Mishneh and Talmudic commentaries and met with Jewish Rabbinical leaders to discuss ways to prevent recurrences of these pogroms and burnings. The decision to censor all references to Jesus of Nazareth from these Jewish sources was a joint decision of the Church and the Jewish leadership. These materials in both Christian monasteries and Jewish libraries were censored. The motive of the Christian and Jewish leaders was to stop supplying ammunition for religious bigots. A bonus for the rabbis was the elimination of the sometimes embarrassing proof from Rambam, the most reliable Jewish scholar, that Jesus of Nazareth had lived, died and fulfilled many biblical prophecies. It was easier to avoid any mention of Jesus and treat the Gospels as Christian myth.

In 1631, a Jewish Assembly of Elders in eastern Europe published a command of censorship. "We enjoin you under the threat of the great ban to publish in no new edition of the Mishneh or the Gemara anything that refers to Jesus of Nazareth." Once the material was removed from copies in Christian monastery libraries and Jewish, rabbinical libraries, most future editions of the Mishneh Torah would omit these censored passages. For many years these passages were indicated by blank spaces or small circles. Eventually, even these indications of censorship were eliminated.

Fortunately, several rare copies of this censored material escaped the hands of the authorities in Europe. One exists in Yemenite manuscripts of the Mishneh Torah discovered at the tip of the Saudi Arabian peninsula. A portion of this was included in a book, *Jesus in the Jewish Tradition*, by Rabbi Morris Goldstein which was published in A.D. 1950. The complete censored portions have now been published with a full fourteen-volume commentary by Rabbi Eliyahu Touger and the Maznaim Publishing Corporation, Jerusalem, Israel. The book jacket of the fourteenth volume on the Messiah has the word "CENSORED" overprinted upon it and the text explains the curious history of these censored portions.

Jesus Christ: CENSORED for over Six Hundred Years

The following is quoted from the censored material from the Mishneh Torah: "Jesus of Nazareth who aspired to be the Messiah and was executed by the court was also [alluded to] in Daniel's prophecies, as (ibid., 11:14) states: 'the vulgar [common] among your people shall exalt themselves in an attempt to fulfill the vision, but they shall stumble.' Can there be a greater stumbling block than [Christianity]? All the prophets spoke of the Messiah as the Redeemer of Israel and its Savior, who would gather their dispersed and strengthen their [observation of] the Mitzvot [the commandments]. By contrast, [Christianity] caused the Jews to be slain by the sword, their remnant to be scattered and humbled, the Torah to be altered and the majority of the world to err and serve a god other than the Lord. Nevertheless, the intent of the Creator of the world is not within the power of man to comprehend, for His ways are not our ways, nor are His thoughts, our thoughts. [Ultimately,] all the deeds of Jesus of Nazareth and that Ishmaelite [Mohammed] who arose after him will only serve to prepare the way for the Messiah's coming and the improvement of the entire world [motivating the nations] to serve God together, as [Zephaniah 3:9] states: I will make the peoples pure of speech that they will all call upon the Name of God and serve Him with one purpose" (Halachah 11:4).

In this amazing censored material, Rambam admits that the basic historical account of the Gospels about Jesus is correct. He states that Jesus of Nazareth was a legitimate teacher; that He aspired to be the Messiah and that He was executed by the Sanhedrin. He declares that He was a legitimate king of Israel in the line of King David and that He was referred to in the prophecies of Daniel. Rambam struggles with the problems posed by the failure of Jesus to establish His kingdom then, His death, and the history of Christianity when the Catholic Church persecuted the Jewish people. However, he refers to the mysterious ways of God and believes that ultimately the deeds of Jesus of Nazareth will be used by God to prepare the hearts of men for the Messiah's glorious coming, the establishing of the Messianic Kingdom and the improvement of the whole world.

Rambam's comment, "Can there be a greater stumbling block than [Christianity]?" is an echo of what the Apostle Paul, twelve hundred years earlier, said about the effect Jesus Christ had upon His people, the Jews. "But we preach Christ crucified, to the Jews a stumbling block and to the Greeks foolishness, but to those who are called, both Jews and Greeks, Christ the power of God and the wisdom of God" (1 Corinthians 1:23,24). It is fascinating to see Rambam use the same word stumbling block in describing the crucifixion of Jesus as Paul the Apostle.

In my discussions with orthodox rabbis and rabbinical students in Jerusalem, the conversation would often focus on Old Testament prophecies that will be fulfilled when the Messiah comes to set up His kingdom. Often they would say things like: "When the Messiah comes, the problems of peace in the world and the Middle East will finally be solved," or "Evil will only be destroyed when the Messiah reigns." When I tried to explore their thoughts about the coming Messiah to find exactly what their expectations were, I often came to a stone wall in the conversation beyond which they refused to venture. After four separate discussions I discovered the problem. These Jewish students of the Bible long for the coming of Messiah and believe that the Bible is correct in declaring that He will change all things forever when He comes. The problem is that they have rejected Jesus partly because of their belief that the Messiah is not the Son of God but rather an anointed Messiah-King. In their understanding of the monotheism of the Old Testament, they believe that God could not have a "Son." Despite the many verses in the Old Testament that refer to the concept of the Trinity, they see this as a contradiction to the basic truth of Deuteronomy 6:4, which has stood as a bulwark for Israel against the paganism of multiplied gods and idol worship: "Hear, O Israel: The Lord our God, the Lord is one!" This passage, known as the Shema, is fundamental to the beliefs of all religious Jews.

However, when I asked what would happen to Israel and the world to come when their Messiah-King became an old man and died, their reaction was pure astonishment. I explained, if they believed that the Messiah will not be the Son of God as Christians believe, but only an anointed human like King David, then he must die after seventy or so years. None of them had ever considered the fact of the death of their coming Messiah-King. The tremendous expectations placed upon the Messianic Age could never be realized in just one lifetime of a normal, human king in Israel. Both the biblical prophecies and the Jewish teaching about the coming Messiah demand that the Messiah be more than just a man and that he must live forever to complete the transformation of all things in the Age of Redemption.

Their response to my question was that God would produce the transformation of the earth into the "world to come" at the time of Messiah's coming, and he would reign forever on David's throne. Their understanding of Messiah's role is closer to Christians' understanding than they know. When Messiah descends upon the Mount of Olives, the veil of spiritual blindness will lift from the eyes of the Chosen People. Then "I will pour on the house of David and on the inhabitants of Jerusalem the Spirit of grace and supplication; then they will look on Me whom they pierced. Yes, they will mourn for Him as one mourns for his only son" (Zechariah 12:10).

After God completes His church, and the time known as "the fullness of the Gentiles," God will turn back to Israel in mercy. Paul the Apostle prophesied: "Has God cast away His people? Certainly not! . . . All Israel will be saved as it is written: 'The Deliverer will come out of Zion, and He will turn away ungodliness from Jacob' " (Romans 11:1,26).

When Will the Messiah Come?

Within the history of Judaism there is a curious parallel to the Christian approach to the coming Messiah. The rabbis warned against trying to set absolute times for the coming of the Redeemer. Yet, in every age, various writers, including the great Maimonides, Rambam, would suggest possible times when he might come. This creative tension includes both a longing for the Messiah and a wise repudiation of date-setting. Judaism evolved the theory that the Messiah could come at any time if Israel's repentance merited it. However, they also teach there is a final point of prophesied time beyond which the Messiah would not delay his coming. Many Jewish rabbis have taught that the Messiah would come before the conclusion of the six thousand years from Adam.

This belief was also widely shared by the church for the first three hundred years following Christ, as shown in my first book. An interesting parallel for the Christians is the apostolic teaching that Christ would come in glory to establish His Millennial Kingdom at the end of the six thousand years. However, the Church was also told to "watch and pray" for the imminent return of Christ for the Church, now described as the Rapture. Both Jews and Christians were faced with this dynamic spiritual tension connected with the promised coming of the Messiah: It could be today; it could be delayed still longer. The certainty of His coming is absolute. The timing of His coming is in the hands of God.

The Messiah and the Muslim World

Arab writings also reflect a strong expectation of the coming Messiah. This belief is derived from both Old and New Testament writings that were partly adopted by Mohammed. This longing for the Messiah, known as the

Mahdi, has played a profound role in the history of Islam. All religious Moslems look for the coming of the Redeemer who will set up a kingdom and establish peace and justice for all. The teachings of the Koran of Mohammed incorporate certain parts of the Old Testament, and while they reject the truth of the divine nature of Christ, they do acknowledge the historical Jesus as a legitimate prophet of God. Shi'ites believe that the last of the Immans, their line of religious leaders, was supernaturally taken away and hidden until the time of his second coming.

Three major religions of mankind trace their beginnings from Abraham and are founded upon the Bible and the Holy Land. Each one is looking for the final resolution of history in the coming of the Messiah. When I was in Israel, peace, security and justice were continually discussed. Conversations with Israeli Jews, Christians and Arab Moslems would often end with their comment that the only solution to the problems of the Middle East will be the coming of the Messiah, the Prince of Peace. While each one obviously has a different concept of the meaning of the Messiah, they all long for a Redeemer who will create a just and perfect society.

As events in Israel and the world accelerate as indicated by the ancient prophecies of the Bible, we shall soon see the fulfillment of all our expectations in the glorious coming of Jesus the Messiah, the Prince of Peace.

CHAPTER 8

Revised and Enlarged

The Ashes of the Red Heifer and the Ark of the Covenant

"The glory of this latter Temple shall be greater than the former, says the Lord of Hosts." (Haggai 2:9).

For twenty-five hundred years the Jews have mourned the loss of their Temple on the ninth day of the month of Av (August). Each year, since the destruction of Solomon's Temple, the Jews would read the Book of Lamentations, written by Jeremiah, and weep for the burning of the Sanctuary where the Lord had promised to commune with them forever. The Lord prophesied that Israel would rebuild the Temple after the Jews returned to the Promised Land. After the second burning of the Temple on the 9th of Av, A.D. 70, by the Roman army, Israel turned to the synagogue, the Torah and rabbinical writings of the Talmud to express their love for God's holy name. Now, after twenty centuries of exile among the nations, Israel stands once more on the sacred soil of the Holy Land and in possession of the sacred city of Jerusalem. However, the land of Israel and the control of the Middle East are of immense strategic importance to America, Russia and other superpowers. In a few years we will witness the climactic struggle for the destiny of mankind between these powers in the valley before the mount of Megiddo, the final Battle of Armageddon.

Israel, especially the city of Jerusalem, stands at the center of the world's spiritual conflict. As the Bible prophesied, the battle for the soul of mankind will reach its conclusion in Jerusalem. The current developments in the Middle East are laying the foundation for the coming Messianic Kingdom. Research projects in Israel are rapidly preparing the way for the rebuilding of the prophesied Third Temple. The building of this Temple must precede the revealing of the Antichrist, the cutting off of the daily sacrifice and the coming of Jesus Christ to set up His Kingdom. Part of this research involves a search for the lost Ark of the Covenant and the last Ashes from the Sacrifice of the Red Heifer. The rabbis say that these two elements are vitally important for Israel to rebuild its cherished Third Temple.

The Ark of the Covenant

"According to all that I show you, that is, the pattern of the tabernacle and the pattern of all its furnishings, just so you shall make it. And they shall make an ark of acacia wood. . . ." (Exodus 25:9,10).

Throughout the years of Israel's wandering, God gave specific directions to Moses to create several sacred objects, patterned after the Temple objects in Heaven, to express His covenant with His chosen people. Israel carried these symbols through the wilderness until they reached the Promised Land and could place them in a Sanctuary befitting their importance. The first of these sacred objects was the rod Aaron used to perform miracles before the Pharaoh of Egypt; next was the manna, the bread from Heaven, which God gave them in the wilderness; the third was the tablets of stone on which God had written the Ten Commandments. These objects not only represented several manifestations of God's presence, they also prophetically pointed to our salvation in Christ.

God gave explicit instructions on the building of the sacred Ark of the Covenant that was to hold these important symbols. The word "ark" comes from the Hebrew word which means a chest, box or coffin. It was built of acacia wood covered with gold within and without. The dimensions were 45 by 27 by 27 inches, with a Mercy Seat of pure gold as the lid. Two gold Cherubim were created by the craftsmen on the Mercy Seat to represent the angelic Cherubim which surround the throne of God in Heaven. The Lord said that His Divine Presence would dwell with the Ark forever. This "Shekinah" glory filled the tribes of Israel with awe and reverence.

God told Moses how the Ark was to be carried and cared for by the Levites and priests, (see Exodus 25:10-22). When it was finished the Ark was placed in the Tabernacle of worship that was moved from place to place as Israel completed their appointed days of wandering in the wilderness. It was carried by the priests to the Jordan River on the 10th day of the month Nisan. When the priests stepped into the river with the Ark, the waters miraculously stopped flowing so that the tribes of Israel crossed over into Canaan on dry land. In the famous battle of Jericho, it was carried seven times around the city. The walls fell and the Israelites conquered the people. They carried the Ark into battle successfully against the armies which opposed them.

Its holiness and Divine Presence was so overwhelming that improper handling resulted in death. It was to be carried by the Levites on their shoulders with the poles extending from the ends of the Ark. Perhaps the years of storing the Ark in Abinadab's house caused his son, Uzzah, to lose his sense of reverence for the holiness of God's presence. When King David violated God's instructions and ordered them to carry the Ark in a cart instead of the way God had told Moses it should be carried, the cattle stumbled and the cart began to tip over. Uzzah reached out to keep it from falling. He died because of his violation of the laws of God regarding carrying the Ark. On another occasion, after the Ark was recaptured from the Philistines, the men of Bethshemesh, out of curiosity, violated its sanctity by opening it which caused more than fifty thousand people to die of the plague.

When the first Temple was finished under King Solomon, the Ark was placed in the Holy of Holies. The First Book of Kings describes this dramatic event: "Then the priests brought in the ark of the covenant of the Lord to its place, into the inner sanctuary of the temple, to the Most Holy Place, under the wings of the cherubim. Nothing was in the ark [at this time] except the two tablets of stone which Moses put there at Horeb, when the Lord made a covenant with the children of Israel, when they came out of the land of Egypt. And it came to pass, when the priests came out of the holy place that the cloud filled the house of the Lord, so that the priests could not continue ministering because of the cloud; for the glory of the Lord filled the house of the Lord. Then Solomon spoke: 'The Lord said He would dwell in the dark cloud. I have surely built You an exalted house, and a place for You to dwell in forever' " (1 Kings 8:6,9-13).

God's special Shekinah glory dwelt on the Mercy Seat upon the Ark of the Covenant and guided and protected Israel. It symbolized the person of Christ, the Messiah, who would fulfill God's covenant with His people. Jesus later explained to Israel His role as their Messiah-King: "I and My Father are one" (John 10:30). He did not come to "destroy the Law or the Prophets . . . but to fulfill" it (Matthew 5:17). The Ark remained in the Temple until the end of King Solomon's reign when it was removed to Ethiopia. From Solomon till now the Bible is strangely silent about the Ark and its location. We know it was not present in the Second Temple after Israel returned from the Babylonian captivity in 536 B.C. Yet according to the prophet Jeremiah, the Ark of the Covenant will play a pivotal role in our future. He prophecies in Jeremiah 3:15-17 that, just before the return of the Messiah, Israel will once more visit the Ark of the Covenant. Then, when the Messiah comes, the Ark will no longer be the central focus of Israel's worship. This prophecy implies that this sacred object must still play a crucial role in the events leading up to the rebuilding of the Temple and the coming of the Messiah.

The Search for the Ark of the Covenant

A recent movie "Raiders of the Lost Ark" was based on a real search for the lost Ark of the Covenant just before World War II. It shows a fictional archeologist, Indiana Jones, looking for it in 1936. The movie tells of the Nazis' fascination with the Ark and other sacred objects and of their search for it in Egypt. Factually, both the German Nazis and the Italian Fascists, led by dictator Benito Mussolini, were intrigued by the Ark and other rare religious objects. Historical records prove that one of the war aims of the Italian army that invaded Ethiopia in 1935 was the capture of the Ark of the Covenant for Mussolini. Why would the Italians search Ethiopia to locate the Ark?

The Ark of the Covenant in Ethiopia

Deep within a complex of underground passages beneath the ancient Church of Zion, in Aksum in northern Ethiopia, is a secret passage that leads to a highly guarded hiding place for the most sacred object in human history. For three thousand years—from the time of King Solomon—this passage to the Holy of Holies has been protected by royal priestly guards of the ancient Ethiopian Jewish monarchy. The last ruling monarch of Ethiopia was Emperor Haile Selassie, who called himself "the Conquering Lion of Judah." The city of Aksum was the ancient capital of the kingdom of the Queen of Sheba.

Within this underground Temple are seven concentric rings of interior circular walls. An ordinary Ethiopian Coptic priest can worship within the areas of the first to the fourth rings. Only the highest priests and the Emperor can enter the fifth and sixth innermost rings. The final seventh central walled circular room is the secret Holy of Holies. The Ethiopians claim that the holy Ark of the Covenant with the Mercy Seat and Shekinah Glory of God has lain in this sacred room of their Temple for three thousand years. Only one person is allowed to enter this room and he is the Guardian of the Ark. This Ethiopian priest-guard is chosen at the age of seven, the age of understanding, from the priestly family. He is trained as a child, in his age of innocence and agrees to guard the Ark for the rest of his life, never seeing the light of day or living a normal life. This guardian fasts for 225 days every year according to the Ethiopian Jewish sacred festival calendar. He prays, meditates and guards the sacred Ark with his life. He never leaves this Holy of Holies until the day of his death, when he is replaced by another chosen Guardian. Each day the High Priest enters the sixth innermost ring to bring the Guardian his food.

The Ethiopian monarchy is the oldest continuous royal dynasty in history. It began with the Queen of Sheba and her son, Menelik the First, the offspring of her marriage to King Solomon of Israel, and continued until the late Emperor Haile Selassie. Prince Menelik the First was educated in Israel. When He returned home at the age of nineteen, he secretly took with him the true Ark of the Covenant, where Ethiopian tradition says it remains. The Ethiopian Royal Chronicles claim he left a perfect replica of the Ark in the Holy of Holies.

In my book, *Armageddon*, I outlined the historical evidence which supports the claim of Ethiopia to possess the true Ark. The evidence is overwhelming that they have an ark of the Covenant which is thousands of years old. The Bible prophecies that Ethiopia will return a special offering to Zion in the last days. Only time and unfolding events will prove conclusively if this object is truly the lost Ark of the Covenant. It is fascinating to note the words of Israel's former chief Rabbi Goren in this regard. He stated to *Newsweek* magazine in November, 1981, "the secret of the location of the Ark will be revealed just prior to the rebuilding of the Third Temple."

Some have asked how the Ark could be in Ethiopia when Revelation 11:19 refers to the Ark of the Testimony being in Heaven. The Ark of the Covenant was built by Moses after the pattern of the Ark in Heaven according to Exodus 25. Therefore, there is no contradiction between a Heavenly Ark of the Covenant and the location of the earthly Ark in

Ethiopia. Others have wondered why famines would occur in Ethiopia if they truly possess the Ark and the blessings usually associated with it. It is interesting to note that Ethiopia was a net exporter of food until the death of the Christian–Jewish Emperor in 1974. The recent famines have been produced by the communist policies of government-controlled farms and the tragic civil war in the last fifteen years.

Although an army coup overthrew the Ethiopian monarchy in 1973, and later the emperor died in prison, several princes survive and live in exile today. Prince Stephen Mengesha, the great-grandson of Emperor Selassie, fortunately was outside the country, studying in Canada at the time of the coup. He escaped the imprisonment or death which befell most of the royal family. His mother, aunts and uncles have been imprisoned by the Marxist regime since that time. Despite the revolution and years of civil war, the Ark of the Covenant stays safely hidden within the Holy of Holies.

According to an article in the Jewish B'nai B'rith *Messenger* magazine in 1935, the Ethiopian priests moved the Ark from its underground temple into the mountains for safekeeping from the forces of Mussolini. The Ark escaped capture by the soldiers of the Italian army. Emperor Haile Selassie fasted and prayed for three days as the Italian invasion began. He was assured that God would grant Ethiopia the final victory. God honored these Ethiopian Jewish remnants of the tribes of Israel who protected the Ark as He had during many other invasions over the last three thousand years. The Lord caused the enormous invading Italian army to fail in its attempt to conquer this ancient Jewish–Christian empire. On May 15, 1941, five years to the day after the Italian invasion of the capital, Addis Ababa, the emperor returned in victory with his troops and the Allied forces. Ethiopia was the first country liberated from the Axis powers in World War II. From that point on the tide of war turned against the Axis powers of Germany and Italy. Once the Italian army had retreated from Ethiopia, the Ark was safely returned to its underground Temple in Aksum, where it remains today.

My Ethiopian sources confirmed that the Ark was guarded by the Ethiopian Coptic priest-guards. Neither the central communist government or the Tigre rebel forces will enter the Church of Zion in Aksum because of fear of repercussions from the population. They have a deep foreboding superstition about the supernatural power surrounding this sacred Ark of the Covenant. In the spring of 1989, the rebel Tigre army forces in northern Ethiopia were victorious and forced the communist government army out of the province for the first time in forty years of warfare.

Prince Stephen's father, Prince Mengesha Sevoum, the former governor-general of Ethiopia, is now the director of an Ethiopian relief operation in the Sudan. He appeared on a national TV program in the United States in the fall of 1988, after the release of my book, *Armageddon – Appointment With Destiny*, to confirm the accuracy of my research and to verify that the Ark is still protected in Ethiopia. He showed pictures of the royal visit in 1965 to Aksum with Emperor Haile Selassie, Queen Elizabeth II and Prince Philip to visit the repository of this ancient Ark of the Covenant.

After the rebirth of Israel in 1948, the Israeli government enjoyed very close relations with Emperor Haile Selassie and supplied considerable technical support and aid to Ethiopia. The royal family has told me that Israeli government representatives helped Ethiopia on many occasions and that Israeli agents repeatedly asked the Emperor about the Ark of the Covenant in Aksum. They suggested that, since Israel had returned from captivity and the Temple Mount was recaptured, it was time for the Ethiopians to return the Ark to its ancient resting place in a rebuilt Temple in Jerusalem. The Emperor is reported to have replied: "In principle, I agree that the Ark should be returned to the Temple, but the correct time has not yet come." He felt that God would reveal the right time for the return of the Ark to Jerusalem.

Israel made an agreement with the Ethiopian government which allowed it to rescue the remaining 60 to 80,000 black Jews from the country in return for Israeli technical aid. My sources told me that the Ethiopian Jews would not leave their precious Ark of the Covenant behind when they returned to the Promised Land. In addition to the lost Ark, the Ashes of the Red Heifer are also vital to Israel's plans for the rebuilding of the Temple.

In 1991 an extraordinary rescue operation was launched by Israel during the chaotic closing days of the Ethiopian civil war. This rescue mission resulted in the return of over 85,000 of the Ethiopian Jews by planes to their ancient homeland that their forefathers had left almost three thousand years earlier. The corrupt military leaders of Ethiopia's Marxist government demanded and received millions of dollars in bribes from Israel during the final months of their rule to facilitate the rescue of these persecuted Ethiopian Jews. Israel flew repeated military cargo flights into the Ethiopian capital Addis Ababa to gather these poor people who had come to the capital to escape the growing persecution in their traditional homeland in the northern province of Gonder. When I first wrote about the black Jews of Ethiopia and the possible location of the Ark of the Covenant in Aksum, Ethiopia in my 1988 book *Armageddon – Appointment With Destiny*, I was challenged by many individuals because they had never heard of these black Jews. However, the events of the last few years have established that my research was accurate. After a great deal of research, debate and counsel, the two Chief Rabbis of Israel accepted the "Falasha" as legitimate Jews who were separated from their brethren in the ancient past.

In the years following this Israeli rescue, known as Operation Solomon, I interviewed three individuals who were knowledgeable about this operation. Two of my sources, one Ethiopian and one Israeli, personally knew about aspects of the rescue. The third source was the Honorable Robert N. Thompson, a former Canadian diplomat and Member of Parliament. He traveled to Ethiopia during the final days of the civil war in a successful attempt to rescue the surviving princes and princesses of the Ethiopian royal family who were imprisoned for fourteen years by the Marxist dictator. I have known Robert Thompson since I was a young boy and have admired his incredible career as a military officer, a missionary, a Member of Parliament, a leader of a conservative political party in Canada, and a diplomat serving as Canada's Ambassador to NATO. For many years following World War II he served as an advisor to the Ethiopian Emperor Haile Selassie assisting in the creation of the country's educational and medical systems. Robert Thompson was the first to tell me when I was a young boy that the true Ark of the Covenant was held in Aksum, Ethiopia. Following his part in the rescue of the remaining members of the royal family in Ethiopia I had the opportunity to discuss these issues with Mr. Thompson. He confirmed that his sources had told him substantially the same story that I will now relate.

All three of my sources confirmed essentially the same account. Apparently, during the final days of the defeated Ethiopian regime negotiations took place between Israel and these government leaders about the Ark of the Covenant in Aksum. The Ethiopian military leaders demanded a bribe of several million dollars to allow the Ark to be taken home to Israel. A number of wealthy Jewish donors put up the necessary funds and a suitcase containing the bribe money was delivered to the corrupt officials who promptly left Ethiopia to fly with their illegal loot to Switzerland. Unknown to the departing officials, the suitcase contained millions of counterfeit dollars. The Israelis phoned the bank in Switzerland to inform them of the dubious value of the money these Ethiopian officials were trying to deposit. Israel took the real money raised by the donors and gave it to the Eritrean rebels who had just conquered the Ethiopian capital of Addas Ababa. Since the outgoing corrupt officials had looted the country's treasury, these millions of dollars from Israel were desperately needed by the new struggling democratic government as they attempted to reconstruct their country after years of mismanagement by the communists.

During the closing days of the Ethiopian civil war a special team of young Israelis flew an Israeli military cargo plane into the northern province of Gonder and secretly entered the sacred city of Aksum at night. Each of these Israelites were from the tribe of Levi as required by the law of Moses to carry the Ark of the Covenant. Jews who have the surname Levi are the only Jews who can be sure of their tribal identity as Levites. According to my sources these specially trained men, accompanied by Israeli elite special forces, secretly removed the Ark from the underground treasury deep beneath the Church of Zion in Aksum. These Levites carried the Ark into the military cargo plane in the biblically prescribed manner with the special staves and covered by a blue dyed covering. After flying home to Israel the Ark was taken to a secure place in Jerusalem where they will hold it until the time arrives to place it in its appointed place within the Holy of Holies of a rebuilt Temple in the future. Obviously, such a story is impossible to document or prove. I have included this new information in this revised edition of *Heaven* because of countless requests from readers for any additional information on the Ark. The people who told me this information are credible and the facts related are consistent with other details that are known to me firsthand. Whether or not the true Ark of the Covenant was returned from Ethiopia, the Bible indicates that the true Ark has a role to play in the final events of this age.

Numerous prophecies declare that there will be a rebuilt Temple in Jerusalem during the final years of this age. In 2 Thessalonians 2:4 the Apostle Paul tells us about the Antichrist, "who opposes and exalts himself above all that is called God or that is worshiped, so that he sits as God in the temple of God, showing himself that he is God." Jesus Christ warned His disciples about the Antichrist's defilement of the future "holy place" within the rebuilt Temple. "Therefore when you see the 'abomination of desolation,' spoken of by Daniel the prophet, standing in the holy place (whoever reads, let him understand), then let those who are in Judea flee to the mountains" (Matthew 24:15,16). Finally, in Revelation 11:1,2 John confirms that there will be a future

Temple and an altar of sacrifice during the Tribulation period. John described his vision of this future Temple. "Then I was given a reed like a measuring rod. And the angel stood, saying, 'Rise and measure the temple of God, the altar, and those who worship there. But leave out the court which is outside the temple, and do not measure it, for it has been given to the Gentiles. And they will tread the holy city under foot for forty-two months' " (Revelation 11:1,2).

The purpose of the Temple and the Tabernacle was to provide a dwelling place for the Ark of the Covenant within the Holy of Holies. "Then David the king stood up upon his feet, and said, 'Hear me, my brethren, and my people: As for me, I had in mine heart to build an house of rest for the ark of the covenant of the Lord, and for the footstool of our God, and had made ready for the building' " (1 Chronicles 28:2 [KJV]). The Scriptures suggest that the Ark will be restored to the rebuilt Temple and that it may be defiled by the Antichrist when he enters the "holy place." The prophet Jeremiah suggests that the Ark still has a role to play in the final events of this age in his prophecy about conditions in Israel after the Messiah establishes His righteous rule. "Then it shall come to pass, when you are multiplied and increased in the land in those days," says the Lord, "that they will say no more, 'The ark of the covenant of the Lord.' It shall not come to mind, nor shall they remember it, nor shall they visit it, nor shall it be made anymore" (Jeremiah 3:15,16). Why would Jeremiah predict that Israelis will stop talking about the Ark of the Covenant and that they will stop visiting the Ark after the Messiah returns and once the Millennium begins? The Jews have not talked about or visited the Ark for almost three thousand years since it disappeared from known history during the reign of King Solomon. Yet Jeremiah prophesied that Israel will stop visiting and talking about the Ark after the Messiah's appearance to set up His kingdom. This prophecy logically suggests that the Ark of the Covenant will be visited and talked about by the Israelites during the climactic years leading up to the return of Christ but they will no longer need the Ark when the Messiah is in their presence. Only time will reveal the true future role of the Ark of the

Covenant in the events that will surround the rise of Antichrist and the return of Jesus as Israel's Messiah to establish His kingdom. It is possible that we will then learn the truth about the mysteries surrounding the location of the Ark during the last three thousand years.

The Ashes of the Red Heifer

One of the most unusual sacrifices in ancient Israel was the sacrifice of the Red Heifer. According to the Talmud and the rabbis, it is essential that Israel resume this Sacrifice of the Ashes of the Red Heifer in order to cleanse the Temple Mount and priesthood. This was the most mysterious of all the sacrifices. Many passages in the Talmud attempt to explore its meaning. While the aim of the sacrifice was to purify the defilement of death, yet it defiled all those who were connected with the offering of the Red Heifer. One commentary states: It purifies the impure, and at the same time renders impure the pure! So inscrutable was its nature—they said—that even King Solomon in his wisdom despaired of learning the secret meaning of the Red Heifer regulations.

"This is the ordinance of the law which the Lord commanded to Moses, saying: 'Speak to the children of Israel that they bring you a red heifer without blemish, in which there is no defect and on which a yoke has never come. . . . Then the heifer shall be burned in his [the priest's] sight: its hide, its flesh, its blood, and its offal shall be burned. . . . Then a man who is clean shall gather up the ashes of the heifer, and store them outside the camp in a clean place; and they shall be kept for the congregation of the children of Israel for the water of purification; it is for purifying from sin' " (Numbers 19:2,5,9).

The blood of the Red Heifer was to be sprinkled opposite the entrance to the Tabernacle during the time the Israelites wandered in the wilderness. When the Temple was later completed in Jerusalem, this sacrifice of the Red Heifer occurred on a plateau on the western slope of the Mount of Olives in view of the Holy of Holies. This plateau was directly across the Kidron Valley from the Temple Gates and the Eastern Gate. During a research trip to Israel, I followed the precise eyewitness description found in the Mishneh Torah by Rambam. There I found the exact spot on the Mount of Olives described as the place for this sacrifice. According to the Mishneh, the ceremonial burning of the Red Heifer happened only seven times in Jewish history: once by Moses, once by Ezra and five other times until the destruction of the Second Temple. Each time, the ashes which remained from the previous sacrifice were added to the new ashes to provide continuity, a perpetual sacrifice. The animal was completely burned with cedar wood, hyssop and scarlet within this huge pyramid-shaped bonfire on the plateau. Then the priest would gather the ashes in a clay vessel and return to the Temple. Because this unusual sacrifice defiled one until sunset, the priest could not be the High Priest or his son. These ashes were sprinkled on the surface of water in a large cistern to provide "waters of purification" to purify people from ritual defilements.

In the Book of Hebrews, the Bible reveals that this sacrifice of the Red Heifer and the waters of purification point to the ultimate sacrifice of Jesus Christ for our sins. In an analogous fashion, Christ became sin for us during His sacrifice on the Cross; that we might become the righteousness of Christ. The Red Heifer was a pure sacrifice, without blemish, sacrificed outside the walls of the city. Jesus became the pure sacrifice for us, without blemish, sacrificed outside the walls of Jerusalem.

A "pure" Red Heifer is very rare. Almost all cattle have some imperfections in their coloring. The Talmud states that even one white hair would disqualify the heifer for this sacrifice. Not only did the heifer have to be 100 percent red, it could not have had a yoke laid upon its neck. *Time* magazine reported on October 16, 1989, that the Chief Rabbi of Israel sent a team of scientists to Europe in August to obtain frozen embryos of a breed of red heifers which will be used to raise a pure Red Heifer on an Israeli cattle ranch. The extraordinary part of this report is that this proves the Jewish authorities have decided to conduct animal sacrifices once more.

For the first time in two thousand years, Israel is preparing to resume the Temple sacrifice system. Obviously, the entire Temple Mount has been repeatedly defiled both by ritual impurity and the deaths of hundreds of thousands of soldiers, priests and others during the intervening years since A.D. 70. These years of desecration and death have made the Temple Mount ceremonially impure for worship as commanded by the Old Testament laws of God. It will be necessary to cleanse the Temple area with the waters of purification on which Ashes of the Red Heifer have been sprinkled. Then a reconstituted Sanhedrin, a group of senior rabbis, can resume the acceptable Temple sacrifice system.

A fascinating copper scroll was found in cave number 8 near Qumran among the Dead Sea Scrolls in 1952. This scroll is located in a museum in Amman, Jordan. It confirms that the last sacrifice of the Ashes of the Red Heifer was offered just before the destruction of Jerusalem in A.D. 70. During the conflict the Ashes were taken in a clay vessel from the Temple by priests and secretly buried with other sacred objects so they could be recovered in the last days to enable Israel to cleanse and rebuild the Sanctuary.

A portion of the copper scroll reads: "On the way from Jericho to Succukah, by the River ha Kippa, in the tomb of Zadok, the priest, which is a cave that has two openings. On the opening on the side by the north, the view toward the east, dig two and one-half cubits under the plaster and there will be found the Kalal and under it one scroll." Sixty-seven Temple objects are mentioned in the copper scroll which were hidden by the Jews before the destruction of the Temple in A.D. 70. Naturally, it is very difficult after this length of time to discover the precise location described in the scrolls but several interesting investigations are being conducted presently under the auspices of the Chief Rabbi and the Israeli museums. Some Christian and Jewish students of prophecy believe that these Ashes will be recovered from their hiding place before the rebuilding of the Third Temple. I am aware of several intensive archeological investigations in Israel that seek to find information about the Ark of the Covenant and the Ashes of the Red Heifer.

The Chief Rabbi of Israel has expressed serious interest in these investigations because they believe that the recovery of the Ashes and the Ark of the Covenant are keys to rebuilding the Temple. There is a curious tradition in the Talmud that Gentiles will assist the Jews in the recovery of these necessary Temple implements. One archeological group has been searching in a cave south of Jericho for several years for these Ashes and further scrolls that would show the location of the lost Temple vessels. Although this particular cave has not yielded the Ashes, another group began some promising investigations near the original Qumran cave site where the Dead Sea Scrolls were excavated by Yigael Yadin in 1947. They found a clay jar in a nearby cave that contained an unusual incense oil. It has been scientifically dated to the time of the second Temple and appears to contain the five special ingredients which the Bible describes as the oil for anointing kings (Exodus 30:22-25). The evidence is still inconclusive, but if this proves to be the oil of anointing described in the copper scroll, it is an important discovery. This would lead credence to other references in the scroll about the secret location of the Kalal (a vessel made with clay and dung from the Red Heifer) that holds the Ashes of the last sacrificed Red Heifer.

The Prophet Ezekiel and the Third Temple

The prophet Ezekiel foresaw the rebirth of Israel and the rebuilding of the Temple as the final events which lead to "the world to come." Ezekiel described an enormous military alliance of Arab and European nations, led by Russia (Gog and Magog) that would attack Israel after she returned to the Holy Land from her worldwide captivity. The prophet declared that God would miraculously intervene to destroy 85 percent of this Russian-Arab army with the greatest earthquake in history (Ezekiel 38 and 39). The devastation

The Temple Mount
*The Eastern Gate was sealed to prevent the Messiah entering through it
into the rebuilt temple. Directly behind this gate stood the four
gates and the Holy of Holies.*

Wilson's Arch
*This ancient arch was uncovered by Wilson a hundred years ago.
It stands on the left side of the Western Wall Plaza
where the Jews pray for the rebuilding of the Temple.*

Interior of Wilson's Arch
An Israeli archeologist is standing with a surveying laser aimed north
into the Western Wall tunnel excavation. Rabbis pray and study
Torah scrolls facing the Wailing Wall.

Entrance to Rabbinical Tunnel
This Western Wall Tunnel revealed enormous Herodian Ashlars,
foundation stones 46 ft. by 10 ft. These are the largest cut stones
in the world.

The Tunnel Excavation

View of the 900 foot long Western Wall archeological tunnel. At some points we were under 150 feet of rubble from the destroyed temple.

Ashes from the burning of the second temple on the 9th day of AV, A.D. 70.

These ashes were recently uncovered hanging in a crack in the foundation stones in the tunnel.

The Secret Underground Western Gate
This gate, when discovered in 1968, led into a complex of tunnels which honeycomb the Temple Mount. In the upper right corner you can see the original arched opening. It was sealed to prevent rioting. Notice the prayer slip of paper inserted in the stones.

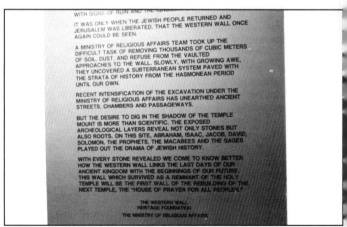

WITH SIGNS OF RUIN AND THE IGNOMINY

IT WAS ONLY WHEN THE JEWISH PEOPLE RETURNED AND JERUSALEM WAS LIBERATED, THAT THE WESTERN WALL ONCE AGAIN COULD BE SEEN.

A MINISTRY OF RELIGIOUS AFFAIRS TEAM TOOK UP THE DIFFICULT TASK OF REMOVING THOUSANDS OF CUBIC METERS OF SOIL, DUST, AND REFUSE FROM THE VAULTED APPROACHES TO THE WALL. SLOWLY, WITH GROWING AWE, THEY UNCOVERED A SUBTERRANEAN SYSTEM PAVED WITH THE STRATA OF HISTORY FROM THE HASMONEAN PERIOD UNTIL OUR OWN.

RECENT INTENSIFICATION OF THE EXCAVATION UNDER THE MINISTRY OF RELIGIOUS AFFAIRS HAS UNEARTHED ANCIENT STREETS, CHAMBERS AND PASSAGEWAYS.

BUT THE DESIRE TO DIG IN THE SHADOW OF THE TEMPLE MOUNT IS MORE THAN SCIENTIFIC. THE EXPOSED ARCHEOLOGICAL LAYERS REVEAL NOT ONLY STONES BUT ALSO ROOTS. ON THIS SITE, ABRAHAM, ISAAC, JACOB, DAVID, SOLOMON, THE PROPHETS, THE MACABEES AND THE SAGES PLAYED OUT THE DRAMA OF JEWISH HISTORY.

WITH EVERY STONE REVEALED WE COME TO KNOW BETTER HOW THE WESTERN WALL LINKS THE LAST DAYS OF OUR ANCIENT KINGDOM WITH THE BEGINNINGS OF OUR FUTURE. THIS WALL WHICH SURVIVED AS A REMNANT OF THE HOLY TEMPLE WILL BE THE FIRST WALL OF THE REBUILDING OF THE NEXT TEMPLE, THE "HOUSE OF PRAYER FOR ALL PEOPLES."

THE WESTERN WALL
HERITAGE FOUNDATION
THE MINISTRY OF RELIGIOUS AFFAIRS

The Western Wall Heritage Foundation Sign

The Dome of the Tablets
The Dome stands over the Bedrock of Mount Moriah, The Temple Mount.
There is ample room to rebuild the temple without disturbing
The Dome of the Rock.

The Foundation Stone
Tradition states that this was the place of the binding of Isaac by Abraham.
The Mishneh Torah describes this foundation stone as the "Even Shetiyah"
where the Ark of the Covenant rested in the temple of Solomon.

The Search For The Ashes of The Red Heifer
This is one of the caves which archeologists are searching
for these ashes.

The Cave of The Dead Sea Scrolls
In 1947, the enormously significant Dead Sea Scrolls were discovered at
Qumran, near the Dead Sea. The copper scroll gave instructions as to
the hiding place of the ashes of the Red Heifer buried before the
Romans burned the temple.

The Place of Sacrifice

For the last offering of the Red Heifer before 70 A.D. this plateau on the Mount of Olives is precisely described in Rambam's Mishneh Torah.

The author Grant Jeffrey and his wife Kaye in front of the Arab Dome of the Rock.

The Tomb of Ezekiel, the prophet in Kafr Al-Kafil, on the Euphrates river in Iraq.

THE EZEKIEL TILES

These inscribed marble tiles are reputed to have come from the traditiona
tomb of the prophet Ezekiel in Kafr al-Kafil, on the Euphrates River in I
They have not yet been dated precisely, but many scholars have suggested
tenth century, at the earliest.

The tomb of Ezekiel is first mentioned in Iggeret Rav Sherira Gaon in 987
C.E. and is described in detail in the accounts of Jewish travellers in the
Middle Ages. Considered a holy place, until recent years Jews visited the to
on pilgrimages, particularly on the holiday of Shavuot.

The story of the acquisition of the Ezekiel tiles extends over a period of sor
40 years.

During World War II, David Hacohen was in charge of Solel Boneh buildin
operations in Syria and Lebanon. His interest in the history of the Middle
East led him to purchase local antiquities. A Lebanese engineer told him of
the existence of a set of marble tiles, on which chapters from the Book of
Ezekiel were engraved in relief Hebrew script. The tiles were in the possessior
of a woman who had acquired them from her father-in-law, a collector of
antiquities.

The Ezekiel tiles description in the museum in Jerusalem.

136

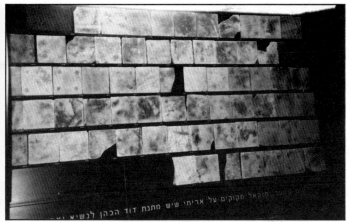

The Ezekiel Tablets
The collection contains 66 marble tablets (some are black basalt).
Two thirds of the text of the book of Ezekiel are present.

Close up of several tablets.

A Single Marble Tablet
Notice the beautiful Bas Relief Script. The workmanship is excellent.

Close up revealing the Bas Relief Script
The letters display an ornate decorative style, using the square,
Aramaic script.

Model of the temple as it looked in the second temple period when Jesus taught in the courtyard.

Yeshiva For Levites
Levites studying the rebuilding of the temple, meet in the Old City of Jerusalem. They have built detailed training models for temple studies.

Bas Relief Carving

An Arab carving a modern script using the same technique as used in the Ezekiel tablets.

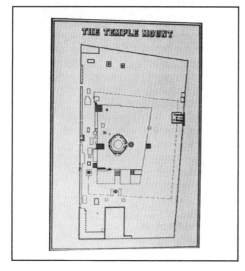

The Temple Mount

A diagram showing the position of the Dome of the Rock (dead center) and the Eastern Gate (higher and to the right). Notice that there is ample room to build the temple north of the dome.

will be so vast that cities around the world will fall and the whole world will be affected. It will take seven months to bury the dead soldiers and seven years for Israel to burn the weapons for fuel. Out of this profound crisis in world history, a political, military and religious transformation will occur. God says: "Then they shall know that I am the Lord" (Ezekiel 28:24). With Russia and her allies devastated, the political-military balance of the world will be changed forever. America will find herself without a Russian enemy for the first time since the end of World War II.

Because of this unique situation, America will possibly withdraw from her role as world policeman and return to her historical position of isolationism. This may be the reason there is so little specific prophecy about America in the events of the last days. When the Rapture takes place, all Christians will be instantly removed from their positions in government, education, business, churches and the military. When the salt is removed, the rot will set in very quickly. As America abandons the spiritual leadership which was the foundation of her greatness, the shift of world power to Europe and the Pacific Rim nations will be overwhelming. The focus of events is quickly turning back to Israel and the Revived Roman Empire of Europe as the Bible prophesied thousands of years ago.

We are entering a very dangerous period of world history. There are heightened expectations of peace but little reduction in the vast armaments available to the dictators. With communist rule in turmoil and America withdrawing from her traditional worldwide peace-keeping role, Europe is uniting for the first time since the end of the ancient Roman Empire. A united Europe will be a true colossus on the world stage. With its huge, well-educated and industrious population, a confederation of the ancient nations of Europe will be the world's major economic and military superpower in the 1990s.

Events are unfolding so quickly that we are witnessing a revolutionary change in the whole course of Western history.

In the light of Bible prophecy, each of the major players are now moving into their appointed places to fulfill the ancient prophecies of the birthpangs of the Messianic Age, the coming Great Tribulation.

"For when they say, 'Peace and safety!' then sudden destruction comes upon them, as labor pains upon a pregnant woman. And they shall not escape. But you, brethren, are not in darkness, so that this Day should overtake you as a thief. You are all sons of light and sons of the day. We are not of the night nor of darkness. Therefore let us not sleep, as others do, but let us watch and be sober" (1 Thessalonians 5:3-6).

Before the Battle of Armageddon and the Return of Christ, the Jews will rebuild the Third Temple on the exact site of the original Temple built by Solomon. There the Levites will resume their ancient sacrifices. The prophet Daniel and Christ both tell us that the coming Antichrist, the leader of the Revived Roman Empire, will abolish this daily sacrifice. He will also enter this rebuilt Temple to claim to be "God" on Earth. Then the world will experience the terrible time of persecution described by the Bible as the Great Tribulation. It will end after three and one-half years of terror and war with the Battle of Armageddon. The only true peace which the world can know before the Millennium is to be found in knowing Christ. "May the God of peace Himself sanctify you completely; and may your whole spirit, soul, and body be preserved blameless at the coming of our Lord Jesus Christ" (1 Thessalonians 5:23). In the next chapter we will talk about an extraordinary archeological discovery concerning the writings of Ezekiel, the prophet of the Exile and the Messiah's glorious return to the rebuilt Temple and the Promised Land.

CHAPTER 9

The Ezekiel Tablets

In a small locked room in Jerusalem lies a treasure that is of tremendous archeological and spiritual importance to the nation of Israel and all those who love the Bible. I had heard rumors about an Israeli discovery of an entire book of the Bible inscribed on ancient marble tablets. Over the past several years, I set about trying to verify the story which was reported in a tantalizingly brief paragraph in an archeological journal. During my most recent trip to Israel, I tracked down the location of this find with great difficulty. As my guide and I approached this small well-hidden museum, four different Israelis who worked there told us that what I was seeking did not exist. They suggested that I was misinformed and must be looking for something else.

As I stood outside this locked room, I knew that my information was correct. But it took several days to find someone who would allow me to see this treasure. Through the good offices of a remarkable Israeli friend who knew the people in charge of this treasure, I was finally privileged to examine in detail these remarkable tablets. My friend had worked daily with these scholars for a year on another project, but they had never shown him their incredible, archeological discovery which they had been secretly studying for years. In the photo section are several pictures of these spectacular stone tablets.

This discovery could change our understanding of the transmission of biblical texts through the centuries. The Israelis who have this treasure call them the Ezekiel Tablets. There are sixty-six marble and black basalt tablets containing almost the complete script of the Book of Ezekiel inscribed in bas-relief. This is a method of carving in which the background is carefully removed, leaving the letters in bold relief. The prophetic Book of Ezekiel has intrigued me for many years. Ezekiel foretold events of profound importance to modern Israel that will occur as the time for the coming of the Messiah draws near. The message of the Exile and the return, of the coming war of Gog and Magog, of the rebuilding of the Temple when the Messiah and the Shekinah glory returns to Israel are imprinted on these sacred tablets. Surely, it is no coincidence that Israel should come into possession of this incredible prophetic treasure now, as we approach the final decade of this millennium and the coming of the Messiah.

In 1947, the year before the rebirth of modern Israel, the world was startled to hear that scholars had discovered an incredible archeological treasure at Qumran, near the Dead Sea. This discovery was the collection of parchments in clay jars known as the Dead Sea Scrolls. These scrolls transformed biblical archeology with their vast amount of information about the beliefs and lifestyles of Jews living during the time of Christ and the Second Temple. Forty years later, the scholastic world is still examining the material from this dig. Now Israel has recovered these extraordinary Ezekiel Tablets which could be equally important.

The stone tablets are located in a small museum in the house of the late Ben Zvi, the second president of Israel, a very religious career diplomat and dedicated amateur archeologist. He became president in November, 1952, when the first president, Chaim Wiezmann, died. He lived in a very simple house which has now been transformed into a religious institute and a museum. The Institute is called Yad Ben Zvi, dedicated to his memory and to commemorate the history of Israel. Within its walls are study halls and a publishing house that deals with Israeli history. The curator of the museum is Yehuda Oppenheim. Research is continuing regarding the origin and meaning of these stones, so there is still much to be learned regarding the reason for their creation and the time of their inscription.

During World War II, a leading Israeli figure was in Syria where he met a French woman who described to him some Hebrew inscribed tablets she had in her possession. She was trying to return to France and the tablets were much too heavy to take with her in wartime conditions. She was concerned about what might happen to them if she left them behind and the war continued. She was hoping that someone would help her place the tablets in proper hands.

One day she came to Jerusalem and spoke with her priest about the inscribed stones. He encouraged her to find a way to return them to the Holy Land because he intuitively believed that the stones were important to the Jewish people. The woman stayed in Syria until World War II ended and kept the tablets with her. Later, during the war of Israel's independence in 1948, she met the Israeli again and was finally convinced to do something with the tablets. The two of them arranged to transfer the tablets from Damascus to Beirut and from there to the northern border of Israel where they would be stored privately. He kept the stones for several years during those uncertain times. When Ben Zvi became president in 1952, the stones were transferred to his home. The stones were stored in a strongroom in the home without serious examination by anyone. The extraordinary political pressures of the day prevented Ben Zvi from devoting the time he wished to resolve the puzzle of these Ezekiel Tablets.

The French woman had stated her father-in-law, a doctor and amateur archeologist, received the stones as payment for medical services he had given to some Arabs while in the desert. Sometimes these Arabs paid him with archeological materials instead of money. They told him that they had taken the tablets from the ancient tomb of the prophet Ezekiel, near the Euphrates River. This tomb of Ezekiel is sixty miles from Baghdad, Iraq, in the small Arab village of Kaffeil Arhut. Like the cave tombs in Hebron, Israel, the tomb is a multiple cave with an upper and lower tomb. These stones were supposedly taken from Ezekiel's tomb to Syria where they were given to the doctor-archeologist some time during the early part of this century. When they finally found a home in the small museum in Israel, a large donation was provided which enabled the museum to establish an exhibit to show the tablets to a few scholars and interested rabbis. Yehuda began to study the tablets personally several years ago.

One reason this is such an important archeological find is the unique nature of the tablets—a biblical text on marble stone tablets, not on scrolls of parchment. A brief mention about the tablets appeared in a professional magazine for archeologists several years ago, but there were no detail or photographs supplied. Aside from a small group of individuals, including my friend, Dr. David Lewis, few people have viewed these stones. Several knowledgeable archeologists and rabbis in Israel told me that it was impossible that such an archeological treasure could exist in Israel without their knowing of it. Until today, no one has been allowed to publish extensive details about the Ezekiel Tablets. Fortunately, because of a providential set of circumstances, my wife Kaye and I received unrestricted access to examine and photograph these sixty-six stone tablets during our recent research trip to Israel. The Israelis in charge of the tablets have decided to allow material to be published to encourage other Hebrew textual scholars and archeologists to assist them in their exploration of this remarkable discovery.

Who Created these Remarkable Ezekiel Tablets?

The small number of scholars who have seen the Ezekiel Tablets are quite divided in their initial conclusions about their origin. While a few of the Israelis believe that the stones may date back to the time of Ezekiel; the majority clearly favor the view that the tablets were created during the Middle Ages. Both groups believe that these unique biblical tablets of stone are extraordinary in their significance to Bible textual scholarship.

Most of the Israeli and North American scholars who examined these stones believe that the evidence indicates they were created about a thousand years ago. The basic reason for their belief is textual, having to do with the shape of the Hebrew letters. The study of writing, known as orthography, suggests that the beautifully decorative style of the chiseled letters on the tablets follows the square Aramaic form that became increasingly common some centuries after the destruction of Jerusalem in A.D. 70. This dating is much later than the sixth century B.C. when the prophet Ezekiel lived in Babylon. If they are correct, some Jewish master craftsman must have created them about one thousand years ago during the Middle Ages. These scholars also point to large areas of "clean writing" in the inscriptions that support a more recent dating. Every one of the twenty-two Hebrew letters are present on the tablets, including several examples of "final Minims" ending sentences that indicate a more recent date.

However, some Israeli scholars connected with the museum hold that these stones could be the original tablets from Ezekiel's tomb, created by the prophet himself or by his pupils after Ezekiel's death. An ancient tradition in the Jewish Talmud says that the original Book of Ezekiel was buried in his tomb at his death and left there to be revealed in the last days. They claim that this would help to explain why such a treasure was hidden for so many centuries. These scholars point to several examples of defective writing in the inscriptions which may suggest an early date, before the birth of Christ.

Whatever the date of their creation, this exciting discovery will throw more light on the accuracy of our present text and on the evolution of the Hebrew script over the centuries. I have supplied competent Hebrew scholars in North America with detailed photos of each stone tablet to allow them to complete an analysis. Over the next few months we hope to learn more from this amazing text. My purpose is to provide evidence about this treasure to those interested in the Bible and to give a brief overview of the two possible conclusions that have been drawn by the scholars who have examined the tablets to date.

Some Unusual Features of the Ezekiel Tablets

The letters are inscribed on the stone tablets in bas-relief. This would take a hundred times more effort and craftsmanship than carving or chiseling in the normal manner. Biblical archeologists in Chicago state there is no known example of any other extensive biblical text inscribed in bas-relief on stone. Nor is there any known book of the Bible that is entirely on stone, even with the normal chiseled engraving method. Israeli scholars who support an earlier date suggest that one of the possible reasons Ezekiel or his students chose bas-relief cutting is that it would prevent any tampering with the text. Not a single letter, "jot or tittle" can be added to such a bas-relief inscription without its being immediately detected.

In my research I discovered that several extensive inscriptions exist from the time of Ezekiel carved in bas-relief on stone. These inscriptions were found in Lebanon on the rocks of Wadi Brissa. They were created by King Nebuchadnezzar's craftsmen on an expedition to conquer Lebanon in 588 B.C. and take enormous amounts of the beautiful cedars back to his capital. In this bas-relief inscription, the King declares his exploits and prays to his god, "O Merodach, my lord, my champion. . . . At thy exalted word, which changes not, may my wood cutting prosper. May the work of my hands come to completion" (*Building Inscriptions of the New Babylonian Empire*, p. 151, Stephen Langdon, 1905, Paris). This wonderful inscription provides additional confirming information about the King Nebuchadnezzar described in the Book of Daniel. It also shows that such bas-relief stone inscriptions were used at the precise time Ezekiel was a captive in Babylon.

Scholars could not determine how ancient craftsmen could produce the entire Book of Ezekiel by this unusually difficult procedure of marble stone-carving. If the artisan made only one mistake, they would have to destroy the entire tablet. The amount of work involved to produce these sixty-six stones in bas-relief script is almost beyond conception, especially if the purpose was purely decorative. The cost and time involved would be prohibitive even for a wealthy patron. If such an incredible treasure is only one thousand years old and existed in some Jewish mansion or synagogue for hundreds of years, why do we have no reference to such a wonderful, priceless object?

The existing tablets contain over two-thirds of the text of the Book of Ezekiel. Less than one-third is missing, and the missing parts are distributed throughout the different chapters. There is some indication that missing stone tablets could be in the hands of private collectors, or might have been taken to France. The scholars in Israel are most anxious to recover them, or at least get photos or rubbings from them, for further research.

There is another curious feature of the stones. While most of the tablets are of marble, a few are inscribed on black basalt. If the purpose for creating the stones was purely for art's sake, why wouldn't the craftsman use pure marble throughout? Anyone with enough money and the expert craftsmen to produce most of the work on marble stones, which is excellent for long-term preservation, would not normally switch to black basalt for the few remaining pieces. They do not match. Black basalt is an inferior stone of less value and will not last nearly as long.

However, some Israeli scholars suggest that if the Jews during the Babylonian captivity inscribed these tablets, it is possible that they could not get enough marble to complete the task and had to use the less expensive, but widely available, black basalt. Normally, in such archeological finds where different material occurs in 10 percent or so of the writing, some damage had happened that called for repairs. If the artisan could not match the original stone exactly, he would usually move up a grade—say, from black basalt to a richer, longer lasting marble—for the replacement pieces. That is not the case in these tablets. The craftsmen used marble throughout until they were forced at some point to use inferior basalt for just a few tablets in scattered areas of the text. If they created these tablets during a captivity, such as the Babylonian captivity, we can easily imagine a situation where they ran out of marble, found it impossible to get any more, and had to switch to basalt to complete the job. One area that must still be explored is the origin of the marble. Since each vein of marble is quite distinct, like a fingerprint, it is possible that this line of inquiry will enable scholars to determine where and when these tablets were created.

The main factor which convinces most scholars the tablets are not from before the time of Christ is the style of script. They ask: if they came from Ezekiel's tomb and were made more than twenty-five hundred years ago when the monarchical script was the common style of writing, why are the tablets written in more modern Hebrew-Aramaic square script? The Israeli scholars suggest that the answer is the original Hebrew letters began to change around the fifth or sixth century B.C. because of a decision by the last great Hebrew leaders, Ezra and Nehemiah. At that time, they claim a new form was given to the Hebrew letter which we now call the square Aramaic script. The two forms are similar but definitely different in their details. As an example of this evolution in the style of letters, a Hebrew inscription from the second Temple period is almost unreadable to a modern Israeli.

The Israeli scholars who support the earlier dating claim that Ezra and Nehemiah introduced the new Aramaic script some seventy years after Ezekiel and they could not have done so unless this type of script was already in common usage. Otherwise, changes would not have been officially accepted by the population or the Great Sanhedrin. They claim that, if this square Aramaic script had first been introduced by the prophet Ezekiel on the marble tablets as the inspired Word of God, this would explain why Ezra and Nehemiah could officially command its acceptance seventy years later, around 520 B.C.

Changes in forms or shapes of letters evolve over hundreds of years and proceed at different paces in different areas. For example, in my own library are English language books written from 1650 onwards. The shapes and uses of the letters change from book to book. At one point the letter "f" was used for an "s" in one country while another country had already switched to the new "s". Some scholars report that the square Aramaic script was introduced gradually from the eighth century B.C. until its universal adoption by the second century after Christ. However, I recently learned of a Hebrew script which appears to be from the sixth century B.C. in Egypt with letters apparently almost identical to those in the Ezekiel Tablets.

Arguments About the Origin of the Tablets

Since the original books of our Bible were copied manually over the centuries, mechanical copying errors were almost inevitable, humanly speaking. Although copies were carefully examined at the time to detect mistakes in copying, most biblical scholars have suspected that our modern translations inadvertently carried over some of these minor errors from manuscripts available then. However, the Dead Sea Scroll of the Book of Isaiah, which was produced in the second century B.C., confirms the tremendous accuracy of the textual integrity of our modern translation of Isaiah. God gave the Jewish Masoretic scribes such an intense love of His Word that they counted every single letter in each book of the Bible to check its copy for accuracy. The Lord has preserved the integrity of His Word over thousands of years in a marvelous way.

The text of Ezekiel on the marble tablets is also almost precisely the same as our modern text. Like other Hebrew texts, there are no chapter breaks as we have in our Bibles now, since chapters and verses were added much later during the Middle Ages when printing was introduced. Nor is there any punctuation or breaks between letters. You have to interpret the structure of the sentence to know where to make the breaks between words. Fortunately, the sentence structure in Hebrew is quite rigid, so there is little possibility of misunderstanding where a sentence should begin and end.

The textual differences found in Ezekiel 1:2 on the marble tablets illustrate a phenomenon which tends to support the view of the Israeli scholars that these tablets may be much older than the Middle Ages. Our modern text states: "On the fifth day of the month, which was in the fifth year of King Jehoiachin's captivity. . . ." However, the Ezekiel Tablets reads, "On the fifth day of the month, which was the fifth year of Jehoiachinis captivity. . ." leaving out the important word "King." If these tablets are simply beautiful but precise copies of the modern text of Ezekiel available in the Middle Ages, why would the artisan leave out the key word "king"? On the other hand, they argue, early copyists would occasionally make marginal notes to better explain a word or phrase in the text. It is understandable why a copyist would include "king" as a marginal notation hundreds of years later to help his readers understand who Jehoiachin was. Since the word did not change the meaning of the text but only clarified it, the missing word "king" could have eventually been included in the section of text instead of in the margin notes. They argue that it is difficult to imagine a cautious, religious craftsman leaving out the word "king" if it was in the material he was copying from. They use this as an argument for the early dating of the tablets before the time of Christ.

There are about fifteen small textual differences between the Ezekiel Tablets and the parchment scripts which were used to produce our current Bible text. Jewish scholars at the institute state that most of these textual variations are similar to the one in Ezekiel 1:2 and tend to support the view that the tablets could have been created in Babylon by Ezekiel's pupils. None of these differences change the general meaning of the text, but they may throw light on when and where the tablets were inscribed.

During some fascinating discussions with the scholars at the institute about the possibility that these tablets may date back to Babylon, the question was asked by someone about their official position of their dating and origin. In light of their obvious enthusiasm, their somewhat surprising answer was: "Our position is that the tablets are only one thousand years old." When asked to explain why they took this position, they replied: "If the stones are only one thousand years old, our institute can keep them. If they are proven to truly date back to the period of Ezekiel, then the government would take them and build their own museum to house them, like the Dead Sea Scrolls. We would then lose the Ezekiel Tablets. So our position is that they are only one thousand years old."

Competent Hebrew scholars have stated that these tablets are one of the most interesting textual finds in the history of archeology. If they were ever proven to date back to the period before Christ, they would be almost as important as the Dead Sea Scrolls. Whether the ultimate decision is that the tablets are a thousand years old or much older, this archeological discovery will have a profound effect upon our understanding of the creation and transmission of biblical texts through the centuries. It is my hope that this newly released material will encourage competent Hebrew textual scholars in Israel and abroad to complete the necessary research to enable us to realize the implications of this wonderful contribution to biblical research.

It is fascinating to consider the message of Ezekiel, the Exile and the Return, in light of the recent discovery of these tablets of stone. The Word of God proclaims the prophetic message inscribed on these ancient tablets so many centuries ago: "I will set My glory among the nations; all the nations shall see My judgment which I have executed, and My hand which I have laid on them. So the House of Israel shall know that I am the Lord their God from that day forward" (Ezekiel 39:21,22).

CHAPTER 10

Special Update Chapter

Exciting New Evidence About The Ezekiel Tablets

Recently I uncovered some fascinating new information regarding the mysterious Ezekiel Tablets described in an earlier chapter. Regarding the possibility that tablets containing the text of the Book of Ezekiel could have been buried in the tomb of a prophet, the Talmud (*Megilla*, 26b) tells about the ancient Jewish custom of burying manuscripts with the body of their sages and scholars. During an examination of some passages in the Talmud I came across some curious references to the tomb of the prophet Ezekiel. As I mentioned in the chapter about the Ezekiel Tablets this was a double tomb designed to hold two bodies such as we find at the tomb of Abraham and Sarah in Hebron, Israel. The texts recount that a Persian Caliph, a prince of Babylon, visited the Jewish Rabbi Solomon because he had heard many remarkable tales about the great prophet Ezekiel. The Caliph requested that Rabbi Solomon take him into the tomb of the famous prophet.

The Tomb of the Prophet Ezekiel

The Talmud states that the tomb of Ezekiel adjoined the tomb of Baruch, the scribe who assisted the prophet Jeremiah by writing down his inspired prophecies. The Bible does not tell us that Baruch ever went to Babylon or that he was buried there. However, it is possible that Baruch traveled in his later life to visit the Jews living in captivity in Babylon some six hundred miles away. The first group of Persians who attempted to break in to the tomb were supernaturally killed according to the Talmud's legends. Then the Persian prince asked the Jews to fast and pray in an attempt to discover the correct way to accomplish his purpose. After many days of fasting the Jewish leaders suggested that they first attempt to open the tomb of the scribe Baruch and then try to enter the tomb of the prophet Ezekiel. Once they successfully entered the second tomb belonging to Ezekiel they were surprised to discover the remains of a body lying on marble tablets. This mention in an ancient text of marble tablets within the tomb of Ezekiel is tantalizing. Could these marble tablets be the same marble stones which the Bedouin Arabs claimed they took from the tomb of Ezekiel more than a thousand years later during the early years of this century? While this account does not prove that the Ezekiel Tablets are from the ancient tomb of Ezekiel it certainly provides some evidence in favor of that argument.

Another fascinating historical footnote is connected to the tomb of Ezekiel. Ginzberg's *Legends of the Jews* (Vol. IV, p. 324-326) describes an attempt by robbers to break into the same tomb in a vain attempt 'to take some books from the grave of Ezekiel.' Again, the legend reveals that the attempt to steal the 'books' was unsuccessful. The word translated 'books' could refer to either 'scrolls' or 'tablets.' The ancient Jews did not have bound books with pages at that time. This reference supports the Arab account that they took these marble tablets from Ezekiel's tomb at a much later date. The Jewish records tell us that King Jehoiachin built this marvelous mausoleum for the prophet Ezekiel's body after Jehoiachin was released from his imprisonment by the Babylonian King Evil-Merodach. Various historical accounts mention the tomb of Ezekiel with the names of thousands of Jews who assisted in building this sepulcher. The famous medieval traveler Rabbi Benjamin of Tuldela also described his visit to the magnificent tomb in his writings in the twelfth century.

A Missing Photo

In 1952 a close friend of Ben Zvi, the second president of Israel, was allowed to view the Ezekiel Tablets. After examining these fascinating stones he turned to the president and said, "You know, I believe that I have seen a picture of one of these stones several years ago." Unfortunately this individual could not remember which book or journal contained the photo. As far as Ben Zvi knew no one had ever been allowed to publish photos of these tablets before. Could this have been a photo of one of the missing tablets? Years of research by those interested in the tablets failed to turn up the photo or reference.

One day in a dark corner of a special library in Jerusalem I was doing research on another project, the Copper Scroll, dealing with the hidden treasures of the Second Temple. This scroll was found at Qumran in 1952 in Cave number 3. It contained an intriguing list of sixty-four locations where the Essenes and priests hid the lost treasures of the Temple from the Roman army in A.D. 68. After hours of following one false lead after another I finally tracked down an elusive reference to the Copper Scroll in an enormous group of documents and volumes covering an entire wall of the library. To my great surprise as I opened a French text dealing with the Copper Scroll, there at the end of the passage, the author J. Milik, one of the major Dead Sea Scroll scholars, included a photo of one of the marble tablets with a partial description of the text and how he had found it. The photo was taken by Jean Starcky, another famous Scroll scholar. Strangely the photo of the marble tablet and text were not listed in either the index or the titles. This important information was simply buried in the unrelated article about the Copper Scroll. This is the reason that no one had ever succeeded in locating the obscure reference to a marble tablet.

Now that I had located the mysterious photo I was able to obtain a translation. The photo revealed a marble tablet with a text in ancient Hebrew script in bas-relief—exactly like the Ezekiel Tablets. However, the mysterious text in the photo did not contain the text of the Book of Ezekiel. Rather, it contains a history of the lost treasures of the Temple (of Solomon) and their secret hiding places located near Mount Carmel.

The article (in French) by J. Milik in *Revue Biblique*, 1959 states:

". . . The copper scroll originating in Cave 3 of Qumran has a catalog of treasures hidden in the underground of Palestine. . . ." Another writing most interesting because it relates in detail the treasures of the Temple of Jerusalem hidden about the time of the destruction by the Babylonians. It was printed in 1853 by A. Jellinek in Bet-ha-Midrash II, Leipzig, pages 26 and 85-91 (which the author of this article did not find available). A duplicate of this "Treatise of the Sacred Vessels" is to be read on the "Plates (Tablets) of Beirut."

A good number of years ago he found in a house in Beirut several marble slabs engraved with letters in relief. It seems they were destined for a synagogue of Syria or Lebanon. They contained the entire text of Ezekiel, but on the two last slabs were found inscribed the history of a treasure of Mount Carmel and the description of the sacred hiding places . . . "these slabs are worth further study to determine the dates of the writing . . ."

This fascinating article tells us that Professor Milik knew that the last two marble tablets regarding the treasures of Solomon's Temple were part of the Ezekiel Tablets collection containing the complete text of the Book of Ezekiel. At some point in the late 1940s Milik had seen the Ezekiel Tablets in Beirut, Lebanon and felt they were worth studying further. Now after all these years they have turned up in Jerusalem. Hopefully the proper scholars will now be able to do the research and determine their true source and dating.

In my book, *Messiah – War in the Middle East*, I share my ongoing research into the secrets of the Copper Scroll's treasures of the Second Temple and these two mysterious marble tablets referring to the treasures of Solomon's Temple. In one of my trips to Jerusalem I met an interesting gentleman who has been fascinated by the Ezekiel Tablets for many years. In his research of the marble text he found a number of very small differences in the letters in the Ezekiel Tablet text. These differ from the normal Hebrew text of Ezekiel found in the oldest biblical manuscripts. As a careful student of the Book of Ezekiel he discovered a curious anomaly. Virtually every one of the ancient prophets of Israel saw the burden of being a prophet as a kind of 'curse' that God had placed upon them. None of these great men of God relished the unwelcome task of preaching repentance to an unrepentant generation. All of the prophets, save one, expressed in their writing within the biblical text that they felt their prophetic call was a terrible 'burden' and a 'curse.' As one example of this phenomenon, the prophet Nahum began his book with these words, "The burden of Nineveh. . . ." The one great exception as noted by the Jewish rabbis was the prophet Ezekiel. He is the only one who did not claim in his writing that his duty as a prophet was a curse or burden to him.

However, in the text of chapter 2, verse 3, found in the Ezekiel Tablets my friend discovered that the marble tablets contained a very small letter reversal in this verse which subtly altered the meaning of the prophet's words. In the normal Hebrew manuscript the text reads: "And He *said unto* me, 'Son of man, I send thee to the children of Israel, to a rebellious nation that hath rebelled against me. . . .' " (Ezekiel 3:2). However, in the marble Ezekiel Tablets the text has two of the letters reversed in verse 2. Instead of ויאמר which means "said unto" the tablet's text reversed these letters to produce the word ויארר that means "cursed." The slight difference in the order of these two Hebrew letters changed the text to read: "And He *cursed* me, 'Son of man, I send thee. . . .' " In other words, the text of the Ezekiel Tablets, if this was the original text, would contain the words that indicate that the prophet Ezekiel, similar to all the other Old Testament prophets, felt the terrible burden of being a prophet as a kind of curse from God. Possibly these two letters were reversed as a simple transposition error at some early point of time in the process of copying this text. This particular type of error could have been quite easily made by a scribe. This new evidence tends to support several Israeli scholars in their belief that the Ezekiel Tablets may be an earlier text than the Hebrew text used to produce the text of Ezekiel in our Bible. As we consider this information, it is important to realize that none of these small textual variations change the vital meaning of any aspect of the message of the prophet. The text of the Bible is so well established that scholars are confident that we have the accurate and full, inspired Word of God.

One final point concerns the fact that the Ezekiel Tablets were written in an Aramæan form of Hebrew script which became increasingly common after the time of Christ and in the medieval period. The presence of this more *modern* Hebrew script style in the tablets convinced many scholars that these tablets were probably created during the last one thousand years. However, the article on Alphabet in the *Dictionary of the Bible* (1901) by Isaac Taylor records, "On the return of the Jews from the Babylonian exile, the ancient ת (and the other letters) of Israel, . . . was abandoned for the more cursive but far inferior Aramæan, which had become the mercantile script of the western provinces of Persia. A Jewish tradition, preserved in the Talmud, attributed the change to Ezra; but there can be no doubt that both scripts were for a time employed concurrently. . . ." This article indicates that the change to the more modern Aramæan script began at the time of the Babylonian captivity and Ezra (536 B.C). Significantly, this is the same time the prophet Ezekiel was writing his prophetic masterpiece in Babylon. In addition, it is interesting to compare the Hebrew script in the sixth century B.C. document found in a Jewish text from the island of Elephantine in the Nile River in Egypt. This script from the sixth century before Christ, the very same period as the prophet Ezekiel, contains letters displaying a very similar style to those found in the Ezekiel Tablets. In light of these findings it is possible to conclude that the Ezekiel Tablets were created before the time of Christ. Some of the scholars in Israel who are closely connected with the Ezekiel Tablets cautiously affirm their belief that the marble tablets might have been created by the pupils of Ezekiel after his death in Babylon to record his inspired prophecies indelibly in stone.

The Vision of Ezekiel About the Fourth Temple

The last nine chapters of Ezekiel contain one of the most extraordinary prophecies in the Bible. The Jewish captives despaired for the loss of their Temple and nation when they were taken in chains to Babylon. While they "wept by the rivers of Babylon" God sent His tremendous message of comfort and hope to the Jews promising that they would someday return to their Promised Land to see their beloved Temple restored to its exquisite grandeur. Despite the hopelessness of their present plight, Ezekiel's prophecy of the building of the glorious Fourth Temple by their Messiah held out the tantalizing hope of a future of freedom and dignity when "the Tabernacle of God would dwell with men."

The unique feature of this prophecy of Ezekiel is the presence of very precise and detailed building instructions about a future Temple which will exist in the Millennium and forever under the reign of the Messiah. These construction details are so specific that most conservative Bible scholars are convinced that the prophet was describing a real future Temple of God, not a symbolic vision. These wonderfully detailed instructions provided an assurance to the Children of Israel in Captivity that God had not abandoned or forgotten them forever. His Covenant with Abraham and his descendants was unbreakable. This Temple structure will be enormous with walls extending over one mile in each direction. In fact this Fourth Temple will be so large that it will not fit on either the existing Temple Mount or even within the boundaries of the old walled city of Jerusalem. These prophetic details confirm that Ezekiel was prophetically describing a future Fourth Temple that will be built by the Prince, the Messiah, during His Millennial reign. In every detail, this Fourth Temple differs from the Third Temple that must be built by the Jews on the present Temple Mount in the Old City of Jerusalem. This Third Temple will be defiled by the future Antichrist and finally, it will be cleansed by the returning Messiah when He enters through the sealed Eastern Gate into the House of God to cleanse the

Sanctuary. The prophet Daniel declared, "then shall the sanctuary be cleansed" (Daniel 8:14).

The Location and Builder of the Millennial Temple

This brings us to the problem of the future location of this Millennial Temple. Where will it be built? Another question concerns its construction. Who will build it—the Jewish people or the coming Messiah? An argument has continued for thousands of years among the rabbis concerning the building of this final Temple. Some Jewish sages held that the command of God in the Torah demands that Israel must rebuild the Temple. Exodus 25:8 declares: "Let them build me a sanctuary; that I may dwell among them." However, other Jewish sages held that they should wait until the Messiah would come to build the Temple Himself. They point to the Messianic message of the prophet Zechariah 6:12 where the prophet predicted: "Behold the man whose name is the Branch; and he shall grow up out of his place, and he shall build the temple of the Lord." The resolution of this apparent contradiction will be found in the fact that the Scriptures declare there must be two Temples in Israel's future. The Third Temple will be built by the Jews in the near future on the Temple Mount. At some point after its construction and the resumption of Temple sacrifice, the prophet Daniel declared that it will be defiled by the Antichrist (Daniel 9:24-27). Finally, the Third Temple will be cleansed by the coming of Jesus Christ as Israel's great High Priest following His victory over the Antichrist in the Battle of Armageddon. The Fourth Temple, described by the prophets Zechariah and Ezekiel, will then be built by Jesus the Messiah during the Millennial Kingdom.

The prophet Ezekiel told us that Israel will finally enjoy its long awaited peace under the reign of the Messiah when He rules from the Throne of David in Jerusalem. Additionally, Ezekiel described a thirteen-fold division of the land "from Dan to Beer-sheba" during the Millennium which will provide each of the twelve tribes of Israel with a parallel portion of land stretching from the Mediterranean Sea to the great Euphrates River. Each strip will be 25,000 rods across (225,000 feet or 43.25 miles wide). In the middle of Israel there will be a special portion called the "Prince's Portion" for the *Nassi*, the Messiah. Ezekiel described the sacred plot of land that will be set aside for God as the Terumah (Ezekiel 45:1-4). This portion called the Terumah will contain the new enlarged city of Jerusalem and the Fourth Temple. The dimensions of the new city of Jerusalem will be 4,500 rods square which will equal 7.75 miles on each side.

A curious feature of this prophecy concerns the position of the Temple between two of the tribal allotments. In the ancient division of the land, Jerusalem and the Temple lay on the dividing line between the portion for Judah and Benjamin (*Yoma* 12a). Ezekiel describes the thirteenth portion of the land for the Temple, city and Messiah as lying between the tribal allotments of Judah and Benjamin once again. While the other tribes will enjoy possession of their tribal portion forever, the prophet declares that the Levites will not inherit a portion of the land. Instead, they will dwell in the Prince's Portion with their beloved Messiah. They will enjoy the tithes of the people as their reward and possession.

The Size of the Millennial Temple

The new Temple Mount area in the Millennium will be enormous. The Bible states: "there shall be for the sanctuary five hundred (rods) in length, with five hundred (rods) in breadth, square round about. . . ." A rod is equal to six cubits or nine feet. Therefore since 500 rods are equal to 4,500 feet—each side of the Temple will be almost one mile long. The world has never seen such a massive structure. This measurement would yield a Temple area of nine million square cubits or 20,250,000 square feet. The Second Temple was the largest Temple enclosure in history encompassing almost thirty-five acres in size. Yet, according to the record in Middos 2:1, the entire Temple Mount area in the Second Temple was only 250,000 square cubits. In other words, Ezekiel's prophecy revealed that this future Millennial Temple will be thirty-six times larger than the enormous

Second Temple area. A detailed analysis of the land measurements given in Ezekiel chapters 40 to 48 indicates that this Fourth Temple will be built by the Messiah approximately twenty-five miles north of the location of the present walled city of Jerusalem.

The glory of this Millennial Temple will be manifested in the eternal presence of the Shekinah Glory of God who will dwell there. Ezekiel had witnessed in his vision (Ezekiel 11:22) the tragic departure of the Shekinah Glory from Solomon's Temple because of Israel's rebellion in the past. Fortunately, God's plan of redemption for Israel and the Gentiles promises that Jesus the coming Messiah will return in His Glory to inhabit the Temple of God forever. When the Divine Presence dwells once again in Jerusalem, Israel will take its true position as God's Promised Land that will bless all of the nations throughout the world. God's promise was given through the words of Ezekiel: "Then will I sprinkle clean water upon you, and ye shall be clean: from all your filthiness, and from all your idols, will I cleanse you." The prophecies reveal that it will not be long until the Messiah will return to fulfill all of the great prophecies of the redemption of Israel and the Promised Land.

One of the great promises of redemption found in Ezekiel's prophecy (47:1-12) declares that God will cause a great river of fresh water to flow from beneath the Temple eastward through the Judean desert to heal the waters of the Dead Sea. God has promised that the desolate land shall be miraculously healed and that the deadly waters of the Dead Sea shall come alive with abundant fish. To illustrate the reality of His glorious promise the Lord declared that a marvelous transformation would occur, including the creation of "a very great multitude of fish" in the previously dead waters of the Dead Sea. The Lord said that there "shall be a place to spread forth the nets" (Ezekiel 47:9,10).

Ezekiel: Prophet of Exile
and the Return to the Land in 1948

As we examine the marble tablets containing the fascinating prophecies of Ezekiel we are reminded of his great prophecy that we are rapidly approaching the "age of redemption," the age of the Messiah. That prophecy found in Ezekiel chapter 37 contains "the vision of the valley of dry bones." This terrible vision tragically describes the desperate experience of the Jewish people who were slaughtered and persecuted for almost two thousand years in the graveyard of the nations. However, this prophecy does not end with Israel left in the graveyard of dry bones. The Lord appeared unto Ezekiel and commanded him to prophesy unto the bones of the Jews that "the breath came into them, and they lived and stood up upon their feet an exceeding great army" (Ezekiel 37:10). The Lord commanded, "I will open your graves and cause you to come up out of your graves and bring you into the land of Israel."

A century ago there were less than 50,000 Jews, and even less Arabs, living in the Land of Promise. Today, in answer to the ancient prophecy, more than four million Jews have returned in fulfillment of God's word. The prophet Isaiah (43:6) said, "I will say to the north, Give up; and to the south, Keep not back: bring my sons from far, and my daughters from the ends of the earth." Over 500,000 Russian Jews have flown out of the north from Moscow and Leningrad returning to the Promised Land. Almost a hundred thousand black Ethiopian Jews flew out of that troubled land from the south where they lived for almost 3,000 years cut off from their brethren. Who can observe the miraculous return of almost a million Jewish exiles to Israel without seeing the Hand of God revealed to our generation? After almost 2,000 years of Exile the Lord has brought the children of Israel back to their land to meet their coming Messiah. Remember the words of King David who prophesied as follows: "Thou shalt arise, and have mercy upon Zion: for the time to favor her, yea, the set time, is come. For thy servants take pleasure in her stones, and favor the dust thereof. So the heathen shall fear the name of the Lord, and all the kings of the earth thy glory. When the Lord shall build up Zion, he shall appear in his glory" (Psalm 102:13-16).

Some people ask, "Haven't all generations longed for the return of the Messiah?" However, the answer is clear. Ours is the first generation that has witnessed the fulfillment of hundreds of Messianic prophecies within the past few decades. Since the rebirth of Israel in 1948 we have witnessed more prophecies fulfilled in our lifetime than any other generation in the last two thousand years. In addition to the return of the Jews to their Promised Land, we have seen "a nation born at once" on May 15, 1948 (Isaiah 66:8). Ezekiel predicted, "I will multiply the fruit of the tree and the increase of the field" and said that "this land that was desolate is become like the Garden of Eden" (Ezekiel 36: 30,35). This tiny desert nation now "blossoms as a rose" providing 90 percent of the citrus fruit consumed by the nations of Europe. Every morning an El Al 747 airplane departs from Ben Gurion Airport to deliver a planeload of tulips to Holland. The incredibly pure fertilizers from the Dead Sea salts now produce awesome yields from the previously parched desert soil. Some scientists believe that the incredible quantity and quality of the chemical salts from the Dead Sea have the potential to fertilize the desolate areas of this planet to allow them to produce the food needed by an ever increasing humanity.

The Book of Exodus (14:31 to 15:2) records "Israel saw that great work that the Lord did upon the Egyptians: and the people feared the Lord and believed the Lord and His servant Moses. Then sang Moses and the children of Israel this song unto the Lord, 'The Lord is my strength and song, and He is become my salvation: He is my God, and I will prepare Him an habitation.' " This Song of Moses will be sung in our future according to the Psalmist David, "O Sing unto the Lord a new song; for He hath done marvelous things. . . ." (Psalm 98:1).

The Book of Revelation (15:3) also promises that those people who are victorious over the Antichrist will then "sing the Song of Moses, the servant of God, and the song of the Lamb, saying, 'Great and marvelous are thy works, Lord God Almighty.'" Now, for the first time since the days of the Second Temple, we can hear the Jews singing at the Western Wall of the Temple.

Since the recapture of the city of Jerusalem and the Temple Mount during the 1967 Six Day War, the Western Wall was opened to Jewish and Gentile worshipers who come to pray and sing. Every Sabbath day and every feast day you can observe thousands of Jews, including yeshiva students and venerable rabbis, coming down from the Jewish Quarter of Jerusalem to the sacred Western Wall. Dancing arm in arm and singing blessings to their people, these worshipers sing praises to the God of Israel who has fulfilled hundreds of prophecies in our day. On January 13th, 1991, only three days before the air war began in the Gulf War, my wife Kaye and I stood at the Western Wall among two hundred thousand orthodox Jews, the "men of God," called there to fervent prayer by their two Chief Rabbis. These devoted men rocked back and forth praying that God would protect Israel against the SCUD missiles aimed at Israel by Iraq. Though hundreds of apartments and houses were destroyed in the Iraqi missile onslaught, the Hand of God was miraculously revealed as only two Israelis were killed when thirty-nine SCUD missiles hit Tel Aviv and Haifa. As these Jews prayed and sang, they called out for the coming of the Messiah and the rebuilding of the Temple in our day.

The message of the Book of Ezekiel has awakened the special attention of both the Jewish people and Christians in our generation through the discovery of these wonderful Ezekiel Tablets miraculously preserved over the centuries. Surely it cannot be an accident or mere coincidence that these strange tablets should be discovered in these momentous days as Israel returns to their land and prepares to rebuild the Temple once again. The inspired words of Ezekiel still speak to those men and women who are open to hear the words of God: "When I have brought them again from the people and gathered them out of their enemies' lands and am sanctified in them in the sight of many nations; Then shall they know that I am the Lord their God. . . . Neither will I hide My Face any more from them: For I have poured out My Spirit upon the House of Israel, saith the Lord" (Ezekiel 39:27-29).

The footsteps of the Messiah are truly resounding on the hills of Judea for those who are listening with their spiritual ears. The voices of the ancient prophets awaken us to the incredible fulfillment of their prophecies in our generation announcing the coming of the Messiah, Jesus Christ. The Age of Redemption is coming soon.

CHAPTER 11

The Millennium

"For unto us a Child is born, Unto us a Son is given; And the government will be upon His shoulder. And His name will be called Wonderful, Counselor, Mighty God, Everlasting Father, Prince of Peace. Of the increase of His government and peace There will be no end, Upon the throne of David and over His kingdom, To order it and establish it with judgment and justice. From that time forward, even forever" (Isaiah 9:6,7).

The Bible's promise of blessing to man has ultimately focused on the prophecy of a Kingdom of God on Earth which will be ruled by the Messiah. From the moment when the Lord made the first covenant with Abraham, God committed Himself to establish a theocratic Kingdom in which man would ultimately enjoy the restoration of the paradise lost by the sin of our first parents, Adam and Eve. Through all the generations leading to the time of Christ, Israel has longed for the coming of the Messiah and his glorious reign from Jerusalem.

The Church has often lost sight of the Scripture's prophesy of Christ ruling on the throne of David forever. In focusing primarily on the role of Christ as the head of the Church, the medieval Church often ignored the prophecies about His coming Kingdom. They set out to change and rule the world themselves. Even today there are many within the Church who believe that our proper role is to Christianize the world. They believe we should politically organize to establish a Christian kingdom now. However, this idea is not consistent with either the Bible's prophecy, nor the tragic reality of past failures to Christianize nations under the Roman Catholic Church. The total failure of all past attempts to politically establish Christian kingdoms should warn us to carefully examine the Bible's prophecies about the last days.

The Bible teaches that in the last days an evil world empire will exist under the Satanic rule of Antichrist. The defeat of this evil world system will not be accomplished by the Church. Jesus Christ, as the conquering Messiah, will return from Heaven with a mighty army to destroy His enemies forever. The prophet Daniel received an interpretation of the dream of Nebuchadnezzar, the King of Babylon, about the future of world political power. God outlined in prophetic detail the last twenty-five hundred years of Gentile world empires. He revealed there would be only four successful Gentile world empires in human history. The fourth empire, Rome, would be revived as a ten nation confederacy in the last days and be led by the Antichrist. Daniel declares that Christ will come and suddenly destroy these kingdoms during the final stage of a revived Roman Empire. The vision in Daniel, chapter 2, shows a huge stone which instantly pulverizes the feet of this great image. The angel explains that the great image refers to the final ten nation confederacy of nations which will arise out of the ashes of the ancient Roman Empire. The stone is the Millennial Kingdom which will emerge suddenly when Christ returns to save Israel from the armies of the Antichrist during the Battle of Armageddon. Christ will judge the nations in the Valley of Jehoshaphat [the valley where Jehovah judges] between the Mount of Olives and the Temple Mount as described in Joel 3:2,12.

The Importance of the Millennial Kingdom

The Millennial Kingdom of the coming Messiah is the most misunderstood subject in the whole field of prophecy. It has become the great dividing issue upon which writers have divided into three great schools: Pre-Millennial, Amillennial and Post-Millennial. The Amillennial and Post-Millennial position holds that either the Millennium (the 1,000 year Kingdom of Christ) is only symbolic or that Christ will only return to establish His Kingdom after the Church has

Christianized the Earth. After many years of study I have concluded that the Pre-Millennial view is the only position which is consistent with the literal prophecies of the Bible. Pre-millennialism was the universal teaching of the Apostolic Church in the early centuries following Christ. The interested reader should examine the excellent comprehensive presentation of the three views and the case for Pre-millennialism by Dwight Pentecost in his book *"Things To Come."* An acceptance of the literal prophecies of the Bible leads to the conclusion that Christ will physically return to the Earth and that He will establish His Millennial Kingdom of Heaven on Earth.

If we want to understand God's unfolding plan for mankind, we must examine the biblical prophecies about the Millennium as revealed by the prophets of both the Old and New Testaments. This prophesied Kingdom is a "real" kingdom, not an allegorical picture of a spiritual state of mind of the believer. As mentioned in an earlier chapter on the Rapture, beginning with the writers Origin and Augustine in the third and fourth century after Christ, a new spiritualizing, allegorical method of interpretation began to enter the teaching of the Church. The Roman Catholic Church gradually abandoned a literal interpretation of the Bible including such foundational beliefs as justification by faith and belief in the Millennium Kingdom. These great truths which were delivered to the early Church through the Bible and the words of Christ were a great treasure. Jude knowing that the Church would someday abandon these principles, wrote the following message: "I found it necessary to write to you exhorting you to contend earnestly for the faith which was once for all delivered to the saints" (Jude, verse 3).

Every single prophecy which was fulfilled in the life of Jesus Christ was fulfilled in a literal, common sense way. The position of many people who reject prophecy is that somehow the future fulfillments will not be "literal." Yet even Amillennial and Post-Millennial scholars admit that the early church universally taught that Christ will someday return to establish His Kingdom. They taught that a personal

Antichrist will arise in the last days to rule for seven years leading to the final Battle of Armageddon. This battle will end in the triumphant victory of the heavenly army of Christ. He will set up His eternal rule from the city of Jerusalem which will ultimately produce the greatest blessings the world has ever known.

The Sealed Eastern Gate

The Messiah will descend to Earth on the Mount of Olives, opposite the Temple Mount, according to the prophet Zechariah. Then a great earthquake will split the earth from the Mediterranean through the Mount of Olives to the Dead Sea. Christ will cross the Kidron Valley as He did on Palm Sunday almost two thousand years ago.

The prophet Ezekiel declared that the promised Messiah would enter the sealed Eastern Gate of the Temple Mount into the rebuilt sanctuary. "And behold, the glory of the God of Israel came from the way of the east. His voice was like the sound of many waters; and the earth shone with His glory. . . . And the glory of the Lord came into the temple by the way of the gate which faces toward the east. The Spirit lifted me up and brought me into the inner court; and behold, the glory of the Lord filled the temple" (Ezekiel 43:2,4,5).

The prophet had told Israel that this Eastern Gate would be sealed to preserve it for the coming Messiah, the Prince. "And the Lord said to me, 'This gate shall be shut; it shall not be opened, and no man shall enter by it, because the Lord God of Israel has entered by it; therefore it shall be shut . . . because He is the Prince' " (Ezekiel 44:2,3). Amazingly, this gate has been shut now for many centuries. The original Eastern gate is also sealed under the accumulated rubble directly in front of the present sealed Eastern Gate which you can see today. The Moslems under Suleiman the Magnificent were aware of the ancient prophecy of the coming Jewish Messiah and they sealed this gate when they rebuilt the city walls four hundred years ago. To prevent the coming of the Messiah through the gate they built a large graveyard in front of it. In their religion a priest or holy man would be defiled by walking through a graveyard so they felt that a grave site would prevent the Messiah fulfilling Ezekiel's prophecy.

Several years ago I approached and touched these ancient stones of the Eastern Gate. On the ground directly in front of the sealed gate the Arabs had placed the gravestones of several children only two inches from the bottom of the huge foundation blocks of the gate. Poignantly, a shell casing from an ejected bullet had fallen onto the child's small grave from the soldier's guard post above the gate. I discovered an amazing inscription which was written on the stones which had sealed the gate for so many centuries. "Ba Ha Moshiach"—"Come Messiah." Some Orthodox Jewish believer, who understood the ancient prophecy of Ezekiel, had secretly approached the Eastern Gate recently and written this welcoming message to the Messiah upon these stones.

Twice in this century an attempt to open the sealed Eastern Gate failed. First, on December 9th, 1917 the Grand Mufti, the Arab leader of Jerusalem, tried to open this gate. He had ordered the other gates to Jerusalem sealed to deter the approaching Allied Expeditionary Army led by the British General, Lord Allenby. Since he needed one gate open, he ordered his workmen to open the mysterious sealed gate. As the workman picked up their sledgehammers, Lord Allenby's biplane flew over the city telling the Arabs to "flee Jerusalem." Miraculously, without a shot being fired the soldiers fled the city. It was delivered into the hands of Britain which had one month earlier promised the Jews "a national homeland" with the famous Balfour Declaration. The workmen fearfully put down their sledgehammers and the gate remained sealed as God had prophesied.

Again in 1967, the ancient prophecy was fulfilled. Tensions were rising in the Middle East as the Arabs commanded the United Nations peacekeeping forces out of the Sinai. Egypt stopped Israeli shipping and moved its forces into attack formations. King Hussein of Jordan had conquered the Old City of Jerusalem in 1948, including the Temple Mount. For the first time in centuries the Jews were forbidden to worship at their sacred Western Wall. The Moslem King Hussein decided to build a hotel for Arab pilgrims on this section of the Western Wall closing off this area to Jewish worship forever. However, the planned hotel would be built over the Magreb Gate which all pilgrims presently use to enter the Temple Mount. The King needed to open another gate to allow Moslem worshipers entrance to the El Aqsa Mosque on the Temple Mount. In violation of the prophecy he ordered his workmen to open the sealed Eastern Gate. On June 5, 1967 as the workmen prepared their air hammers to shatter the huge stones, Israeli aircraft pre-emptively responded to the Arab war preparations. The warplanes flew out of their underground air bases to devastate their enemies' air forces and armored formations. As the stunningly successful Six Day War began, the workmen put down their tools. The Eastern Gate is still sealed. The gate will remain sealed until the day when the promised Messiah will enter into His kingdom.

The First Thousand Years
of Christ's Eternal Kingdom

Most people have thought of the Millennium and the Kingdom of Christ existing for a period of only one thousand years. The Bible teaches that Christ's Kingdom will be an eternal one which will never end. The Millennium is simply "Chapter One" of the eternal kingdom of Christ. John refers to this first period of Christ's rule as one thousand years, six times in Revelation 20. He described specific events which would begin and end this defined period of time. It is a mistake to believe that the complete promises of the Kingdom could ever be totally fulfilled in such a short time. The Old and New Testaments both prophesy that the Kingdom begins with the Coming of the Messiah in glory and will continue forever.

"Then I saw an angel coming down from Heaven, having the key to the bottomless pit and a great chain in his hand. He laid hold of the dragon, that serpent old, who is the Devil and Satan, and bound him for a thousand years, and he cast him into the bottomless pit, and shut him up, and set a seal on him, so that he should deceive the nations no more till the thousand years were finished. . . ." (Revelation 20:1-3). Following the rebellion of Adam and Eve, Satan was given the dominion of this world from Adam and became "the god of this age" (2 Corinthians 4:4). However, in the Millennial Kingdom, the righteousness and justice of God will finally be experienced in this world. Man will be tested during this period as he lives under the government of God, without the active temptation of Satan. Any sin will be dealt with judicially by Christ as He rules with "a rod of iron." Even in this ideal condition, the Bible prophecies that man will fail this final test.

After the Millennium, Satan will be allowed to go free for "a little season" in which he will gather the rebels of all nations for a last great battle against "the beloved city" Jerusalem. He will be defeated by God and sent to the "lake of fire" forever. Revelation prophesies that God will renew the Earth and the Heavens with fire after this final rebellion of Satan is defeated. In the same manner that God cleansed the world from the effects of sin with a flood in the days of Noah, He will cleanse the Earth and Heaven with fire from the polluting effects of thousands of years of sin. Then the ageless Kingdom of Christ, with Israel and the surviving Gentile nations, will continue throughout eternity enjoying the blessings of God.

God's Covenant Promises to Israel

The covenant which God made with Abraham and the kingdom promises to David, Solomon and all the prophets will be finally realized in the Millennial Kingdom. These promises of peace, justice, prosperity and eternal blessings for Israel and the nations will find fulfillment when Christ sets up His throne in Jerusalem. In addition to the material promises, the Lord promised a new covenant with Israel in which He would give them "a new heart," forgiveness of sin, and the infilling of the Spirit to the renewed nation. This promised kingdom will provide the fulfillment of all the hopes and dreams of the Chosen People forever.

Jesus Christ in the Millennial Kingdom

Israel and the nations will see the manifested glory of Christ exhibited when Jesus returns from Heaven to establish His kingdom. His glory will include both His humanity and His divinity. His multiple roles as Judge, King, Teacher, Shepherd and Redeemer of mankind will be revealed in the sight of all men. As the true "son of David" He will take His rightful place upon the throne of David. Jesus is both perfect man and perfect God. Christ will show His righteousness, holiness, mercy and goodness as He rules the planet. He will receive the worship of men and fulfill each of the remaining prophecies of the Old Testament. A perfect and just peace will flow from Jerusalem "the City of Peace" because the Prince of Peace will rule forever.

Some have rejected the reality of this Millennial Kingdom in their mistaken view that somehow this biblical "reality" is carnal, material and less spiritual than some imaginary kingdom in their mind. However, the literal prophecies of the Bible demand a real Kingdom of Christ on this Earth. The promises of the Bible are of a spiritual and a material kingdom. The problem we face today when we contemplate this real kingdom is similar to the problem faced by the Jews in the life of Jesus. While they strongly believed that God would send the Messiah to the Earth at that time, when Jesus stood before them in the flesh, many had a difficult time accepting His reality. The tremendous truth that God revealed Himself to man in the form of "the Son of Man" with a "real" material body was shocking to the Jews. Let me suggest that, this same difficulty they experienced with the reality of a "flesh and blood" Jesus Christ, is paralleled in some measure by the difficulty many people have today when they contemplate a "real" Heaven and Millennial Kingdom. This kingdom of Christ will be visible and concrete, yet it is also spiritual in its context. A totally material and natural kingdom, divorced from the spirit, is unscriptural. However, a purely spiritual Kingdom, without a tangible and material element, is contradicted by the plain declarations of the Word of God. God has promised in the clearest language possible that He will establish His kingdom of righteousness on Earth in the near future.

The Unique Qualities of Life in the Millennium

After the Second Coming of Christ, He will rule the nations from the "throne of David" in Jerusalem. Sin will not be totally eliminated from the universe until the final defeat of Satan after the Millennium. However, during this period it will be severely limited because any outward rebellion and crime will be dealt with immediately by Christ.

One of the most wonderful characteristics of life during this period is that God's Holy Spirit will be poured out on Israel and the Gentile nations to transform mankind. "And it shall come to pass afterward that I will pour out My Spirit upon all flesh; your sons and your daughters shall prophesy, your old men shall dream dreams, your young men shall see visions. And also on My menservants and My maidservants I will pour out My Spirit in those days" (Joel 2:28,29). The infilling of the Holy Spirit which gave birth to the Church on the day of Pentecost almost two thousand years ago was only the foretaste of the Millennial Kingdom in which the spirits of all natural men who are believers will be renewed by the Spirit. The transforming Holy Spirit will manifest himself in the glorious praise, joy and worship of men in those days. The barriers which separate believers will be removed by the unity and fellowship of God's Holy Spirit. As the Lord pours out His Spirit upon Israel, her heart will overflow with the joy of a bride who finally sees her bridegroom. The Gentile nations will bask in the overflowing blessings of Israel and will share in the glory of Christ's Kingdom.

The Government of the Millennium

One of the greatest blessings which will flow from the Kingdom of God will be the introduction of a true and lasting world peace. For the first time in human history, soldiers will put down their weapons secure in the knowledge that their countries are safe at last.

"He shall judge between many peoples, and rebuke strong nations afar off; they shall beat their swords into plowshares, and their spears into pruning hooks: nation shall not lift up sword against nation, neither shall they learn war anymore" (Micah 4:3).

The guns of war will then be silenced. For the last four thousand years of recorded history there have been thirteen years of war for every year of peace. This year the nations will spend over one trillion dollars on weapons and soldiers in a futile search for an elusive security. When the prophet Micah declares that "they shall beat their swords into plowshares" I believe he is referring to the enormous release of financial, scientific, material, and human resources from the task of war which can then be utilized to meet the needs of human beings. The allocation of such unimaginable sums for the military today, while we cannot find the money to provide for either the homeless in our cities or the starving millions in the Third World, is a sad indictment on our national priorities. In the aftermath of the Great Tribulation and the terrible Battle of Armageddon there will be an enormous need to rebuild a ravaged planet. Then, the energies of the world can be turned to the positive rebuilding of the planet's environment and the feeding of its precious children.

Under the direction of Jesus Christ, the resurrected believers of the Church will provide the leadership necessary to create a just society for mankind. Some have imagined that the verses which promise that the Church will "reign and rule" suggest a passive rule from a throne. However, when you consider the practical nature of God's plan and the large number of believers, it is probable that we shall provide leadership in a multitude of roles, including government. Someone who has spent their lifetime learning to communicate and educate children may find that their assignment will be the provision of education for the natural children in the Millennium.

As a writer and communicator, I may have the opportunity of sharing the results of my future research in seminars and books, etc. The interests and skills which the Lord has led you to develop in this life may be the first stage of a tremendous career which you will enjoy forever. Today we so often experience frustration because we would like to explore many more careers, friendships and vacation trips than our limited time and finances will permit. Have you ever wanted to be an explorer, a doctor, a naturalist or a teacher? With all eternity before you, everyone of these careers could be explored and many more. In the Millennium and beyond, we shall have all the time in the world to explore every one of the possibilities of our vastly expanded abilities and interests. The greatest adventure we could ever imagine awaits us in the reality of the Kingdom of Christ.

Under the Millennial rule of Christ, man will find the perfect justice which has eluded him since the first rebellion in the Garden. Christ will accomplish Isaiah's great prophecy of peace, judgment and just government which we celebrate each Christmas: "Of the increase of His government and peace there shall be no end, upon the throne of David, and upon His kingdom, to order it, and to establish it with judgment and with justice from henceforth even forever." Jesus Christ, as Messiah and the mighty God, will rule the Earth from the throne of David. His perfect and just government will never end, The oppression of evil governments will be replaced by the benevolent protection of a just and loving Savior.

The religious, ethnic and political conflicts which characterize human society today will be resolved in the unifying reign of Jesus Christ. Ultimately every human has an appointment with destiny to meet Jesus Christ. Either we shall meet Him as our Savior or we shall meet Him as our Judge. God declares "that to Me every knee shall bow, every tongue shall take an oath" (Isaiah 45:23).

The curse which was placed upon the earth following the sin of Adam and Eve will be lifted when the Kingdom is established. The deserts will blossom and the earth will produce abundantly under the care of God. According to Isaiah 33:24 all sickness will be eliminated. The deaf and the blind will be cured as Christ heals the men and women in that wonderful day the Millennial Kingdom begins. Even the devastated land of "Lebanon shall be turned into a fruitful field" as the Messiah renews the land from the curse of sin (Isaiah 29:17,18).

Many have assumed life in the Kingdom of Christ will involve boredom and idleness. Nothing could be further from the biblical truth or from the nature of God's creation. Everything in the universe has purposeful activity. Even in the Garden of Eden, before man's rebellion, Adam and Eve did not sit around idly. God gave man intelligence, purpose, emotions, curiosity and desires. He gave him a spirit, a soul and a body to use in fulfillment of God's command to have dominion over the Earth. Adam was responsible for the Garden under the Lord's direction and named each species. In the Millennium, the Lord declares that man will have a just economy which will provide joyous and purposeful employment of the gifts and skills of men (Isaiah 62:8,9).

Some have imagined that life in the Millennium will be an eternal 24-hour-per-day church service where the most exciting thing will be turning to hymn number two. There is not one verse in the Bible which suggests that Heaven or the Millennium will be boring or uneventful. God did not ask Adam and Eve to hold church services 100 percent of the time. The Word of God tells us that they walked with God in "the cool of the day." Their relationship was a daily living walk with God which included every aspect of their exciting and purposeful life. In addition to a perfected industrial society, the Earth will produce an abundant agricultural harvest of "wheat, and the new wine and oil, for the young of the flock, and the herd" Jeremiah 31:12). The Bible describes a joyful life without fear or poverty. "Then shall the virgin rejoice in the dance, both young men and old together: for I will turn their mourning into joy, and will comfort them, and make them rejoice from their sorrow. And I will satiate the soul of the priests with fatness, and my people shall be satisfied with my goodness, saith the Lord" (Jeremiah 31:13,14). All the hopes and dreams of men for a just and perfect society will find their fulfillment in the Millennial Kingdom under Christ.

CHAPTER 12

The Mysterious Role of Angels

Throughout human history men have been fascinated with angels and their role as messengers from Heaven. Many people have misconceptions about these spiritual beings. They imagine that they are cherubic figures such as we find on a Valentine's Day card. This image is contradicted by the teaching of the Bible that angels are powerful creatures who have a significant role to play in God's unfolding plan for mankind. Millions of people are fascinated by the concept of angels. *Time* magazine ran a cover story in their December 27, 1993 issue discussing the virtually universal interest in angelic beings. The article declared, "If there is such a thing as a universal idea, common across cultures and through the centuries, the belief in angels comes close to it." The mysterious role of angels is presented numerous times in the Jewish and Christian Bible as well as passages in the Islamic Koran. Angels were present at pivotal points in the spiritual history of man, including the creation of the universe, the proclamation of the birth of Jesus and will also return with Christ's heavenly army to establish His Millennial Kingdom.

Despite their presence in religious literature, until quite recently, the topic of angels received little interest. However, we are experiencing a tremendous surge in interest in the subject of angels in the last decade. Everywhere we look, the images of angels confront us in art, book covers and television. Naturally, much of the recent information about angelic beings is heavily influenced by Hollywood movies as well as the rising popularity of New Age cults. It is important that we examine the clear teaching found in the Word of God to enable us to understand the true role of angels in God's spiritual kingdom. A large motivation for the growing fascination with angels comes from the fact that they stand in an intermediate position between heaven and man. While many people find it difficult to imagine heaven clearly, they can imagine an angelic being appearing in a human form to assist a person in need. The concept of angels is a comforting one to many people and helps account for their universal popularity. A careful examination of the Scriptures reveals an astonishing range of angelic activities has occurred in the course of history as recorded by the Bible.

It was angels who announced the wonderful news to the shepherds that the promised Messiah was born in Bethlehem. In Luke 2:8-14 the Scriptures record the most important message ever delivered by these messengers. "Now there were in the same country shepherds living out in the fields, keeping watch over their flock by night. And behold, an Angel of the Lord stood before them, and the glory of the Lord shone around them, and they were greatly afraid. Then the angel said to them, 'Do not be afraid, for behold, I bring you good tidings of great joy which will be to all people. For there is born to you this day in the city of David a Savior, who is Christ the Lord. And this will be the sign to you: You will find a Babe wrapped in swaddling cloths, lying in a manger.' And suddenly there was with the angel a multitude of the heavenly host praising God and saying: 'Glory to God in the highest, and on earth peace, goodwill toward men!' "

The Role of Angels

Who are these angels? What is their mysterious role in Heaven and in our lives? Are some of them "fallen angels?" The Bible specifically refers to them 294 times showing that they were notable beings with an important role to play. One of the Hebrew words translated "angel" in the Old Testament is mal'ak, and it means "to dispatch as a deputy, ambassador or messenger." In the New Testament the Greek word *angelos* is the word from which we form our word "angel" and it means "a messenger" whether from God or man. They are spiritual beings, but they take on human form to complete their role as messengers of God.

We have all heard of "guardian angels." The Lord Himself warned people to cherish children when He said, "In Heaven their angels always behold the face of my Father." Angels still intervene to protect men, women and children from harm. When we get to Heaven and look back on our life with the complete spiritual insight of God, I believe we will be astonished to discover the many times angels have intervened to protect us without our awareness. Only Heaven will reveal how often assaults and accidents have been prevented by the supernatural actions of these angelic messengers of God. In Hebrews 13:1 God tells us that we should not "forget to entertain strangers: for thereby some have entertained angels unawares."

We also find them called guardians, sons of the Mighty, sons of God, the congregation of the Mighty, saints, hosts, spirits, and the elect. They have names, but we know of only five whose names are recorded in Scripture: Satan, the fallen angel; Apollyon, also a fallen angel called the "Destroyer" named by John in Revelation; Michael, the archangel, and Gabriel who appeared to Daniel and who announced the birth of both John the Baptist and Jesus and lastly, Palomi, the "Numberer" named in the original language of the Book of Daniel, tells Daniel how long it will be before Christ comes to cleanse the defiled earthly sanctuary.

The Characteristics of Angels

As spirit beings, usually angels are invisible to humans; but they are sometimes visible to animals such as happened with the donkey of Balaam (Numbers 22:22-27). They usually take on human form as they deliver messages from God and minister to people. Various places in Scripture tell about their physical features including heads, faces, eyes, mouths, hair, hands, and feet. Angels have emotions, appetites, passions, desires, willpower, language, intelligence, knowledge and wisdom. They also have patience, meekness and modesty. The Bible says the angels who serve God are holy (Matthew 25:31).

The fallen angels who rebelled with Satan display hate, anger, lust, pride and vengeance. There are many similarities between men and angels but also profound differences. Many have assumed they are robot-like creatures without emotions or moral choice. However, the Bible states that they do have the option to sin. We are told that one third of the angels joined Satan and rebelled against God. The Bible does not describe them ever repenting from their rebellion. Possibly the fact that they already have complete spiritual knowledge means that their decision to rebel is final and not subject to change.

They are not to be worshiped or prayed to. Whenever men like Daniel or John have mistakenly bowed to angels, they have immediately rejected such homage and stated that only God is to be worshiped. In the light of this command, it is tragic to see the worshiping of images, shrines, saints, angels and even Mary. The Bible describes such false worship as idolatry. The Book of Hebrews tells us that the angels worship Jesus Christ. We are "created a little lower than the angels." Today we have capacities less than these messengers of God. After the resurrection, when we receive our new bodies and enhanced capacities, we shall judge the angels and have a position above them. Their role is to serve God and man. The Scriptures tell us that they are vitally interested in the affairs of mankind, salvation and most of all, the subject of prophecy. According to Ephesians 3:10 they are taught wisdom through their observation of God's unfolding plan in the Church.

The Bible records one hundred and four times when angels showed themselves to men. One day when Abraham was sitting in his tent door he looked up and saw three "men" coming toward him. These men were actually Jesus Christ and two angels, who visited Abraham on the day which would later become the Feast of Passover. Their purpose was to tell Abraham and Sarah about the birth of their son Isaac which would happen at "this set time" next year, on Passover. They looked like men, talked like men in Abraham's language, and they ate veal, bread, milk and butter which Abraham offered them. (see Genesis 18). The two messengers then went to Sodom that evening to see Lot, Abraham's nephew. Lot treated them in the same hospitable way. He fed them a meal of unleavened bread and asked them to spend the night (Genesis 19). On another occasion an angel cooked a meal for Elijah after the prophet had escaped from the wicked Queen Jezebel (1 Kings 19:5-8). In Psalm 78:24,25, David tells us that the manna supplied in the wilderness is the "angel's food," the "corn of Heaven." This proves that angels eat in Heaven.

Heavenly messengers have appeared at times as soldiers. When Joshua was ready to attack Jericho, he saw an angel in battle array, standing with his sword drawn. He introduced himself to Joshua as the "Commander of the army of the Lord" (Joshua 5:13-15). As the prophet Elisha and his servant were surrounded by a huge army, God allowed Elisha's fearful servant to have his eyes opened to the spiritual reality. He was privileged to see a "mountain" full of "horses and chariots" that were angelic beings (2 Kings 6:17). They are tremendously powerful. On one occasion a single angel destroyed 185,000 Syrian soldiers.

They are created beings (Psalm 148:2,5; Colossians 1:16), but can never die because they are immortal (Luke 20:36). Angels have a hierarchy; at the highest level is Michael, the archangel who contends with the devil (Jude 9). He will announce the Lord's return. The cherubim (Ezekiel 1:5-14), and seraphim (Isaiah 6:1-7) are a special class of angels which surround the throne of God in Heaven. The Ark of the Covenant contained gold cherubim modeled after these "Living Creatures" seen by the prophets Ezekiel and John. There is another group of angels that has fallen into sinful rebellion, which we will discuss a little further into this chapter.

The Ministries of Angels

They have many responsibilities in the government of God. They minister to men, execute judgments of God, and rule the nations. Far from being the pacifistic angels of medieval art or of greeting cards, angels wage actual physical warfare against the enemies of God, the Antichrist and his fallen angels. Ephesians 6:12 reminds us of this continuing spiritual warfare: "For we do not wrestle against flesh and blood, but against principalities, against powers, against the rulers of the darkness of this age, against spiritual hosts of wickedness in the heavenly places." They will participate in the climactic Battle of Armageddon. The Bible says that angels sometimes ride heavenly horses, as described in Zechariah 1:7-11 and in the Book of Revelation. One of their roles is to guard the gates of New Jerusalem to prevent anything unholy from entering. Their numbers are described as "myriads of myriads" or "millions of millions."

Angels worship God in praise, word and song (Revelation 5:11); they give laws, joyfully witness the repentance of men, and lead sinners to those who will bring them to Christ. It is fascinating to note that the martyr Stephen declared that angels were used by God to provide His divine laws to the Israelites. Speaking about the ancient Israelites in the Exodus Stephen declared, "Who have received the law by the disposition of angels, and have not kept it" (Acts 7:53). They help and protect individuals in times of need, strengthen us in trials, and greatly help ministers in their preaching and witnessing to sinners. Angels can appear to men in dreams to warn or encourage them; sometimes God uses them to bring answers to our prayers. The angels wear robes of white raiment showing their righteousness.

Often when angels appear to people they encourage some type of action. When the angels appeared to Lot and his family they told them to leave the city before the angels destroyed Sodom. The time Sarah wanted Abraham to send Hagar and Ishmael away, God told Abraham to do as she asked. Abraham gave Hagar food and water and sent her into the desert, trusting God to care for her. After their food and water expired, Hagar put her son under one of the bushes to die. As she sat crying a few yards away, an angelic messenger came and told her to "arise, lift up the lad and hold him with your hand, for I will make him a great nation" (Genesis 21:18). The angel told Gideon to "go in this might of yours, and you shall save Israel from the hand of the Midianites" (Judges 6:14). When the angel woke up Elijah as he lay under a tree he told him to "arise and eat." An angel appeared to Joseph and told him to "arise, take the young Child [Jesus] and His mother, flee to Egypt, and stay there until I bring you word; for Herod will seek the young Child to destroy Him" (Matthew 2:13). The angel told Philip, the deacon: "Arise and go toward the south along the road which goes down from Jerusalem to Gaza" (Acts 8:26). When Philip did as the angel commanded he led the Ethiopian eunuch to faith in the Lord. As Peter sat with his hands and feet in chains, having been imprisoned by Herod, an "angel of the Lord stood by him . . . and he struck Peter on the side and raised him up, saying 'Arise quickly!' " (Acts 12:7).

At other times God sent them to protect His people. David said that the "Angel of the Lord encamps all around those who fear Him, and delivers them" (Psalm 34:7). Shadrach, Meshach, and Abed-Nego were protected by an angel when they were thrown "into the midst of the burning fiery furnace" (Daniel 3:21). When the servants of the king looked into the furnace they saw four men in there instead of three. So was Daniel protected when King Darius reluctantly threw him into a den of lions. When the King came to check on him "he cried out with a lamenting voice to Daniel . . . 'Daniel, servant of the living God, has your God, whom you serve continually, been able to deliver you from the lions?' Daniel could answer: 'O King, live forever! My God sent His angel and shut the lions' mouths, so that they have not hurt me, because I was found innocent before Him' " (Daniel 6:20-21).

In the ninety-first Psalm, David describes how God is our refuge and fortress in whom we can trust. "Surely He shall deliver you from the snare of the fowler and from the perilous pestilence. He shall cover you with His feathers, and under His wings you shall take refuge; His truth shall be your shield and buckler. You shall not be afraid of the terror by night, nor of the arrow that flies by day, nor of the pestilence that walks in darkness, nor of the destruction that lays waste at noonday. A thousand may fall at your side, and ten thousand at your right hand; but it shall not come near you. . . . Because you have made the Lord, who is my refuge even the Most High, your dwelling place, no evil shall befall you, nor shall any plague come near your dwelling; for He shall give His angels charge over you, to keep you in all your ways. In their hands they shall bear you up, lest you dash your foot against a stone."

Angels are sent to comfort. When Joseph discovered that Mary, the young Jewish girl he intended to marry, was pregnant, he decided to quietly break their engagement. As he worried about his decision, an angel appeared to him in a dream and comforted him with these words: "Joseph, son of David, do not be afraid to take to you Mary your wife, for that which is conceived in her is of the Holy Spirit. And she will bring forth a son, and you shall call His name Jesus, for He will save His people from their sins" (Matthew 1:20-21). Paul had a visit from "an Angel of the God to whom I belong and whom I serve," when he was a prisoner on a ship that was ready to capsize in the great storm. The angel told him, "Do not be afraid, Paul; you must be brought before Caesar; and indeed God has granted you all those who sail with you' " (Acts 27:23-24).

The Fallen Angels

Lucifer, an angel whom Isaiah calls "Son of the Morning," said in his heart, "I will ascend into Heaven, I will exalt my throne above the stars of God; I will also sit on the mount of the congregation on the farthest side of the north; I will ascend above the heights of the clouds, I will be like the Most High" (Isaiah 14:12-14). This he tried to do. When he failed, he recruited many angels to leave Heaven with him in his rebellion. Isaiah goes on to say that, eventually, Lucifer "shall be brought down to Sheol, to the lowest depths of the Pit" (v. 15).

Scholars believe that Ezekiel is also speaking of this chief of fallen angels under the title "Prince of Tyre" in chapter 28. He describes this as "the seal of perfection, full of wisdom and perfect in beauty. You were in Eden, the garden of God; every precious stone was your covering. . . . You were the anointed cherub who covers; . . . you were on the holy mountain of God; you walked back and forth in the midst of fiery stones. You were perfect in your ways from the day you were created, till iniquity was found in you . . . You became filled with violence within, and you sinned" (vv. 12-16). Ultimately, Lucifer-Satan, the devil, "the god of this world," will be "cast into the lake of fire and brimstone" to be "tormented day and night forever and ever" (Revelation 20:10).

These fallen angels fall into two different groups. The first category consists of those angels "who did not keep their proper domain, but left their own abode," as Jude 6 describes them, and who are now chained in darkness.

The Fallen Angels of Genesis

Genesis chapter 6 recounts how fallen angels were the reason God had to destroy the Earth with a great flood in the time of Noah. Among those who rebelled against God were a number who chose also to violate the law of God involving the prohibition of sexual relations with mankind. "The sons of God saw the daughters of men, that they were beautiful; and they took wives for themselves of all whom they chose" (v. 2). This, was an abomination to God. He determined then to destroy the offspring of this unholy union of angels and men; but in mercy He promised that generation He would delay His judgment "one hundred and twenty years" in which He gave them time to repent (v. 3). During the next one hundred and twenty years Noah preached righteousness to this wicked and violent generation. But the people rejected his call for repentance and mocked as Noah built a boat to save his family and those animals that God told him to take on board.

The Bible describes Noah as "a just man, perfect in his generations. Noah walked with God" (v. 9). We know that no man is perfect. What does the Bible mean in this passage? It says that Noah was "perfect in his generations," or reproductive history. Because of the unholy union of these angels, almost all mankind's families had been infected by this demon seed by the time of the Flood. The last remaining family that had not succumbed to this appalling demonic infestation was the family of Noah, "perfect in his generations."

Satan's purpose in this wholesale corruption of humanity was to create a situation in which there would be no pure, undefiled genetic line through which Jesus, the Messiah, could be born. If Satan had been successful in this attempt to demonize all humanity, salvation would have been impossible. Jesus the Messiah could not, as holy God, be born into a human family line that had been defiled by demons. Genesis 6:4 describes the "giants on the earth in those days, and also afterward, when the sons of God came in to the daughters of men and they bore children to them. Those were the mighty men who were of old, men of renown." It is possible that these offspring of angels led to the "demigods" of Greek literature and the many legends of ancient history of "gods" coming to earth and mixing with mankind. The phrase "and also afterward" shows that, after the Flood some fallen angels again tried to mate with human women to prevent the birth of the Messiah.

The children of these alliances were those "men of great stature" which the twelve Israeli spies told about. "And there we saw the giants, the sons of Anak, which come of the giants: and we were in our own sight as grasshoppers, and so we were in their sight" (Numbers 13:33 [KJV]) David slew Goliath (1 Samuel 17) and his brother (2 Samuel 21:19) who were giants. Some of these giants had six fingers and six toes and were over ten feet tall. Bashan was known as the land of giants.

The term "sons of God" in Genesis 6, verses 2 and 4, is used five places in the Old Testament, and each time it refers to angels. Many translations use the word "angels" in this passage instead of the "sons of God." Job 1:6 and 2:1 also use this term. Daniel 3:25 describes the fourth "man" in the fiery furnace as appearing like "the Son of Man." Many Jewish commentaries on the Torah say that Genesis 6 refers to fallen angels. Flavius Josephus, in his *Antiquities of the Jews* (Book I, chap. 3), says, "Many angels of god accompanied with women, and begat sons that proved unjust, . . . these men did what resembled the acts of those whom the Grecians called giants." He notes in Book V, chap. 2 that the bones of these giants were still available for inspection in his day.

In the first few centuries, early Church writers wrote of these beings. Justin Martyr said: "But the angels transgressed . . . were captivated by the love of women, and begat children." Peter in his second Epistle reports that "God did not spare the angels who sinned, but cast them down to hell and delivered them into chains of darkness, to be reserved for judgment; and did not spare the ancient world, but saved Noah, one of eight people, a preacher of righteousness" (2 Peter 2:4-5)

The Bible describes only male angels. The Hebrew word for angel is masculine. The Scriptures clearly state that the fallen angels of Genesis 6 were physically capable of reproduction. If these angels were not male, they could not have produced giants as children from their unholy union with the "daughters of men." Satan cannot create; he can only twist the creation of God into something sinful. Therefore these fallen angels, the "sons of God" must have been created originally as male angels by God.

Many Christians, upon reading the account of the Israelites taking possession of the Promised Land, have been troubled by God's command to totally annihilate all the inhabitants of Canaan. If these people of Canaan were the offspring of demonic angelic-human relations, no wonder God said to wipe them out. There are many Scriptures which show that these people were not normal humans (Numbers 13:32-33; Deuteronomy 2:10, 20).

The Canaanites indulged in awful idolatry and pagan practices, such as offering their firstborn sons as burnt sacrifices before their idol Moloch. They engaged in temple prostitution and perversion of every kind. God knew that Satan's plan was to infiltrate and defile the Chosen People. It was the mercy of God which resulted in the stern command. Israel's failure to remove the people of Canaan from the Promised Land as God told them to do, caused Israel trouble for the next thousand years.

The second category of fallen angels did not participate in that sin before the Flood and are still free to wage spiritual warfare with the believers (see Ephesians 6:12). The last group will be defeated at the Battle of Armageddon when Christ returns to defeat Satan's plan to conquer Earth. They will be judged at the Great White Throne Judgment after the Millennium. Matthew 25:41 tells us that God prepared Hell for those angels who rebelled with their leader Satan.

These fallen, sinful and rebellious angels who work with Satan will finally be judged by Christ at the end of the Millennium at "the judgment of the great day" according to Jude, v. 6. They now have access to some parts of Heaven as the Book of Job (1:6-12) records that Satan appeared in Heaven. However, these fallen angels and Satan will finally be cast out of Heaven at the mid-point of the seven-year tribulation period (Revelation 12:79) by the archangel Michael and the angels of the Lord. This event will trigger the Great Tribulation on Earth because Satan knows from the Bible's prophecies that when this happens he has only 1,260 days of freedom left before he and his angels are defeated by Christ and His heavenly army.

Revelation 20:1-3 tells us that after the Battle of Armageddon an angel of God will bind Satan with a chain and consign him to "the bottomless pit" for a thousand years. Angels have a role to play in the final regathering of Israel and will return in great numbers in the heavenly army of Christ to establish His eternal kingdom. When Adam and Eve were sent out of the Garden of Eden, an angel with a flaming sword was put on guard at the gate to prevent them from re-entering. God's purpose was not simply to punish them for their sin. In His great mercy He kept them from eating of the Tree of Life that grew in the garden. If they had eaten of the fruit of the tree in their sin, they would have achieved immortality without salvation through the blood of Jesus Christ. Mankind would have been locked into an eternity without hope of salvation forever had this happened.

The angels of God are vitally interested in the salvation of men and women. In Luke 15:10 the Bible tells us: "Likewise, I say to you, there is joy in the presence of the angels of God over one sinner who repents." When a Christian dies he is not alone. The angels of God now receive the departed spirits of those who accept Christ as their Savior (Luke 16:22.) These holy angels will participate with Christ in the Judgment of the Nations after Armageddon. In the New Heaven and New Earth we shall have the joy of fellowship with the angels of God forever.

The Protection of Guardian Angels

Over the course of my life I have been involved in numerous accidents and dangerous incidents that could have prematurely ended my life. I have often sensed the presence of God's supernatural protection when I have escaped serious injury or death. Several times I felt that an invisible angelic presence had awakened me to danger or helped me avoid a potentially life-threatening accident. My wife, Kaye, lived with her brothers and sisters in a home with her mother and father, who was a pastor in several different towns in the province of Ontario, Canada. In one particular town, her family moved into a house just up the street from a hotel bar and dance-hall. Before they moved to town, drunks were accustomed to using the verandah and laneway by the side of the empty house as a place to party after midnight, when the hotel bar had closed its doors. However, once the preacher and his family moved into the house, they felt it took away the freedom for their "after hours" parties, but they would still hang around. One particular night, the bar patrons were quite angry and rowdy after the hotel bar closed. As their anger grew, the men came onto the verandah swearing, blaspheming, and threatening the preacher and his family. They began to pull on the door in their attempt to break into the house.

Kaye's dad had put the children to bed, but everyone was fearful as they could hear the drunks yelling loudly that they were going to "get the preacher and his family." Her father gathered the whole family into the upstairs front bedroom to pray for God's divine protection. As her dad prayed for his family's safety, the Lord showed him a vision of a large guardian angel standing guard on the porch in front of their main door. At that very moment, the family heard the sounds of a big commotion and the men started running for their lives away from the house.

When the sun came up the next morning, the body of one of the drunken men was found lying on the ground at the side of the house: he had died of a heart-attack. When the drunks were questioned, they claimed that while they were yelling threats, suddenly a large man appeared, guarding the front door. They claimed they were so afraid for their lives that they simply ran away as their friend fell to the ground. The drunks never came back to bother the preacher's family during the rest of the time they lived in that town. Kaye's family believes that God sent a guardian angel to protect their family in response to their prayers.

CHAPTER 13

The Judgments
and the Rewards

"Then I saw a great white throne and Him who sat on it, from whose face the earth and the heaven fled away; and there was found no place for them. And I saw the dead. small and great, standing before God, and books were opened . . . which is the Book of Life. And the dead were judged according to their works, by the things which were written in the books" (Revelation 20:11,12).

The prophet John was given a vision of the great Judgment of the wicked dead which will take place at the end of the age. Poets and painters have often thought of this Judgment Day as one single Judgment in which all men, both evil and righteous, living and dead, would be judged together at one time before the Throne of God. However, the Bible tells us in detail about seven separate judgments of God in which He will judge all who have ever lived. If we wish to understand the justice of God we must examine what the Scriptures reveal about these seven judgments.

The Judgment of the Believer's sin

Everyone who becomes a believer and enters Heaven must have his personal sin judged and punished according to the holy law of God. The Bible assures us that "the wages of sin are death" and therefore, it was necessary that Jesus Christ die on the cross and bear the eternal punishment for our evil rebellion. This judgment happened in time almost two thousand years ago on Calvary. But its benefits are applied today to the hearts of men and women when they personally believe in Christ and accept God's pardon based on the perfect atonement of the Cross.

Jesus Himself refers to this judgment of our sin and His defeat of Satan as follows: " 'Now is the judgment of this world; now the ruler of this world will be cast out. And I, if I am lifted up from the earth, will draw all peoples to Myself.' This He said, signifying by what death He would die" John 12:31-33). The basis of this judgment is the finished and perfect atoning work of Christ's crucifixion which resulted in the actual death of the sinless Son of God on the Cross and the gift of eternal life in Heaven to all those who accept this pardon from God.

The Judgment of the Believer's Walk

"For if we would judge ourselves, we would not be judged. But when we are judged, we are chastened by the Lord, that we may not be condemned with the world" (1 Corinthians 11:31,32).

This is a continuing judgment of our daily walk through the Holy Spirit awakening our Conscience to an active obedience to the will of God. The chastening of God is a mark of His manifested love for us. Its purpose is to redirect us to an even closer walk with Him. While we sometimes resent this chastening, just as children resent the chastening of their parents; it is done out of a profound love for us and a desire for our best interests. In the Book of Hebrews 12:11, Paul assures us of the value of these experiences: "Now no chastening seems to be joyful for the present, but painful; nevertheless, afterward it yields the peaceable fruit of righteousness to those who have been trained by it."

The Judgment of Israel

"And I will bring you into the wilderness of the peoples, and there I will plead My case with you face to face. . . . I will make you pass under the rod, and I will bring you into the bond of the covenant. I will purge the rebels from among you and those who transgress against Me" (Ezekiel 20:35,37,38) .

" 'Alas! For that day is great, So that none is like it; And it is the time of Jacob's trouble, But he shall be saved out of it. . . . For I am with you,' says the Lord, 'to save you; Though I make a full end of all nations where I have scattered you, . . . But I will correct you in justice, And will not let you go altogether unpunished' " (Jeremiah 30:7,11).

God has prophesied repeatedly that Israel would face persecution and tribulations because of her rebellion against the words of the prophets and her rejection of God's commands. Israel's destiny as the Chosen People has truly been a two-edged sword. On the one hand she has been blessed with the custody of the Word of God and the revelation of God over many centuries. While most of the world suffered in spiritual darkness, God continued to reveal His truth and purposes to mankind through a continuous chain of Jewish prophets. Then, the greatest blessing was given to mankind through the coming of the prophesied Messiah, Jesus of Nazareth, who was born as the Son of David. All the apostles, with the possible exception of Luke, were Jews who evangelized the world with the good news of the resurrection of Jesus Christ.

However, these blessings put a great responsibility upon Israel to be true to the revelations of God. When they failed, because of the greater light which Israel had received, God held them to a higher standard than the pagan nations which surrounded them. The result of Israel's rejection of the prophets and of the prophesied Messiah has been exactly what Moses predicted in Deuteronomy 28. For centuries the Jews have suffered persecution. Tragically, the prophets of both the Old and New Testament tell us that just before the return of Jesus Christ as Messiah, the world will know a time of terrible persecution under the Antichrist, which is described by Christ as the Great Tribulation. While this period of tribulation will involve the whole world, its worst persecution will be focused upon Israel during the last three and one half years before the Battle of Armageddon. Yet even then, the Lord will not leave Israel without a witness. The Two Witnesses and the one hundred and forty-four thousand Jewish witnesses will evangelize the entire world beginning in Israel during the Tribulation period.

While the biblical prophecy that Israel still faces a future time of intense judgment is understandably unpalatable to Israelis; the prophecies in the Word of God have never yet been mistaken. The good news is that all those who live through this prophesied period of trouble will be saved and blessed for eternity according to the Bible. Twenty-five centuries ago the prophet Zechariah prophesied of that blessed day when the Messiah would come to save Israel from her enemies. "It shall be in that day that I will seek to destroy all the nations that come against Jerusalem. And I will pour upon the house of David, and on the inhabitants of Jerusalem, the Spirit of grace and of supplication; then they will look on Me whom they pierced. Yes, they will mourn for Him, as one mourns for his only son, and grieve for Him as one grieves for firstborn" (Zechariah 12:9,10). He continued, "In that day a fountain shall be opened for the house of David and for the inhabitants of Jerusalem, for sin and for uncleanness. . . . 'It shall come to pass in all the land,' says the Lord, 'that two-thirds in it shall be cut off and die, but one-third shall be left in it. I will bring one-third through the fire, will refine them as silver is refined, and test them as gold is tested. They will call on My name, I will answer them. I will say, This is my people;' And each one will say, 'The Lord is my God' " (Zechariah 13:1,8,9). The Lord has promised that in the future Israel will finally enjoy the great blessings and prosperity that have been the hope of the Chosen People for some four thousand years.

The Judgment of the Gentile Nations

"When the Son of Man comes in His glory, and all the holy angels with Him, then He will sit on the throne of His glory. All the nations will be gathered before Him, and He will separate them one from another, as a shepherd divides his sheep from the goats. And He will set the sheep on His right hand, but the goats on the left. Then the King will say to those on His right hand, 'Come, you blessed of My Father, inherit the kingdom prepared for you from the foundation of the world' " (Matthew 25:31-34).

The nations of the world will face Jesus Christ as their Lord and King following their defeat at the Battle of Armageddon. All the nations of the world will take part in the titanic struggle for world control. On the one side will be the nations of Asia with a two hundred million man army led by the Kings of the East. Revelation 16:16 tells us that the nations of the West will be gathered by the Antichrist, the leader of the revived Roman Empire in Europe, to face this colossal Eastern army "to a place called in Hebrew, Armageddon." This huge plain in northern Israel has known more historical battles than any other place on Earth save for Jerusalem itself. There, before the ancient city of Megiddo, these armies will meet to destroy Israel and each other in a bloody struggle for world supremacy. However, Jesus Christ will interrupt this battle by returning to Earth at that very moment with His heavenly army of angels and Christian saints. Revelation 19:19 says, "And I saw the beast [the Antichrist], the kings of the earth, and their armies, gathered together to make war against Him [Jesus] who sat on the horse, and against His army." Both armies will turn from fighting each other to attack Christ but will be defeated in the greatest military disaster of history. The Bible states that the whole valley will be turned into a quagmire of blood and mud so the horses will sink into it "even to the horse's bridle."

During this terrible Battle of Armageddon, Christ will destroy the Antichrist who has caused Israel and the nations so much devastation and persecution during the period known as the Great Tribulation. "And then the lawless one [the Antichrist] will be revealed, whom the Lord will consume with the breath of His mouth and destroy with the brightness of His coming" (2 Thessalonians 2:8).

The nations will be judged by Christ on the basis of their treatment of both the Jews and the Gentile believers according to Matthew 25:31-46. Those nations which have protected God's people will be termed "sheep nations" and will be preserved to enjoy the blessings of the Millennial Kingdom and Eternity. Those nations who have despised and persecuted the people of God will be judged on that day by Christ as "goat nations" and will be cast unto the dust heap of history. Those nations will cease to exist in the future. Individuals must be judged as individuals by God on the basis of their acceptance or rejection of the pardon of Jesus Christ. As nations, God will either bless or curse them for their collective acts on the day of the Judgment of the Nations.

Many have assumed all nations will cease to exist once Jesus sets up His eternal Kingdom of God upon Earth. Nothing could be further from the truth. God specifically described the future of mankind in terms of the continuation of both Israel and those "sheep nations" which have blessed God's people, especially during the Great Tribulation. The prophet Zechariah declares that the nations will send their representatives to the city of Jerusalem to worship the Messiah King forever. "And it shall come to pass that everyone who is left of all the nations which came against Jerusalem shall go up from year to year to worship the King, the Lord of Hosts, and to keep the Feast of Tabernacles" (Zechariah 14:16). We are told in the Book of Revelation that nations will exist and be ruled by the saints during and after the Millennium. After the renewing of the Earth with fire, the Kingdom of God, Israel and the nations will enjoy peace forever. John describes the wonderful future in which the Heavenly City, the New Jerusalem, will descend from Heaven to the renewed Earth. The angel shows John "that great city, the Holy Jerusalem, descending out of Heaven from God." He then says, "And the nations of those who are saved shall walk in its light, and the kings of the earth bring their glory and honor into it" (Revelation 21:24).

The Bible tells the followers of Christ that they shall reign and rule with Christ forever. Revelation 5:10 tells us that Christ has redeemed us and has "made us kings and priests to our God; And we shall reign on the Earth." This reigning will involve more than governmental functions. Leadership during the Millennium may be exercised by Christians in other areas such as education, hospitals and social organizations. There must be nations in the future, both in the one thousand years of the Millennium and in the future New Earth, to fulfill these prophecies. It should be the prayer of every believer that even after the Rapture of the Church, the seeds that we have sown in our witness will cause our nations to be protectors of the future Tribulation saints and not their persecutors. If our countries will bless Israel and the Gentile believers in Christ during that terrible time of persecution, when they will be judged by Jesus as "sheep nations," they will be allowed to continue their existence under the Kingdom of God forever.

The Great White Throne Judgment

"Then I saw a great white throne, and Him who sat on it, from whose face the earth and the heaven fled away. And there was found no place for them. And I saw the dead, small and great, standing before God; and the books were opened. And another book was opened, which is the Book of Life. And the dead were judged according to their works, by the things which were written in the books. The sea gave up the dead who were in it, and Death and Hades delivered up the dead were in them. And they were judged each one according to his works. Then Death and Hades were cast into the lake of fire. This is the second death. And anyone not found written in the Book of Life was cast into the lake of fire" (Revelation 20:11-15).

This judgment will occur after the Millennium and will involve the final judgment of two distinct groups of sinners: (1) all the rebellious angels and (2) all the wicked dead who have ever lived. Since it happens after the Millennium all unrepentant men and women who have lived since Adam until that point will stand before the Throne of God. The prophet John described earlier the Battle of Armageddon and the defeat of Satan. He is chained in the bottomless pit for a period of one thousand years which allows mankind to enjoy the peace and prosperity of the Kingdom of God. John prophesied that, after the Millennium, Satan would be released to lead a final rebellion against God. He would then be cast into the Lake of Fire forever. Immediately after that John tells us that the final judgment of wicked angels and men will take place in Heaven.

The Judgment of Fallen Angels

All the angels who joined in Satan's rebellion will stand before the Great White Throne. These wicked angels belong to two classes. One group of fallen angels sinned in a particular manner before the Flood and attempted physical relations with women. They were chained by God in a special prison to be held there until the day of this judgment. "God did not spare the angels who sinned, but cast them down to hell, and delivered them into chains of darkness, to be reserved for judgment" (2 Peter 2:4). The Book of Jude tells us that, the "angels who did not keep their proper domain, but left their own abode, He has reserved in everlasting chains under darkness for the judgment of the great day" (v. 6). The second group of rebellious angels who did not sin in that way were allowed to follow Satan. On this final judgment day they will be imprisoned forever in the lake of "everlasting fire prepared for the devil and his angels" (Matthew 25:41). Note that in this passage Christ says that the lake of fire was originally prepared for the devil and his angels. If man had never rebelled against God or all men had repented of their sins, then the Gates of Hell would never have opened to mankind.

The Judgment of the Wicked Dead

The purpose of this dreaded Great White Throne judgment day is to give every man a fair trial before God the

Father and Jesus Christ. The Psalmist David in Psalm 9:7,8 states: "But the Lord shall endure forever; He has prepared His throne for judgment. He shall judge the world in righteousness, And He shall administer judgment for the people in uprightness." The souls of all men who have died in their sins will be released to join their resurrected bodies for that ultimate judgment day. The Bible says that the grave and even the sea will give up their bodies and Hell will surrender their souls so that they can stand before Jesus.

"And I saw the dead, small and great, standing before God; and books were opened. And another book was opened, which is the Book of Life. And the dead were judged according to their works, by the things which were written in the books" (Revelation 20:12).

Everyone who appears there will be judged by the works of their life. Each will be found to have sinned against God and each failed to repent of their sins. When the books are opened of the works of men, every secret thought and deed will be revealed once and for all. The deeds of their life will stand in judgment against men on that day.

One of the most tragic verses in the Bible is this verse which describes that when men stand before God without any further evasion "the books were opened; and another book was opened, which is the Book of Life." The Book of Life contains only the names of those who have won eternal life because they have accepted the pardon of Jesus Christ for their sinful rebellion. There is a tragic reason that the Book of Life must be opened on that awful judgment day when only unrepentant sinners will stand before God. There will be many who will, even then, falsely claim to be Christians. They will point to their public religious life and their words, but God will point to their heart and the Book of Life where their name will not be found. Jesus warned His listeners that in that final day He would examine their heart, not their outward works. "Not everyone who says to Me, 'Lord, Lord,' shall enter the Kingdom of Heaven; but he who does the will of My Father in Heaven. Many will say to Me in that day,

'Lord, Lord, have we not prophesied in Your Name? Cast out demons in Your Name? And done many wonders in Your Name?' And then I will declare to them, 'I never knew you: depart from Me, you who practice lawlessness!' " (Matthew 7:21-23).

All man-made religion is merely "words and works." Men vainly hope these will make them acceptable to a Holy God and fit for a Holy Heaven. The flaw in this theory is that no amount of good works will ever erase the sinful rebellion which exists in the heart of every son of Adam. The only cure for our sin and our guilt is to be miraculously transformed by the blood of Jesus Christ into that perfect righteousness which alone makes us acceptable to God and fit for an eternity in Heaven. Those who reject the salvation of God will all be judged and sentenced to an eternity without God.

The Bema Judgment Seat of Christ

"For we shall all stand before the judgment seat of Christ. For it is written, 'As I live', says the Lord, 'Every knee shall bow to Me, and every tongue shall confess to God.' So then each of us shall give account of himself to God" (Romans 14:10-12).

This judgment will take place before Jesus Christ and will involve all Christians who have ever lived. It will take place in Heaven after the Rapture of the Church and will involve the giving or the loss of rewards for our service to God. This judgment will not affect anyone's salvation because only those saved by the blood of Jesus Christ will appear before this judgment. The Apostle Paul uses the Greek word "Bema" to describe this judgment and the word is derived from the crown or wreath given to the victorious athlete after a tournament. All Christians will have their lives judged by Jesus on the basis of their works. Those whose lives have revealed true spiritual gold and silver will receive eternal rewards in Heaven. Those whose lives reveal only spiritual "wood and stubble" will not receive the rewards and crowns of glory. But they will still be saved by the blood of Christ. We are saved by the atoning finished work of Christ applied to our heart, not by our subsequent works. However, the Lord has promised eternal rewards for those who have lived in holiness and obedience to His commands.

To reign and rule with Christ is part of the reward which will belong to Christians in the Millennium and the New Earth. Every believer has an opportunity to qualify for positions of leadership in the world to come by our obedience to Christ today. David will be resurrected as the King of Israel, in a special position as Prince-Regent in Jerusalem, with Jesus Christ ruling as the King of Kings. The Apostles will rule the twelve tribes of Israel and many Christians will be given positions of ruling various cities throughout the world. Other leadership roles will belong to faithful Christians. The positions of rule will be given as a reward to those whose spiritual life has reflected the fruits of the Spirit and the true spiritual gold and silver. While we are saved by the blood of Christ, we will not earn the right to rule simply by accepting salvation. The judgment seat of Christ will show that: "Each one's work will become clear; for the Day will declare it, because it will be revealed by fire; and the fire will test each one's work, of what sort it is. If anyone's work which he has built on it endures, he will receive a reward. If anyone's work is burned, he will suffer loss: but he himself will be saved; yet so as through fire" (1 Corinthians 3:13-15).

All the descriptions of Heaven tell us that our eternal destiny will have a hierarchy of rewards and glory. While all will be saved solely by the atonement of Christ, there are rewards which will be enjoyed forever for those who follow the Lord in obedience and holiness. We are told in the great chapter of faith, Hebrews 11:24-26 that, "By faith Moses, when he became of age, refused to be called the son of Pharaoh's daughter, choosing rather to suffer affliction with the people of God than to enjoy the passing pleasures of sin, esteeming the reproach of Christ greater riches than the treasures in Egypt; for he looked to the reward." The motive of Moses in rejecting the pleasures of Egyptian royalty for the persecution of following God was his understanding of the tremendous eternal reward which God offered to all believers.

It is my conviction, after hundreds of discussions with Christians, that one of the great reasons for the lack of holiness in the Church today is that we have lost sight of the rewards of Heaven. People have so often said, "We can become so heavenly minded that we are no earthy good." The tragedy in the Church today is the opposite error. We have become so Earthly minded that we are in serious danger of being no Heavenly good. One of my motivations in this study is to help restore a proper balance in our outlook and to re-emphasize the reality and promises of our Heavenly rewards as we follow Christ.

The Bible promises that when we get to Heaven God will honor Christians with crowns and rewards for their service to Him during our life here on Earth. Those who "have fought the good fight" will receive the rewards and justice eternally which so often eluded them while in this earthly life. The Scriptures describe five crowns which are granted at the Bema Judgment Seat of Christ.

The Crown of Life

This crown is promised to all those who have withstood the tribulations, including martyrdom for Christ. In Revelation 2:10 God promises: "Be faithful until death, and I will give you the crown of life." Though to the world the believer often appears to lose; in the eternal world to come, those who follow Christ will receive the glorious martyr's Crown of Life. Those who have chosen martyrdom rather than to renounce their faith in Christ will be honored in Heaven forever.

The Crown of Glory

Those who have served Jesus Christ in the role of elders in the Church and pastors will receive their reward from God. Though they have often given thanklessly of their time and resources here, in Heaven they shall receive a Crown of Glory. Christ tells us: "The elders who are among you I exhort, I who am a fellow elder and a witness of the sufferings of Christ, and also a partaker of the glory that will be revealed: Shepherd the flock of God which is among you, serving as overseers, not by compulsion, but willingly . . . and when the Chief Shepherd appears, you will receive the crown of glory that does not fade away" (11 Peter 5:1,2,4).

The Crown of Rejoicing

Those who have won others to faith in Jesus Christ as their Savior are promised a special reward in Heaven. In the same manner in which society today offers honors to those who save people from a burning house; we are promised that God will honor those who have faithfully witnessed to their friends and neighbors about Christ. "For what is our hope, or joy, or crown of rejoicing? Is it not even you in the presence of our Lord Jesus Christ at His coming?" (1 Thessalonians 2:19) If a Christian chooses to be silent to those around him about his faith in Christ, then we must draw one of three possible conclusions: (1) He does not truly believe that the friend that continues as an unrepentant sinner will spend eternity in Hell. Or (2) He believes this, but does not love his friend enough to risk the loss of his friendship by telling him the truth about our eternal destiny. Or (3) He believes in his salvation through Jesus Christ but has received so little teaching about the reality of Heaven or Hell that he hesitates to venture into discussions about these eternal matters. Often today, I am convinced that the third conclusion is the real reason so few will witness about their faith. Once we receive an understanding of the biblical truths about the reality of Heaven and Hell, it should motivate us to tell others the good news about salvation through Jesus Christ.

The Crown of Righteousness

"Finally, there is laid up for me the crown of righteousness, which the Lord, the righteous Judge, will give to me on that Day, and not to me only but also to all who have loved His appearing" (2 Timothy 4:8).

This crown is to be given to all Christians that long for the return of Christ. Too many Christians today are so caught up in their own life plans that they have lost sight of the glorious truth that Jesus is going to return soon to set up His Kingdom. Throughout the New Testament, Christians are told again and again to be watchful for the imminent return of their Lord and Savior. While we must be watchful we are also told to occupy until He comes. We must live in a spiritually creative tension in which we should plan as though we have a hundred years till He returns but live as though He will return before the next dawning.

The Incorruptible Crown

"And everyone who competes for the prize is temperate in all things. Now they do it to obtain a perishable crown, but we for an imperishable crown" (1 Corinthians 9:25).

There is a crown of purity for the victors in the daily spiritual struggle which we wage in our life. The Bible tells us to "put on the whole armor of God" to be prepared for this spiritual warfare. Paul tells us that we must exercise spiritual discipline, like an athlete, if we are to find victory in Christ. "Therefore I run thus: not with uncertainty. Thus I fight: not as one who beats the air. But I discipline my body and bring it into subjection. . . ." (vv. 26,27). He uses the imagery of an athlete who practices running in preparation for the race or a boxer who prepares for a real fight; not just shadow boxing. Paul declares that our spiritual rewards and Heaven's crowns are worth the fight.

The wonderful truth is that God is vitally concerned about our life and our spiritual struggles. He promises us that He intends to reward us with the crowns we have earned when Christ returns for His Church. Christ encourages us to strive for the best in our spiritual life and that we will become an overcomer to achieve the heavenly rewards. "Behold, I am coming quickly! Hold fast what you have, that no one may take your crown. He who overcomes, I will make him a pillar in the temple of My God, and he shall go out no more. I will write on him the name of My God, and the name of the city of My God, the New Jerusalem, which comes down out of heaven from My God. And I will write on him My new name. He who has an ear, let him hear what the Spirit says to the churches" (Revelation 3:11-13).

In this life we often are appalled at the injustice that surrounds us. Daily we see evil, powerful men go free while innocent people are hurt and destroyed. The heart rebels against the injustice of it all and cries out to God, "Where is the justice?" King Solomon, the wisest man who ever lived, struggled with the same dilemma. "I returned and saw under the sun that the race is not to the swift, nor the battle to the strong, nor bread to the wise, nor riches to men of understanding, nor favor to men of skill, but time and chance happen to them all" (Ecclesiastes 9:11). Then Solomon muses about the ultimate judgment of Heaven: "I said in my heart, God shall judge the righteous and the wicked: for there is a time there for every purpose and for every work" (3:17). But Solomon ultimately ends his deliberations: "Let us hear the conclusion of the whole matter: Fear God, and keep His commandments: For this is man's all. For God will bring every work into judgment, including every secret thing, Whether good, or evil" (12:13,14).

As this chapter has shown, God will ultimately judge fairly all the deeds of men and angels. Justice will be done. Someone once said, "I don't want justice; I want mercy." There is a mercy for those who will accept it on God's terms; not their own. God's great mercy is manifested to us in the offer of salvation to all who will repent of their sin and accept Jesus as their personal Savior. Then, and only then, can any of us look forward to seeing the justice of God handed out. Those who insist on having an eternity on their own terms, rather than God's terms, will finally receive it, but at the cost of their salvation. As Milton wrote in his *Paradise Lost*, the choice of Satan and every soul who rejects salvation is really this: "my choice to reign is worth ambition though in Hell: Better to reign in Hell, than serve in Heaven." In the end, someone has to be the God of your life. If you will not accept God's will; then He will accept your will for your life with all its tragic consequences.

The invitation of God is still open to all who will accept. In Revelation 3:20,21 Christ declares: "Behold, I stand at the door and knock: if anyone hears My voice, and opens the door, I will come in to him, and dine with him and he with Me. To him who overcomes I will grant to sit with Me on My throne."

CHAPTER 14

Special Update Chapter

The Gates of Heaven: Coming Home

To Gain the World and Lose Your Soul

Two thousand years ago Jesus Christ asked one of the most profound questions that has ever been uttered: "For what shall it profit a man, if he shall gain the whole world, and lose his own soul? Or what shall a man give in exchange for his soul?" (Mark 8:36,37). Most men and women spend their whole lives planning and working to achieve material success or the respect of others. Yet after the passage of only a few years, all that we have worked for and achieved will turn to dust. The only things that we do in our life that will last through eternity are the relationships we build, the souls we have led to faith in Christ and the faithful works that we have done for our Lord. We need to examine our lives in light of eternity and consider whether we are in danger of exchanging our soul for worldly success.

The newspapers and television are filled with advertising and programs that proclaim our happiness and value depend on our material success and acquisitions. Nothing could be further from the truth. Material success may give you momentary pleasure but no one has ever yet found joy in the possession of things. Joy, that pure emotion that uplifts our spirit, comes from God alone.

Despite our knowledge that joy does not come from worldly success many of us look at those in the media who have achieved great wealth and believe that they "have it made." Sometimes we think that if only we had their degree of wealth that it would solve all of our problems. We need to remember that wealth apart from God's blessing usually turns out to be a curse. Several years ago Ann Landers wrote a column that appeared in *The Toronto Star* newspaper on January 29, 1994 which was entitled *Eight tragic stories shed light on the super-rich.*

"For those folks who believe that a huge amount of money and power are essential to happiness: Consider this:

1. Ivar Krueger was the head of one of the world's greatest monopolies, International Match Corp. However, the 'Match King' either killed himself or was murdered. The truth was never established.

2. Jesse Livermore was a 'boy wonder,' one of the most successful speculators on Wall Street. He died a suicide.

3. Charles Schwab was the president of Bethlehem Steel, the largest independent steel company in the United States. After a lifetime of success he died broke.

4. Samuel Insull was a chairman of Commonwealth Edison Co., one of the largest utility companies in the U.S. He was acquitted on embezzlement and mail fraud charges. He died in Paris in poverty.

5. Howard Hopson was a former president of Associated Gas and Electric Utility, the largest gas company in the U.S. He went to prison on mail-fraud charges before dying in a sanitarium.

6. Richard Whitney a man who was once the president of the New York Stock Exchange. He served time in Sing Sing for grand larceny.

7. Leon Fraser, a former president of the World Bank for International Settlements died a suicide.

8. Albert Fall was a Secretary of the Interior in President Warren Harding's cabinet. He served a prison term for accepting a bribe."

The Last Words of Some Who Rejected God

The words of a dying person have been accepted in many societies as having the same legal importance of a written last will and testament. The reason is simply that common sense and experience have shown that men will seldom consciously lie when they know they are facing the prospect of eternity and their final appointment to meet God as their judge. In the light of this knowledge that such dying words will likely reflect men's truest thoughts; consider some of the last testaments of some famous people who knew they were dying without Christ. Despite the bravado and contempt of death that men pronounce when all is well in their life "eat, drink and be merry, for tomorrow we die!"; when death stands at the door, their words often change to reflect the utter bankruptcy of their vain philosophy

Julian The Apostate

As emperor of Rome, Julian the Apostate arrogantly hated the Christians and their Scriptures. He passed brutal laws condemning Christians to death if they would not deny their faith in Jesus. Julian closed churches and reopened the pagan temples that had been left in ruins as the majority of the Roman Empire had turned to faith in Jesus Christ. In a vain attempt to prove the prophecies of Jesus Christ were wrong, Emperor Julian gave orders for his workmen to rebuild the Temple in Jerusalem. When flames shot out of the tunnels and holes in the surface of the Temple Mount, the workmen were so afraid that they abandoned their tools and refused to continue the project. Julian was defeated in his plans to oppose God's will. Finally as he lay dying, Julian acknowledged his defeat, "Thou hast conquered me, O Galilean!"

Cesare Borgia

Cesare Borgia was a church leader and general who ruled Italy during the fifteenth century. He was known and feared due to his deadly reputation for poisoning his enemies, violence and debauchery. Despite a lifetime of extraordinary worldly success and immense wealth, Borgia discovered as he lay on his deathbed that he had provided well for his body but he was woefully unprepared spiritually to meet His Creator. His last recorded words were these: "When I lived, I provided for everything but death; now I must die. I am unprovided to die."

Cardinal Wolsey

Cardinal Wolsey was the infamous chief minister of the government of England in the days of Henry VIII who was known for his cruelty and contempt of true believers. Although Wolsey was a church cardinal he did not know Christ as his personal Savior. When he lay dying he said, "Had I been so diligent in serving my God, as I have to please my king, he would not have forsaken me now in my gray hairs."

François Voltaire

The great French philosopher was an enemy of the church and spent his whole life ridiculing and attempting to destroy the truth of the gospel of Christ. Yet as he lay on his deathbed Voltaire continually cried out that he was, "abandoned by God and man." He often called out in utter despair: "O Christ! Oh Jesus Christ!" His doctor was so terrified that he abandoned his patient. Voltaire's closest friend, the Marshal de Richelieu, another cynic, was so appalled that he fled as well. His nurse, who was hired to care for him as he approached his death, refused to care for the dying the rest of her life because of "fear of witnessing another such scene as the death of Voltaire."

Edward Gibbon

The great English historian who wrote the *Decline and Fall of the Roman Empire* had dismissed the reality of the truth of Christianity. At his death Gibbon said: "The present is a fleeting moment, the past is no more, and my prospects of the future are dark and doubtful."

Such examples could be multiplied endlessly. The tragic reality is that most men and women, after a lifetime of saying no to God, even as they face death knowing they will soon give an account of their rejection of Christ, still cannot turn from their stubborn rebellion against the Lord.

The Dying Words of Some Christians

In contrast to these words of those who died in unbelief, there are multitudes of examples of the dying words of Christians which illustrate the tremendous gulf which separates the spiritual state and attitude of believers from those who have never known the touch of Jesus Christ in their lives. Jesus Christ warned His disciples about the persecution that would afflict them wherever the Gospel was preached. There is a natural hatred of divine truth that rises within the heart of those who reject God's law. They form a deep contempt for the holy lives and the selfless love possessed by the followers of Christ. Objectively, the Christians were the best citizens of the countries which persecuted them. As a group the disciples of Jesus in every generation have been law abiding, tax paying citizens who have prayed for the good of their persecutors. Yet the evil leaders of this world are driven by a satanic hatred to persecute the Church because they view the existence of a dynamic Christianity as a reproach against their sins and corruption. However, the blood of the martyrs ultimately inspired a whole generation to leave paganism to follow the One who could inspire such selfless devotion in men and women facing a martyr's death. While the Christians during the last few centuries in North America have known freedom from the horrors of persecution, throughout the world our faithful brothers and sisters are called upon to prove their faith with their life's blood every day around the world. A recent study concluded that on average over 300,000 Christians die as martyrs worldwide every year. In the south of Sudan in East Africa, Moslem army units have raided Christian villages for the last decade. Hundreds of Christian Sudanese men have been crucified while their wives and children are sold as slaves in parts of the Saudi Arabian peninsula. Throughout the last two thousand years many believers have been forced to endure incredible tribulations through which they gained an entrance into the Heavenly City of God. As the Apostle Paul warned, "We are persecuted on every side, yet not forsaken; cast down, but not destroyed" (2 Corinthians 4:8,9).

Consider the testimony of these dying words of those who loved Jesus Christ even at the cost of their lives:

St. Stephen

This deacon of the Jerusalem church was one of the seventy disciples of our Lord. Stephen was martyred by stoning in the early days of the Christian church. After giving witness to his faith by one of the most stirring messages ever preached as recorded in the Book of Acts, those standing around him began to execute him. Rather than appeal for mercy or cursing his oppressors, Stephen looked up steadfastly towards his home in Heaven and said: "Lord Jesus, receive my spirit."

Ignatius

Ignatius was considered one of the early fathers of the Church. He was a disciple and close friend of the Apostle John who wrote the Gospel and the Book of Revelation. Ignatius had also worked with Peter and Paul. After forty faithful years as bishop of the great Church in Antioch in the Roman province of Syria, Ignatius was condemned to death as a Christian by Emperor Trajan. As he approached the moment of martyrdom some of his friends were praying that he might be spared such a painful death due to his advanced years. However, Ignatius replied, "Let nothing of things visible or invisible, grudge me the attainment of Christ. Fire and the cross, or beasts tearing my limbs asunder, or crushing my whole body—let all such afflictions come upon me, provided I only win Christ."

St. Polycarp

Polycarp was the bishop of Smyrna (in present-day Turkey). He was personally taught the Gospel by the Apostle John. When the persecution was at its greatest, the Roman proconsul threatened him with death unless he would deny his faith in Christ. The proconsul demanded that he worship Caesar, "Swear and I will release thee; blaspheme Christ." Polycarp replied, "Eighty and six years I have served Christ, and He has never done me injury; how can I then blaspheme my King, my Savior?" As they prepared to burn him, Polycarp said, "I fear not the fire that burns only for a moment, but thou hast heard of that which burns for ever and ever."

John Huss

John Huss was a great reformer who helped to return the Church of Jesus Christ to the foundational truths of the Bible. He upheld the necessity of personal faith in the atonement of Jesus Christ. After a thousand years of growing apostasy, the Roman church used the Inquisition and the stake to destroy any who refused to bow to Rome. As men and women began to search the Scriptures for themselves they found that many of the practices and doctrines of the church were not supported by the commands of God as found in the Bible. When he rejected several of these doctrinal errors, Huss was martyred for his faith in Jesus in 1414. As he lay sick in a dungeon waiting for the moment of his execution he declared, "I take God to witness, I preached none but his own pure doctrines and what I taught I am ready to seal with my blood." As they led him to the stake John Huss uttered these words, "Lord Jesus, have mercy on me! Into Thy hand, O God, I commend my spirit."

Jerome of Prague

Jerome was a great reformer in Europe during the same period as his friend John Huss. After a faithful career as a pastor and witness to Jesus Christ he was martyred at the stake for his stand that the Bible was the source of doctrine, not the church councils and traditions. As he was dying, Jerome uttered these words, "This soul in flames I offer, Christ, to thee."

Bishop Latimer

Bishop Latimer was a reformer in the church in England who ultimately restored the Bible to its place of honor in the churches and in the nation. He called men to salvation and affirmed the need for a personal faith in Jesus. The persecution against true believers brought many leaders of the Reformation to a martyr's death for Jesus Christ. As Latimer was being tied to the stake with his friend and fellow preacher, Bishop Ridley, he said: "Be of good cheer, Brother Ridley, for we shall this day light such a candle in England as will, I trust, by God's grace, never be put out." The Gospel message and martyrdom of these two saints were used by God to awaken the Reformation spirit in England.

Martin Luther

Though Martin Luther had been trained as a priest and Catholic theologian he could not find assurance of personal salvation in the religious duties and works demanded by the medieval church. Finally, after years of agonizing works, doubt and suffering, Martin Luther found the truth of salvation in the words of the Holy Scriptures. "The just shall live by faith" was the radical but fundamental teaching of the Word of God found in both the Old and New Testaments. This biblical doctrine of justification by faith in Jesus Christ's atoning work on the Cross became the rallying cry and foundation of the Reformation that released untold millions from the shackles of dead religion. Luther became the father of the Protestant Reformation in Germany in A.D. 1520. As Luther approached death he said, "Thou hast redeemed me, O Lord God of truth. I will die steadfast, clinging to Christ and to the doctrine I have so constantly preached."

Ludwig van Beethoven

Ludwig van Beethoven was a brilliant composer who created numerous memorable symphonies which have thrilled audiences around the world for centuries. Many people do not realize that this incredible musical genius could not hear his own music except when he held his head against a musical instrument to feel the physical vibrations. Beethoven was deaf. Yet this man of faith expressed his own confidence in the promises of Jesus Christ that He would restore all things. As he lay dying, Beethoven said, "I shall hear in Heaven."

George Washington

George Washington was the first president of the United States of America. He was a committed Christian, though many secular humanist critics try to deny his deep faith in God. Often he would be found praying during the greatest crises of the Revolutionary War to free the colonies from England. On his deathbed, Washington expressed his deep and abiding faith in his eternal home in Heaven with Jesus Christ, in these dying words, "It is well."

CHAPTER 15

Special Update Chapter
Hell: The Final State of Those Who Choose to Reject Salvation

"Hell is an abiding place, but no resting place."
Thomas Watson.

The Bible declares that this is "the day of salvation." As long as we live and until the day when Christ returns to set up His kingdom men can still turn from their sin and accept His salvation. "For he saith, I have heard thee in a time accepted, and in the day of salvation have I succoured thee: behold, now is the accepted time; behold, now is the day of salvation" (2 Corinthians 6:2). However, as surely as God declared that this is "the day of salvation," He also warned that there would come a day in the life of every man and woman when the open door to heaven would close forever. We will then face the inevitable prospect of an eternity in darkness in Hell. Jesus Himself announced the dreadful words of final judgment that will face everyone who in the end says, "No" to God. Christ warned, "Then shall he say also unto them on the left hand, Depart from me, ye cursed, into everlasting fire, prepared for the devil and his angels: And these shall go away into everlasting punishment: but the righteous into life eternal" (Matthew 25:41,46).

The Reality of Hell

"The Scriptures tell us that in Hell there are these three things: there is darkness, there is fire, and there are chains."

Thomas Watson.

While there are many things about Hell that have been hidden from us in the plan of God, the Bible has declared to all who accept the Word of God that Hell is absolutely real and that it will last forever. The punishment of Hell is affirmed in numerous verses throughout the Scriptures. "He that believeth and is baptized shall be saved; but he that believeth not shall be damned" (Mark 16:16). The Bible repeatedly states that those who reject God's salvation will endure an eternity in Hell where they will experience "fire and brimstone." John wrote in Revelation 14:10, "The same shall drink of the wine of the wrath of God, which is poured out without mixture into the cup of his indignation; and he shall be tormented with fire and brimstone in the presence of the holy angels, and in the presence of the Lamb." Jesus warned the people listening to Him to turn from their sins to escape the "furnace of fire." Matthew recorded this warning by Jesus, "And shall cast them into a furnace of fire: there shall be wailing and gnashing of teeth" (Matthew 13:42). In addition to the terrors of Hell itself, one of the most horrible things will be the knowledge that they have refused forever Christ's forgiveness and the glorious "kingdom of God." The Apostle Paul warned, "Know ye not that the unrighteous shall not inherit the kingdom of God?" (1 Corinthians 6:9). Some theologians have tried valiantly to escape the clear teaching of the Scriptures about the terrors of Hell by assuming that it might involve the annihilation of the sinner's soul or at least that they might be unconscious of where they were throughout eternity. However, the Scriptures clearly declare that those who reject Christ's mercies today will then endure an eternity in Hell while fully conscious. Jesus declared, "But the children of the kingdom shall be cast out into outer darkness: there shall be weeping and gnashing of teeth" (Matthew 8:12). It is hard to say whether the physical torments of Hell will be worse than the spiritual pain of knowing that they are cut off from light, love and peace forever in that place filled with equally unrepentant sinners. However, the suffering in Hell, both physical and spiritual, is declared in numerous passages of the Word of God.

The Bible's Description of Hell

The Scriptures declare repeatedly that Hell is a real place, though perhaps in another dimension. Three different words are used throughout the Bible to describe Hell. The first word is 'Hades' which describes the place where all departed spirits wait until the Day of Judgment. However, even before the resurrection of Christ, Hades was divided into two portions that were divided by a great gulf. On one side was that part of Hades known as Abraham's Bosom which held the souls of all those who died in faith in the Old Testament. Those souls in Abraham's Bosom were in a pleasant place of waiting until Jesus Christ descended into Hades to preach to the spirits in prison. When these departed saints of the Old Testament finally heard the words of Jesus, the Son of God, they could understand fully for the first time what they had only perceived in part due to their lack of knowledge about Jesus Christ's part in God's plan of salvation. However, those souls who rejected whatever of God's truth was presented to them, went to the part of Hades known as the place of torment.

Another word associated with Hell is the word 'Tartarus' which appears in only one passage of Scripture. "For if God spared not the angels that sinned, but cast them down to hell, and delivered them into chains of darkness, to be reserved unto judgment" (2 Peter 2:4). This passage indicated that there is a special place in Hell in which God imprisons those fallen angels who chose to defile mankind in the ancient past by having sexual relations with the women of Earth. Their great sin was the violation of God's prohibition of breaking the barrier between angels and mankind through illicit sexual relations. The Book of Jude reveals the nature of their sin at the dawn of man's existence on the Earth. "And the angels which kept not their first estate, but left their own habitation, he hath reserved in everlasting chains under darkness unto the judgment of the great day" (Jude 6). The final word translated repeatedly as Hell in the Bible is the word 'Gehenna' which occurs in numerous passages such as Matthew 5:22-30 and Mark 9:43-47. For example, in Matthew 5:22 we read these words, "whosoever shall say, Thou fool, shall be in danger of hell fire." The words translated 'Hell' in the Bible appears in the original Greek manuscripts as 'Gehenna.' In every passage that used the word 'Gehenna' they all refer to pain, torment, and punishment. The visual image of Gehenna was the horrible, burning garbage pit whose fire never ceased in the Valley of Hinnom outside the walls of Jerusalem on which they threw the garbage and the bodies of criminals to rot and burn. Significantly, Jesus Himself used the word Gehenna to describe Hell in every one of twelve passages in the New Testament where the word appears.

Degrees of Punishment in Hell

Are there degrees of punishment for sinners in Hell, or will all sinners drink from the same cup of punishment regardless of their wickedness? The holiness and justice of God demands that there will be a different degree of punishment that will reflect the evil deeds and motives of those who reject Christ's salvation. While the Bible tells us repeatedly that all those who enter Hell will endure its flames forever, the justice of God and the clear teaching of the Scriptures assure us that "Shall not the Judge of all the earth do right?" Genesis 18:25). God's holiness demands that He will justly judge all sinners. That is why every sinner from Cain to the last rebel who joins Satan's rebellion at the end of the thousand year Millennium will appear before the Great White Throne Judgment to be judged by God for their sins.

The Apostle John wrote of the final judgment of sinners. "And I saw a great white throne, and him that sat on it, from whose face the earth and the heaven fled away; and there was found no place for them. And I saw the dead, small and great, stand before God; and the books were opened: and another book was opened, which is the book of life: and the dead were judged out of those things which were written in the books, according to their works. And the sea gave up the dead which were in it; and death and hell delivered up the dead which were in them: and they were judged every man according to their works. And death and hell were cast into the lake of fire. This is the second death" (Revelation 20:11-14). Since everyone who appears at this judgment before the throne of God in Heaven is an unrepentant sinner, there would be no need for this judgment to occur unless individual sentences were to be handed out by man's final judge, God Almighty. Notice that the books contained God's record of men's deeds will be opened and "they were judged every man according to their works." The Judge of all the earth will judge the deeds of Adolph Hitler more harshly than those of a woman who lived a good life but still rejected Christ's salvation in her religious pride. Yet both will endure an unimaginable eternity in Hell forever because they rejected the only hope of salvation offered by God to atone for our sins. Jesus Himself affirmed that there will be differences of punishment for those in Hell when He condemned the sinful deeds of some hypocritical religious leaders. "Woe unto you, scribes and Pharisees, hypocrites! for ye devour widows' houses, and for a pretence make long prayer: therefore ye shall receive the greater damnation" (Matthew 23:14).

The Company of Sinners in Hell

We have all heard people jest who say that "when they die they will go to Hell but they will hold a great party because all of their friends will be there as well." These jokes reflect the almost total absence of realization of the reality and the horror of an eternity in Hell. The Bible describes Hell as "a lake of fire" with burning forever in a body that cannot be destroyed. "And if thine eye offend thee, pluck it out: it is better for thee to enter into the kingdom of God with one eye, than having two eyes to be cast into hell fire. Where their worm dieth not, and the fire is not quenched" (Mark 9:47). One of the worst things about Hell is that the resurrected bodies of sinners will never die. "And whosoever was not found written in the book of life was cast into the lake of fire" (Revelation 20:15). Yet consider for a moment who will be the companions who will share Hell with those who stubbornly resist God's mercy to the end . . . Hitler, Eichmann, plus every other murderer and torturer in history. Hell will be filled with untold billions of sinners who will still have bodies that can feel pain but can never die. They will curse God and all others in their pain and rage against His justice. Their desire will be to revenge themselves on God but they cannot succeed. It is more than likely that they will exact revenge for their punishment on their companions in Hell.

Think for a moment of what a normal human would experience in torment at the hands of wicked perverted prisoners in our worst penitentiary in America. Imagine that there were no guards or cell bars to protect you from the cruelty of the monsters who shared your jail. The most you could hope for would be a swift death. However, those who reject the salvation of Jesus Christ to the last will face a situation far more horrible than the one I have just suggested. Those who have chosen to spend eternity in Hell will include every murderer, rapist, pervert, torturer and vile person who ever lived. Those sinners who tormented their fellow citizens while on earth will not suddenly change their behavior for the better when they are imprisoned forever in Hell and have no hope of release for good behavior.

The Duration of Hell

"The damned shall live as long in Hell as God Himself shall live in Heaven."

Thomas Brooks.

Among the liberal theologians who accept the reality of Hell we still find many that seek to minimize its horrors by supposing that those who enter Hell will finally emerge at some point in the future and take their part among the blessed of the Lord. Others suggest that the Bible really intended to communicate the idea of the annihilation of the souls of those who reject Christ's salvation rather than condemn them to an eternity in the torments of Hell. Anyone who has spent an hour in careful thought about the reality of an eternity in Hell for sinners will understand fully the desire of theologians to escape the horror of the thought of a Hell that will never end for sinners who reject God. However, a careful reading of the pages of the Scriptures reveals that God intended us to understand that Hell will last forever and that the souls of those who reject Christ's mercy will not be annihilated but will be conscious forever. While the Scriptures declare that both Heaven and Hell will last an eternity that continues forever, there is a great difference between the two. The eternity of Heaven for those who love God will be the glory of a beautiful day that has no sunset. On the other hand, the eternity of Hell for sinners will be the horror of a night that will never end in sunrise.

Those philosophers and theologians who deny that God created man in His image now dare to create a god in their own image. They deny the validity of the Scripture's declaration that a holy and just God will condemn unrepentant sinners to Hell forever. In other words, they suggest that, if only God were like their image of Him, He would be compassionate and never send men and women to an eternity in Hell. What these theologians fail to understand is that God is not only more compassionate than we can ever understand, but He is also absolutely just and holy. His compassion motivated God to send His only Begotten Son, Jesus Christ, to die on the cross to bear the punishment of the sins for everyone of us. However, His absolute holiness and justice demands that, if men reject His blood-bought pardon, then they must themselves bear the eternal consequences of their rejection of God and His salvation.

The Scriptures use the word 'forever' over thirty times in the New Testament alone to describe the duration of Hell. It is significant that even a theologian who rejects this conclusion was forced to admit that twenty-nine of the thirty references to Hell cannot possibly be interpreted as anything other than 'forever' (Oxenham, *What is Truth as to Everlasting*

Punishment?, p. 101.) It is significant that the same words used to describe the eternal nature of the duration of Hell are used in other passages of the Bible to describe the eternal duration of Heaven. The concept of forever is almost impossible for the human mind to grasp. The puritan writer Thomas Watson suggested that "The torments of hell abide for ever. . . . If all the earth and sea were sand, and every thousandth year a bird should come, and take away one grain of sand, it would be a long time ere that vast heap of sand were emptied; yet, if after all that time the damned may come out of hell, there were some hope; but this word *EVER* breaks the heart."

Finally, we need to consider the sacrifice of Jesus Christ on the cross for our sins. Would Jesus have chosen to die in agony on the cross to enable sinners to escape Hell if it was only of limited duration? It defies common sense that God would have sent Jesus to the sacrifice of crucifixion if He knew that sinners would eventually survive a period in Hell and qualify for Heaven. The truth which is declared from Genesis to Revelation is that Hell is real and it will last forever. That is why it is so important that people turn from their sins while there is still time to repent and find salvation through faith in Jesus Christ.

CHAPTER 16

A New Heaven
and a New Earth

"Now I saw a new heaven and a new earth, for the first heaven and the first earth had passed away. . . ."
(Revelation 21:1)

Heaven is the last frontier. Like other frontiers in human history, it will challenge us with new opportunities, possibilities and experiences. Unlike the previous frontiers on Earth, Heaven will be unlimited in time and space. It will inspire us to join as participants in the dynamic, creative plans of Jesus Christ as we embark on a greater adventure than any we have ever dreamed of. The eternal quest of our human spirit yearns for a Heaven in which we can explore the infinite possibilities of an unlimited universe. Our future blessings in Heaven will begin with the ending of all evil, suffering and adversity. But it will also provide the fulfillment and enhancement of all the real joys and happiness of human life. The language in the Bible describe our rest after satisfying labor and the elimination of toil and grief. These passages do not suggest a life of inactivity or boredom. The promises are of an active, purposeful and joyful life in a creation filled with beauty, fairness and justice.

In our present earthly life, it is difficult to reconcile the goodness and power of God with the apparent triumph of evil and death. However, in the New Heaven and New Earth we will see the final reconciliation of the accounts of life in which evil will be judged and good will triumph forever. The spiritual warfare which exists in the hearts of men between our good and evil natures will finally end. Believers will enjoy their newly resurrected bodies with their heart, mind and spirit cleansed from the taint of sin. We shall be purified and made ready as "the bride of Christ" to become citizens of the City of God.

Our study of Heaven and the Coming of the Messiah is similar in nature to the unusual character of prophecy in the Book of Daniel. The Bible's passages about Heaven simultaneously reveal and conceal the truth about "the world to come." After a long passage of very specific prophecy about the future kingdom of God, the angel told Daniel to, "Shut up the words and seal the book until the time of the end" (Daniel 12:4). The angel continues with the admonition: "Many shall run to and fro, and knowledge shall increase." This puzzling dual nature of prophecy, both revealing and concealing, is even more apparent when we examine those prophecies which deal with the timing of the Second Coming and the details of the New Heaven and Earth.

God's unfolding purpose throughout human history is that His will and nature will be reflected in a perfected humanity in which evil will be annihilated and good will triumph. The age-old prophecy of God is, "The kingdoms of this world will become the Kingdoms of our Lord and Savior, Jesus Christ." There is an obvious contradiction between our desire for justice and the tragic injustice which continuously assaults us at present. Some day the wrongs will be righted and the good will be rewarded. The underlying theme of prophecy is that the justice of God will triumph in the end. Behind the detailed predictions of the rise and fall of empires lies the theme that all of these events are unfolding toward the final goal in which the Kingdom of God will prove victorious.

Some students have assumed the Bible suggests that the very nature of time, duration and causality will end in Heaven. A verse in Revelation 10:6 in the King James Version states: "There should be time no longer." However, the original language states: "There should be delay no more." Tragically, many have developed a concept of a static, boring Heaven of total inactivity from a misunderstanding of this

Scripture verse. However, the verse only states, at that point in the unfolding sequence of prophetic events in the Great Tribulation, time (or delay) will be no more. The very nature of man and the specific predictions of the many activities of Heaven prove that time will exist in the eternal New Heaven and Earth.

Eternity is not the absence of time; it is an infinity of time. The tragic consequence on this boring view of Heaven is that many people have lost all desire to go there. It is my desire to awaken in Christians an active interest and discussion of our future in a real life in the New Earth and the New Heaven. When we begin to study the passages on Heaven in the Bible we will find that all the best things of life here will find a dynamic fulfillment in our eternal home in Heaven.

After the Millennium the existing Earth and Heavens will be cleansed with fire and renewed from the pollution of sin. Even Heaven has experienced sin's pollution according to the biblical description of Satan appearing there before the throne of God. When God cleansed the Earth from sin in the days of Noah with a worldwide Flood, He promised that He would never again use water to destroy the Earth. However, in several passages, the Lord prophesied that at the end of the Millennial Kingdom He will release the atomic forces of creation to melt the elements and recreate the surface of the Earth. The Earth will not be annihilated as some believe. It will be renewed. There are many verses which prove that the Earth will continue forever in its renewed form.

However, Peter describes this renewal as follows: "But the heavens and the earth which are now preserved by the same word, are reserved for fire until the day of judgment and perdition of ungodly men. . . . But the day of the Lord will come as a thief in the night in which the heavens will pass away with a great noise and the elements shall melt with fervent heat; both the earth and the works that are in it will be burned up. Therefore, since all these things will be dissolved, what manner of persons ought you to be in holy conduct and godliness, looking for and hastening the coming of the day of

God, because of which the heavens will be dissolved, being on fire, and the elements will melt with fervent heat? Nevertheless we, according to His promise, look for new heavens and a new earth in which righteousness dwells" (2 Peter 3:7,10-13).

It is fascinating to read the research of nuclear scientists who claim that the enormously strong electrical forces within the atom are repulsing each other so strongly that only a huge force equal to 900,000 volts for each atom is holding all atomic structures together. Scientists now agree that the elements can melt with a fervent heat. When God releases the staggering powers of the atoms "kept in store by the same word, reserved for fire until the day of judgment" we shall see the fulfillment of this prophecy. Yet the promise is not simply of destruction, but it holds the promise of "a new heaven and a new earth in which righteousness dwells." Sin will cease to have dominion forever in the New Earth.

John prophesied in the Book of Revelation that Satan would be released for "a little season" after the Millennium to test mankind one last time. Many of those born during this period to the natural men and women will choose to join this final rebellion of Satan. God will destroy Satan and his army with fire. Though the Bible does not give us details of how God will transfer the people of Earth safely from the Old Earth into the New Earth, they will be protected like Noah's family during the Flood, and live in peace forever in the New Earth.

"Then He who sat on the throne said, 'Behold I make all things new' " (Revelation 21:5). After the cleansing of sin's pollution by fire, the New Jerusalem, the home of the Believers, will descend to the New Earth for eternity. Its enormous size of 1,500 miles by 1,500 miles will cover an area equal to half the size of the United States. It will be the headquarters and home of the Church as we reign and rule with Christ on the Earth forever. The curse of sin will be eradicated from the planet forever. Creation will then be transformed into a worldwide Garden of Eden. Men will no longer fear the violence of animals because God will restore animals to their original state before the Fall when they all eat vegetation. Isaiah the prophet tells us that, "The wolf and the lamb shall feed together, the lion shall eat straw like the ox . . . they shall not hurt nor destroy in all My holy mountain" (Isaiah 65:25). In this future Paradise, natural men will flourish in joyful and purposeful living under the rule of Christ and the Church. "For behold, I create Jerusalem as a rejoicing, and her people a joy, I will rejoice in Jerusalem and Joy in My people: the voice of weeping shall no longer be heard in her, nor the voice of crying" (Isaiah 65:18,19.) The cause of weeping, sin and evil, will be ended to allow men to enjoy the wonderful creation of God.

Life on the New Earth will be productive, enjoyable and finer than all the dreams of mankind, "they shall build houses, and inhabit them; They shall plant vineyards, and eat their fruit" (v. 21). The prophet promises that men will enjoy the fruits of their labor, "They shall not labor in vain, nor bring forth children for trouble; for they shall be the descendants of the blessed of the Lord, and their offspring with them" (v. 23). These natural men, Jew and Gentile, will have offspring forever in the New Earth and God promises that He will always hear their prayer. He will communicate again with men as He did with Adam as He walked with him "in the cool of the day." Isaiah describes the prayer life of the blessed men of that day: "It shall come to pass that before they call, I will answer; and while they are still speaking, I will hear" (v. 24). With sin eradicated there will be no impediment to perfect communication with God.

Moses prophesied of this future blessed time for Israel and the nations. "And you will again obey the voice of the Lord, and do all His commandments which I command you today. The Lord your God will make you abound in all the work of your hand, in the fruit of your body, in the increase of your livestock, and in the produce of your land for good. For the Lord will again rejoice over you for good as He rejoiced over your fathers" (Deuteronomy 30:8,9). This marvelous prophecy confirms that in the New Earth the natural men who survived Armageddon, Jew and Gentile, will enjoy children, crops, cattle and fruit throughout eternity.

The promise to the Church is that we, as Christians, shall be transformed at the Rapture into a resurrection body similar to the resurrected body of Jesus Christ. "Beloved, now we are children of God, and it has not yet been revealed what we shall be, but we know that when He is revealed, we shall be like Him, for we shall see Him as He is" (1 John 3:2). As the Sons of God we shall see Jesus face to face and enjoy His Divine Presence for eternity. John tells us that the knowledge of this will purify our spiritual walk, "And everyone who has this hope in Him purifies himself, just as He is pure" (v. 3).

In his letter to the Corinthian Church, Paul talked about the transformation in knowledge which we can eagerly await after our resurrection. "For we know in part, and we prophesy in part. But when that which is perfect has come, then that which is in part will be done away. When I was a child, I spoke as a child, I understood as a child, I thought as a child; but when I became a man, I put away childish things. For now we see in a mirror, dimly; but then face to face. Now I know in part; but then I shall know just as I also am known. And now abide faith, hope and love, these three; but the greatest of these is love" (1 Corinthians 13:9-13). The love of God and our love for each other will surround us in the heavenly city.

With all the limits removed our capacity for knowledge and experience will be phenomenal. We shall enjoy direct knowledge of God's creation and will understand our brothers and sisters in an authentic, transparent love which transcends our earthly experience. Faith, hope and most of all, love, will exist forever. If there are elements in our present life not present for us in Heaven; I believe that Paul shows that the essence of these things will be experienced there on a much higher level. An adult often looks back fondly on his memories of building sand castles on a beach, but he does not miss it because now he builds beautiful houses and skyscrapers. We shall not have regrets in Heaven for the loss of anything which has enduring value. All that is worthwhile in this life will find its highest expression in Heaven.

The New Heaven and the New Jerusalem will be the final home of all the righteous sons of God from Adam to the last member of the Church. We shall enjoy and have access to the "pure river of life, clear as crystal, proceeding out of the throne of God and of the Lamb." The "Tree of Life" was removed from the Earth after Adam's sin. It will be available to all who live in Heaven. One of the promises is that those who obey the commandments of God will have the privilege of eating from the Tree of Life and may freely enter the gates of the New Jerusalem forever (Revelation 22:14). The Tree of Life will yield "twelve fruits, each tree yielding its fruit every month" which shows that we shall still enjoy the taste of various kinds of fruit. The mention of months shows that the phenomenon of months and seasons will exist in Heaven to provide some variety of climate in our new home.

As the servants of God, we are promised a life of meaningful service to our Lord and "they shall see His face and His name shall be in their foreheads." There will be no night in the New Jerusalem because the Divine light of God Himself will illuminate the City of God. Some have mistakenly believed that the sun will cease to exist because Revelation 22:5 says, "they need no lamp, nor light of the sun; for the Lord God gives them light." Note that it does not say that the sun doesn't exist; simply that in the city we won't need either lamps or the light of the sun.

Christ told us to "Lay up for yourselves treasures in Heaven, where neither moth nor rust destroys and where thieves do not break in nor steal. For where your treasure is, there your heart will be also" (Matthew 6:20,21). If you talk to a man for only thirty minutes you will quickly learn where his treasure is. Do his eyes light up when he discusses his business? Does her voice change when she talks about her children? Can you hear the excitement in his voice when he speaks about Jesus? In Matthew 6:33 Christ told us, "Seek first the Kingdom of God and His righteousness, and all these things shall be added to you."

One of the reasons for the disappointments of life today is that we have been deceived by the rampant materialism of our world. It is folly to even try to measure our spiritual life by the standards of material prosperity. The Christian life is often presented as a "better lifestyle" and as an opportunity to "live like a King's kid." They have lost sight that the King we follow is the Son of Man who had nowhere to lay His head, was rejected by men and ultimately crucified as a criminal. The blindness of this gospel of materialism has caused some to suggest that, "If Paul had only had enough faith; he would not have experienced his thorn in the flesh and persecution." We are promised riches, perfect health and freedom from troubles. However, these promises belong to our future life in Heaven with Christ. In this life we will experience trials and tribulations, which will often prove to be the place of our greatest spiritual victories. Christ promised us victory in our battles, not the absence of battles. He promises "And he who overcomes, and keeps My works until the end, to him will I give power over the nations" (Revelation 2:26).

Honors and rewards will be given to those who follow the commands of Christ. "To him who overcomes I will give some of the hidden manna to eat. And I will give him a white stone, and on the stone a new name written which no one knows except him who receives it" (Revelation 2:17). Jesus knew that the Christian walk would be difficult but He promised that we would never walk alone. He promises that we will receive from Him the "hidden manna," the bread of eternal life and our relationship with God will be so special, and so intimate a friendship that He will know each of us by a secret personal name which He shall give us. "I am He who searches the minds and hearts: and I will give to each one of you according to your works." Though we often think that no one is aware of our life and our deeds, Christ assures us that He is following our activities with the same loving care of an earthly father.

There is a registry in Heaven for the names of those who are followers of Jesus. The promise of eternity is that our personal identity continues there, as manifested by this registry, our individual crowns, rewards and treasures.

If Heaven is real, it must occupy an actual location somewhere in the infinite universe. The natural tendency of people to deny this tends to show that many do not really believe the promises about the physical reality of Heaven. Often the biblical writers refer to Heaven as being in "the north" and in a direction "above" the Earth. The Scriptures insist on a "real" Heaven and Christ declares that He has gone to prepare mansions for us. While Heaven may occupy a different dimension than ours; the Bible does not state this.

The descriptions of Heaven are very precise and "real." Jesus told His followers there is enough room in these mansions for all Christians, "In My Father's house are many mansions; if it were not so, I would have told you. I go to prepare a place for you. And if I go to prepare a place for you, I will come again and receive you to Myself; that where I am, there you may be also" (John 14:2-4). The description of the New Jerusalem is quite detailed, but there is much which the Bible has not even mentioned. God created the beautiful world we see around us in only six days. Christ has now had almost two thousand years to "prepare a place for you." He also told us there is only one way to enter His Father's House. "Jesus said to him, 'I am the way, the truth, and the life. No one comes to the Father except through me' " (John 14:6).

Revelation 7:9 promises that we shall be clothed with white robes to symbolize the righteousness of God. Palm branches are waved before the throne of God. This description of palm branches, the Tree of Life, fruit, and leaves proves that Heaven contains a variety of vegetation. The Scriptures, including Exodus 25, describe Tabernacle worship objects on Earth which were designed after the blueprints of the original heavenly items. It is more than probable that all the pure and good things of this Earth have their original counterparts in Heaven. God declared in the Book of Genesis that man was created in His heavenly image. John and Paul both saw in their heavenly visions a wonderful Paradise that contains the pure original forms of many things we enjoy here on Earth. Paul tells us in Hebrews 8:5 that God told Moses, "See that you make all things according to the pattern shown you on the mountain." In the Book of Revelation, John describes Christ giving rewards to every man according to their works on Earth (Revelation 22:12).

The Infinite Possibilities of Heaven

What would you dream of doing if you knew you could not fail? What projects would you embark upon if you knew you would have forever to complete them? What subjects would you study if all the information of the universe was at your fingertips? Can you imagine the wonderful conversations you will have in Heaven when you can meet all the great historical and biblical characters? What countries and places would you visit with your loved ones if time and money did not restrict you? Would you like to talk to Jesus about the unanswered questions of life when you have the joy of sitting at His feet?

One of the great joys of eternity will be the great reunion with our long-lost friends and family who have passed on before us to await us in the eternal city. The joy of parents at the birth of their firstborn is just a small foretaste of the happiness we shall experience when we begin to discover the things which Christ has prepared for His disciples. All the trials, persecutions and pains of life will fade away in the light of His countenance.

In the Book of Ephesians 2:6,7, the Apostle Paul tells us that Christ has "raised us up together, and made us sit together in the heavenly places in Christ Jesus that in the ages to come He might show the exceeding riches of His grace in His kindness toward us in Christ Jesus." Paul was blessed by the Lord with a foretaste of the glory to come when he was "caught up to the third heaven." He tells us that he saw things when "he was caught up into Paradise and heard inexpressible words, which it is not lawful for a man to utter" (2 Corinthians 12:2-4). Like John in the Book of Revelation, Paul had part of his vision sealed because it was too glorious to reveal until the day of the Rapture of the Church. The glory of his vision was so great that God allowed Paul to receive "a thorn in the flesh" to afflict him and prevent his becoming puffed up in pride at the great privilege he had received. The mention of the "third Heaven" suggests there are at least three Heavens; some have suggested there may be seven. The first is the atmosphere above the Earth. The second is the heavenlies, among the stars, which is available to all spiritual creatures, including Satan, who appeared in Heaven occasionally according to the Scriptures. Paul was raptured to the Third Heaven which contains the angelic host, the New Jerusalem and the throne of God.

One of the glories will be the ethereal music of Heaven. The twenty-four elders around the throne of God will produce music on harps which shows that our Heavenly Father enjoys the beauty of melodious music (Revelation 5:8,9). They will sing a new song in glory, "Thou art worthy. . . ." These elders represent the Church, they wear white raiment and they will have golden crowns upon their heads which they will receive at the Judgment Seat of Christ following the Rapture. Before the throne of God is a beautiful crystal sea. The four living creatures, the highest class of angels, surround the throne of God and continually sing, "Holy, Holy, Holy, Lord God Almighty, Who was and is and is to come!" (Revelation 4:8-11). In response to this anthem of praise, the elders cast their crowns at the feet of Jesus to give Him glory and call out, "You are worthy, O Lord, to receive glory and honor and power; For You created all things, And by Your will they exist and were created." The golden vials full of incense near the throne of God also show that we will be able to experience the aromas of beautiful fragrance.

The voices of 100 million angels ("ten thousand times ten thousand") surround the heavenly throne with a glorious anthem: "Worthy is the Lamb who was slain to receive power and riches and wisdom, and strength and honor and glory and blessing!" (Revelation 5:11,12). This proves that in Heaven these qualities will be present under the governing of Jesus Christ, the Lamb of God. Power, riches, wisdom, strength, honors, glories and blessings will be the birthright of the sons of God in the New Heaven and New Earth. John saw the Temple of God in Heaven which God had shown to King David to give him the pattern for the First Temple. A heavenly Ark of the Covenant, a Holy of Holies, golden censers, trumpets and a golden altar are elements of the worship there. Many martyred saints will have the privilege and joy of serving God within this heavenly Temple.

One of their great privileges will be the experience of dwelling where Jesus lives in the city of God. John declares that these martyrs will, "serve Him day and night in His Temple, and He who sits on the throne will dwell among them." The pain and suffering of their persecution and martyrdom will be rewarded as Christ promises to "feed them, and shall lead them unto living fountains of waters: and God shall wipe away all tears from their eyes."

Those who are followers of Christ receive the name of God as well as the recording of their name "written in the Book of Life of the Lamb slain from the foundation of the world" (Revelation 13:8). A special group of one hundred and forty-four thousand believers will sing "a new song" of praise to God on the Mount Zion in Heaven. "These were redeemed from among men being the firstfruits to God and to the Lamb" (Revelation 14:1-4). We shall live forever in the most beautiful city of pure gold and walls of jasper. "The foundations of the wall of the city were adorned with all kinds of precious stones." As one small example of the unparalleled riches of Heaven, God used twelve kinds of gemstones to decorate the foundations of the city. The streets we shall walk upon there shall be composed of pure, transparent gold.

Many have wondered if animals will exist in Heaven. The Bible describes the heavenly horses and chariots of fire in both the rapture of Elijah and the description of horses and horsemen in the heavenly army of Christ at the Battle of Armageddon. "The armies in heaven, clothed in fine linen, white and clean, followed Him on white horses" (Revelation 19:14). While the Scriptures do not describe other animals specifically, there are no verses which suggest that animals will not exist there. It is quite possible that all the tremendous varieties of created animals will have their place in the New Heaven. Certainly the Bible does describe animals during and following the Millennium as flourishing on the Earth. All pure and good created things will have their appointed place in the New Earth. Since the resurrected believers will have access to both the New Heaven and the New Earth we shall enjoy all God's creation in the world to come.

The cumulative effect of the study of these biblical promises about the New Earth and the New Heaven creates an overwhelming impression of the exciting reality of our future life in Heaven. While our eternal life contains many mysteries which shall only be revealed in Heaven, the Bible also speaks clearly about a definite location called Heaven; not merely a condition of spiritual happiness. Though Heaven will surely contain much more than the wonderful, biblical descriptions I have detailed in this book; it will not contain less. The greatest adventure of man's history lies before us if we will only turn from our sin and accept God's offer of eternal life. The Word of God tells us that, "the gift of God is eternal life in Christ Jesus our Lord" (Romans 6:23). We do not have to wait until we die to receive eternal life. The moment we accept Christ's pardon, we are transformed from spiritual death to eternal life.

There is a profound eternal choice which every human must make. In the end we will either choose to accept Christ's salvation or we will turn away from Heaven's pardon in a false and fatal pride. The choice is clear. At the end of our life's journey we shall meet Jesus Christ face to face. We will stand before Him on that day as our Judge or as our Savior. If you have accepted the evidence of history, fulfilled prophecy and your conscience, then you have accepted that you are a sinner in need of forgiveness and cleansing through your acceptance of Jesus Christ as your Savior. If you have not yet accepted Him, I appeal to you to honestly consider the truths about Jesus Christ and our eternal destiny in this book.

The Old Testament saints longed for the day when they would enter Heaven, the true Promised Land of God. Abraham "looked for a city which has foundations, whose builder and maker is God." They were transformed by their belief that someday they would inherit the promises. In Hebrews, chapter 11, it is recorded that "these all died in faith, not having received the promises, but having seen them afar off were assured of them, embraced them and confessed that they were strangers and pilgrims on the earth. For those who say such things declare plainly that they seek a homeland. . . . But now they desire a better, that is, a heavenly country. Therefore God is not ashamed to be called their God: for He has prepared a city for them."

When John received his wonderful vision of Heaven while a prisoner on the isle of Patmos, he saw Jesus in His glory as the Son of God. He fainted and Jesus revived him and said, "Do not be afraid; I am the First and the Last. I am He who lives, and was dead, and behold, I am alive forevermore, Amen. And I have the keys of Hades and Death. Write the things which you have seen, and the things which are, and the things which will take place after this" (Revelation 1:17-19). Jesus came once to this Earth to suffer and die on a Cross to pay the supreme judicial penalty for rebellion and sin. He came as a suffering Messiah and still holds open to every man and woman the invitation to accept His pardon and citizenship in the city of God. However, the same Scriptures which tell of His First Coming also assure us that He is coming again. He is coming as King of Kings and Lord of Hosts. With His mighty heavenly army He will destroy the armies of the world and establish an eternal throne in Jerusalem.

Many people have said in their hearts that at the right time they will turn from their sin and accept Him. However, for many people, that time will never come. Without warning, you may face your death or you may arise one morning to find that every single Christian believer on the planet has been raptured to Heaven. The invitation to eternal salvation is not open-ended forever. It is "subject to cancellation without further notice." No one knows how long the Lord will continue to call.

As we approach the climax of human history, the invitation of Christ is clear. "And He said to me, 'It is done! I am the Alpha and the Omega, the Beginning and the End. I will give of the fountain of the water of life freely to him who thirsts. He who overcomes shall inherit all things; and I will be his God and he shall be My son' " (Revelation 21:6,7).

CHAPTER 17

Questions You Always Wanted to Ask About Heaven

In the course of my teaching in prophecy seminars, many participants have asked fascinating questions about our life in Heaven. Several of these questions have already been answered through the various chapters of the book. Some answers to difficult questions will only be revealed when we get to Heaven. Here are some of the most perplexing of these questions with answers from the Scriptures.

1. Why is there a veil over some truths about Heaven?

The Lord repeatedly told His disciples that they could not fully understand the things about Heaven if they did not understand the truths He had already taught them about earthly things. Paul said that "For now we see through a glass, darkly; but then face to face: now I know in part; but then shall I know even as also I am known." In our present state the Bible is our only sure source of knowledge about eternity and Heaven. While there are many things we cannot presently understand, the major aspects of our eternal life with Christ are revealed. The Lord declared: "The secret things belong to the Lord our God: but those things which are revealed belong to us and to our children forever, that we may do all the words of this law" (Deuteronomy 29:29). My purpose is to bring together in an organized manner the scriptural truths about Heaven and the "world to come."

2. Will we enjoy our life in Heaven as we enjoy our life on Earth?

The Bible describes our life in the resurrection as a life of pure joy, worship and purposeful activity. We shall have all the good things that the Lord created for Adam and Eve, and none of the bad things like sin, pain, worry or death. Can you imagine what a joy life will be in Heaven when we will be able to work in harmony with God to complete His purposes? There will be no misunderstandings, no sins of pride, no gossip and no violence there. With all eternity before us then we shall be able to explore all the gifts and talents which our Heavenly Father gave to us. In the limits of time and resources on Earth today, every choice we make ends all sorts of other possibilities. For example, if you choose to be a teacher you normally cannot also be a world explorer, a minister and a scientist in only one lifetime. In Heaven, with all eternity before us, every interest and gift of God can be utilized and explored.

With unlimited resources and eternity before us, we shall then be able to explore and develop all the abilities which God has given to each of us. The fall of sinful man resulted in disease, death and a diminishing of the tremendous abilities which God created within mankind. Adam and his immediate descendants had more intelligence, longer lives and abilities than those men born after the Flood in the days of Noah. Archeologists confirm that Middle Eastern societies appeared almost instantly five thousand years ago in a very advanced level. These ancient civilizations created some of the most astonishing engineering feats in history, including the Pyramids. The Bible tells us that Cain, the son of Adam "went out and built a city." In the New Heaven and Earth the limits and problems associated with the sinful fall of man will disappear. When we receive our resurrected bodies we will actualize all the tremendous potential which God has created in everyone of us.

3. Will our souls sleep until the time of the Rapture?

Some imagine that when a person dies, their soul sleeps until the great judgment day. However, the Bible teaches that the soul is neither annihilated at death, nor does it sleep. The body is described as sleeping in a sense because it rests until God resurrects it into a new immortal and incorruptible form for eternity. However, the Bible never speaks of the soul as sleeping. Quite the contrary, the clear teaching of Scripture is that Christians immediately join Christ in Heaven once we die. When the thief on the cross turned in faith to Jesus he said: "Lord, remember me when thou comest into thy kingdom." And Jesus said unto him, "Verily I say unto thee, Today shalt thou be with me in paradise" (Luke 23:42,43 [KJV]). Here is the clearest possible statement that the soul passes immediately from consciousness in this life to a conscious existence in Heaven. Christ also taught His disciples that the rich man who died in sin was totally conscious, not only of his torment, but also of his brothers who were in danger of hell. Paul tells us that "to be absent from the body is to be present with the Lord."

John prophesied in the Book of Revelation that those in Heaven, "rest not day and night" but serve God day and night in joyful worship. In the Old Testament several passages speak of death as sleep and Sheol as a condition of unconsciousness; but upon closer examination you find that, each time, the passage refers to the body, not the soul. As one example, which is sometimes quoted in favor of the position of "soul-sleep" consider the words of Solomon: "Whatsoever thy hand findeth to do, do it with thy might; for there is no work, nor device, nor knowledge, nor wisdom, in the grave, whither thou goest" (Ecclesiastes 9:10 [KJV]). Here Solomon is clearly referring to the body in the grave, not the soul. In confirmation of this interpretation, in the final chapter of Ecclesiastes, King Solomon affirms the different destiny of the soul as opposed to the body: "Then shall the dust return to the earth as it was; and the spirit shall return unto God who gave it" (v. 7 [KJV]).

The Hebrew word "sheol" appears sixty-five times in the Old Testament and is translated in the King James Version thirty-one times as "hell" and thirty-four times as "the grave" or the "pit." Each time the verse refers to the grave or the state of the body, never to the condition of the soul. The New Testament Greek uses the word "Hades" eleven times and ten of those clearly refer to the place of the dead body not the spirit.

4. What happens to babies and children when they die?

Jesus Christ gave an intriguing clue about Heaven when he held the little children who came to stand beside Him as He taught the multitudes. Small children intuitively recognized in Jesus the love and acceptance which adults so often could not see because religious prejudices blinded them. His tender love and affectionate interest in children often manifested itself. Christ tells us that these children have a birthright in the world to come when He said: "Of such is the Kingdom of Heaven."

Christians believe that if children die before the age of accountability, when they can recognize the meaning of sin, they shall inherit that birthright as children of God. Even when a child dies before the age of accountability when he could even begin to understand the meaning of sin and forgiveness, somehow in the spiritual economy of God there must be a point where they accept salvation personally. At some point the atonement of Christ's blood must be applied to the heart of that child to enable him to receive a new spiritual life in Jesus so that he can partake of the joys of eternal life in Heaven. This is one of those areas where we must trust the love and justice of God until we see His unfolding purpose and plan in Heaven.

Even as a child develops in his earthly life, we can believe that in Heaven such children will develop into fully mature members of the family of God. In Heaven there will be abundant opportunities for the fullest development of all the gifts which God has given humans. These children will enjoy the tender love of Christ and of angels while receiving their celestial education. Though temporarily parted from their parents and family, these children have gone ahead to await the glorious day of joyous family reunion in the heavenly city. Death cannot defeat our love; it can only delay it.

King David spoke of his tender love as a bereaved parent and his faith that God would reunite his child to him in the resurrection at the last day, "I shall go to him, but he shall not return to me" (2 Samuel 12:23). David's inspired words assure us that we will recognize our loved ones as he will be reunited with his beloved son. This passage proves that children who die are taken to Heaven. In addition, the verses about John the Baptist being "filled with the Holy Spirit in his mother's womb" also prove that a fetus has an eternal soul. Heaven will contain hundreds of millions of children who have been destroyed before their birth. When you consider the billions who have died as infants and unborn babies over the thousands of years, it is probable that this group forms a majority of the human inhabitants of Heaven.

5. How shall we live in Heaven?

The Bible describes our life in Heaven as purposeful and joyful. We will serve God and reign and rule with Him forever (Revelation 7:15 and 22:3-6). While the home of the Church will be the New Jerusalem, we shall also have access to Earth to reign with Christ. This reigning will not necessarily be solely governmental rule, but will probably involve teaching, guiding, building and supplying leadership to the natural men on Earth forever. While we will enjoy purposeful activity, the pain and weariness of toil will end. In Heaven we shall "rest from our labors." Life there will involve eating and drinking, including the Marriage Supper of the Lamb. God will provide a tree with real fruit including taste sensations for us to enjoy it.

A rainbow surrounds the throne of God (Revelation 4:3) which shows that an atmosphere with water vapor also exists there. The New Jerusalem, as the capital city of Heaven, rests on a foundation of beautiful stones. From these descriptions it is probable that the materials which God used to create the Earth have their original counterpart in Heaven. The city has gates, streets and a wonderful river of pure water. Christ said that we would not drink of the fruit of the vine until He drank it again with His disciples in Heaven. This tells us that vegetation including grapes will be grown in our future home. The Scriptures describe "the armies which were in heaven followed Him upon white horses, clothed in fine linen, white and clean" (Revelation 19:14). These horses also appear in the Old Testament account of the chariot of Heaven coming for Elijah and the vision of the prophet Zechariah. If horses exist in Heaven then it is only logical to many to believe that other animals will also be there.

We shall enjoy a wonderful relationship with Jesus Christ, our Heavenly Father and the Holy Spirit in a life of pure worship and obedience to His perfect will. Some imagine a boring existence floating on clouds or sitting in eternal church services. Actually, an exciting, active and diversified life will be ours as we walk with God in the heavenly city as Adam once did in the Garden of Eden. We shall have eternity to worship our Savior and learn from Him as His disciples did on the road to Emmaus: "beginning at Moses and all the prophets, He expounded unto them in the scriptures the things concerning Himself." Revelation 6:9-13 and 14:2 tells us that we shall offer "prayers of adoration" and "praises in song" as we enjoy the eternal city.

6. What will our homes be like in Heaven?

Christ promised us "many mansions in My Father's house" (John 14:2) which we will inhabit in the New Jerusalem. The Book of Revelation describes the city in very real terms including the actual building materials. Its enormous size would allow each person to have a spacious living area if he wanted. Since we will recognize our earthly family and friends, plus those saints we never knew on Earth, we will have tremendous opportunities to relax and enjoy relationships. We shall visit the Earth continually and be able to enjoy the beauty of God's creation of animals, waterfalls and forests which will exist on the Earth both during the Millennium and beyond. All the good things of Earth will continue to be experienced by natural men and women who are descendants of those who survived the Tribulation and the Battle of Armageddon.

7. Will bodies which have been destroyed be raised intact at the Rapture?

The Bible says that "the sea gave up the dead who were in it" (Revelation 20:13). The God who created all that we see out of things invisible is also able to recreate the body we once had, now transformed into a new resurrected, spiritual body. Scientists tell us that the human cells of our bodies are replaced continually and change completely every seven years. During seventy years your body reproduces the cells needed to form a complete human body repeatedly. Yet there is a continuity of identity throughout our life. The Lord said, "But even the very hairs of your head are numbered. Fear not therefore" (Luke 12:7 [KJV]). We can safely trust that the God of creation knows the location of every atom of our bodies and He will resurrect and transform them at the last day.

8. Will we have an opportunity to explore the enormous universe?

The twenty-four elders around the throne of God declare, "You are worthy, O Lord to receive glory and honor and power: for thou hast created all things, and for thy pleasure they are and were created" (Revelation 4:11 [KJV]). "The heavens declare the glory of God" according to Psalm 19:1. The staggering majesty and complexity of the heavens declares the glory of God to all who are not blinded by rebellious atheism.

While God has shown us many things in the Bible there is far more that He has chosen to conceal until we meet Him face to face in Heaven. "In the beginning God created the

Heaven and the Earth" is the first verse in the Bible. We know that everything created had a purpose in the plan of God. Scientists tell us that the universe may expand forever. It contains an infinity of space, stars and probably billions of planets. Several years ago astronomers detected the first proof of a nearby star with several planets. This is important because, before this discovery, scientists thought that our solar system might be the only one with planets. Now we know that even if only one star in a million has a solar system of planets, then millions of other suns must contain planets. It is possible that, after sin is eradicated from the universe after the Millennium, man will explore and settle in distant galaxies. The continued population growth throughout the universe of a population of the sinless, natural sons of Abraham would finally fulfill the promise made to Abraham by God in the Book of Genesis: "In blessing I will bless thee, and in multiplying I will multiply thy seed as the stars of the heaven, and as the sand which is upon the sea shore. . . ." (Genesis 22:17 [KJV]). Even the renovated New Earth would not hold an infinitely growing population such as the Bible describes. God might have created the infinite universe as a home for man under the rule of Jesus Christ and His Bride, the Church.

All the spiritual and intelligent life of a vast universe will join in a song of worship to God. "And every creature which is in heaven and on the earth and under the earth, and such as are in the sea, and all that are in them, I heard saying, Blessing and honor and glory and power, be unto him that sits on the throne, and to the Lamb forever and ever!" (Revelation 5:13)

9. What is the alternative to Heaven?

The gate to eternal darkness lies in front of all who choose to reject the invitation of God to repent from their sin. In this century the only topic discussed less than Heaven is the topic of Hell. There is almost a conspiracy of silence on this subject which prevents most ministers from preaching about this ultimate destination of all those who choose to continue in their sin. However, the Lord Himself talked more about Hell than He did about Heaven. It was the reality of the horror of Hell that motivated the Son of God to atone on the Cross for the sins of all men that would accept the pardon and escape spiritual death. Those who in the end reject God's pardon will have to experience the consequences of their rebellion against God. The prophet John tells us that after the Millennium the bodies of the wicked dead will also be resurrected so that their spirits from Hades will have a spiritual body for eternity. The descriptions of Hell are of total darkness, isolation, and the awful scene known as "the lake of fire." While it is not possible to understand all the details about Hell, it is absolutely real and indescribably terrible. The unrepentant souls who take part in the Great White Throne Judgment will spend their eternity isolated from God.

The ultimate tragedy is that all those who end in Hell will have chosen it. Instead of accepting that we are all sinners in need of the salvation of Jesus Christ, their pride condemns them to spiritual death. In the end, someone must be the god of our lives. If we insist on being our own god, we shall succeed, but at the cost of an eternity in Hell. The final proof that pride is the first and greatest sin is displayed in this stubborn sinful pride which insists on having its own way, at the cost of eternity. In his epic poem "Paradise Lost," Milton declared that in the end either we shall say to God, "Thy will be done" or in the end God will say to us, "Thy will be done."

Some day each of us will recognize that Jesus is the Son of God and that we are sinners; now, while salvation is available or at the great judgment of God when it is too late to repent and accept salvation. To those who continue to reject Him, let me offer this thought: Either Jesus Christ is right or you are. The suggestion that "all this is only opinion" is simply an evasion of the issue, it does not settle it. The Bible, our conscience and fulfilled prophecy prove that Jesus was not mistaken. The choice for each of us is to decide if we will continue to be.

10. Are There Degrees of Glory in Heaven?

There will be different measures of reward and glory given to the saints in Heaven as well. The Apostle Paul declared that "we shall all stand before the judgment seat of Christ. For it is written, As I live, saith the Lord, every knee shall bow to me, and every tongue shall confess to God. So then every one of us shall give account of himself to God" (Romans 14:10-12). While the punishment for our sins was paid for completely by Christ's death on the cross, every Christian will be judged by Christ in Heaven after the Rapture as to their faithfulness to God's commands in their daily walk. Many Christians will receive crowns and rewards, including mansions, for their faithful works. Others will receive nothing as a reward because, while they were saved by accepting Christ as their Savior, they failed to put Him first in their life. Throughout eternity those who have faithfully witnessed to others, worked in the Church or on a mission field, or lived in purity will wear a golden crown. As Christians walk down the streets of the heavenly city, every other saint will know at a glance whether they put Jesus first in their daily life because they will either wear a crown of glory or they will not.

The degrees of glory and happiness in Heaven are like different sized buckets that children cast into the ocean. Some larger buckets will hold more than smaller ones, yet all of the buckets will be full of water to the brim. Among the saints of Heaven, although some like the Apostle Paul will receive more glory than another saint, yet all, without exception, will be full of God's glory which is inexhaustible.

11. How Can I Receive God's Pardon for My Sins?

The greatest gift that God could ever bestow upon repentant sinners is the gift of eternal life through the forgiveness of our sins by the blood of Christ shed for us on the cross. While He paid the full price of our pardon, the choice is still ours as to whether or not we will confess our sins and ask Him to forgive us and be our Lord and Savior. I remember reading years ago about a man condemned to death row in New York State for the murder he had committed in a fit of passion years earlier. At the last minute the governor of the state wrote a pardon releasing him from the sentence of death passed by the court. Yet, when the warden of the prison told the man of his pardon, the prisoner refused the governor's pardon. In his overwhelming sense of guilt, despite the free pardon extended to him, the prisoner felt that he must die to pay for the murder he had committed. The warden had no legal choice but to carry out the death sentence of the court. In order to be effective, a pardon must be accepted. Although Jesus Christ pardoned us by His death on the cross two thousand years ago for your sins and mine, unless we confess our sins and repent, asking Him to forgive us, we will still have to pay the price of our sinful rebellion against God by spending an eternity in Hell.

God commands that all of us repent of our sins and turn to follow Christ. Yet many of us have forgotten the nature of the true repentance that God demands before He will forgive us and write our name down in the Book of Life in Heaven. Many believe that repentance means sorrow for being caught in our sins. This is not repentance, it is only remorse. Some people ask God to forgive their sins while explaining to Him why they sinned. I once heard a man confessing his sin of hatred of his brother while explaining to God that his brother had grievously injured him. This is not repentance, it is only an excuse and explanation. True repentance and confession consists of agreeing with God about the nature of our sinful disobedience without excuse or explanation. Too often men delay their repentance until it is too late. None of us have a lease on life. Someday, without warning, God will call us to an accounting for our decision regarding Jesus Christ. Whenever a man delays his prayer of repentance, in effect, he is pawning his soul to Satan, hoping that he will someday be able to redeem it before it is too late. As the sixteenth century writer Thomas Fuller once wrote, "You cannot repent too soon, because you do not know how soon it may be too late."

12. How can I know that I will go to Heaven?

The choices we make in time will determine our destiny in eternity. God has not left us in doubt regarding the only way by which we can know that we will become citizens of the heavenly city. The Bible declares that God is holy and that His home in Heaven cannot contain sin or rebellion. It also confirms what each of us knows by observation, that "all have sinned, and come short of the glory of God" (Romans 3:23 [KJV]). Every man has disqualified himself from Heaven by his choice to rebel against his Creator. No amount of good works can ever erase this stain of sin upon our lives. The demand of some philosophers that God allow unrepentant sinners into Heaven displays a sinful contempt for God's absolute holiness and justice. He declares that "the wages of sin is death." Since the fall of our first parents in the Garden of Eden, spiritual and physical death has been the lot of all men. Yet God in His infinite mercy supplied a way for man to become holy and sinless so that we might enjoy an eternal home in Heaven with Christ forever. He allowed Jesus Christ to be born and then die on the cross to pay the ultimate penalty for the sins of all mankind. Like any other pardon, in order for it to be effective, the prisoner must accept it. "For the wages of sin is death; but the gift of God is eternal life through Jesus Christ our Lord" (Romans 6:23 [KJV]).

"For all have sinned, and come short of the glory of God, Being justified freely by his grace through the redemption that is in Christ Jesus: Whom God hath set forth to be a propitiation through faith in his blood, to declare His righteousness for the remission of sins that are past, through the forbearance of God; To declare, I say, at this time his righteousness: that he might be just, and the justifier of him which believeth in Jesus" (Romans 3:23-26 [KJV]).

Jesus took upon Himself the complete penalty for the sins of mankind and bore their just punishment on the Cross in His death and through three days and nights in Hell before His Resurrection. He stood in our place judicially to receive the penalty of the full "wages of sin" for each one of us. If we, by faith, recognize our sinful nature and accept His pardon, then we will have the privilege of one day standing before God forgiven and clothed in the perfect righteousness of Jesus Christ.

The very word "justified" is a judicial word which defines a situation where a judge declares that a man is innocent and free; just as though he had never committed the act he was justly accused of. At the Rapture, when God the Father looks at believers, He will not see the sins of our life but He will see the righteousness of His only begotten Son. Then, as adopted sons and daughters of God, being "justified by faith," we will enter the gates of Heaven forever.

The command of God to Christians is that we live upright lives and obey the grace and law of Christ in our hearts. Grace is the only thing that enables us to live an obedient life. However, we must never make the mistake of believing, after our conversion to Christ, that we can ever "earn" or justify our salvation. Only the blood of Jesus Christ saves us from our sin. As Jesus Christ judicially "became sin for us" upon the cross, each believer in Him becomes judicially righteous before God so that we might enter the joys of Heaven. Our only qualification to stand in righteousness before God is the holiness of Christ which God places to our account because of our faith in His finished work on the cross.

The invitation is still open to all who are tired of their sinful life and are willing to turn from sin and accept Jesus as their personal Savior. "Behold, I stand at the door, and knock: if any man hear my voice, and open the door, I will come in to him, and will sup with him, and he with me. To him that overcometh will I grant to sit with me in my throne, even as I also overcame, and am set down with my Father in his throne. He that hath an ear, let him hear what the Spirit saith unto the churches" (Revelation 3:20-22 [KJV]).

The privilege of becoming members of the Bride of Christ, the Church, and participating in the Marriage Supper of the Lamb in Heaven belongs to everyone who accepts His pardon. John saw this magnificent scene in his vision and records the voice of the multitude of Heaven saying: "Let us be glad and rejoice and give Him glory, for the marriage of the Lamb has come, and His wife has made herself ready." And to her it was granted to be arrayed in fine linen, clean and bright, for the fine linen is the righteous acts of the saints. Then he said to me, Write: 'Blessed are those who are called to the marriage supper of the Lamb!' " (Revelation 19:7-9).

SELECTED BIBLIOGRAPHY

Armstrong, Amzi. *Lectures On The Visions of The Revelation.* Morristown: P. A. Johnson, 1815.

Atter, Gordon, F. *Rethinking Bible Prophecy.* Peterborough: College Press, 1967.

Auerbach, Leo. *The Babylonian Talmud.* New York: Philosophical Library, 1944.

Bacon, Francis. *The Advancement Of Learning.* London: 1605.

Barnes, Rev. Albert. *Notes On The Book Of Revelation.* Edinburgh: Gall & Inglis, 1852.

Baylee, Rev. Joseph. *The Times Of The Gentiles.* London: James Nisbet & Co., 1871.

Bettenson, Henry. *Documents Of The Christian Church.* London: Oxford University Press, 1967.

Bloomfield, Arthur, E. *A Survey Of Bible Prophecy.* Minneapolis: Bethany Fellowship, Inc., 1971.

Bloomfield, Arthur, E. *The End Of The Days.* Minneapolis: Bethany Fellowship, Inc. 1961.

Boston, Thomas. *Human Nature In Its Fourfold State.* Philadelphia: Ambrose Walker, 1814.

Bounds, E. M. *Catching A Glimpse Of Heaven.* Springdale: Whitaker House, 1985.

Boyd, Robert. *The World's Hope.* Chicago: J. W. Goodspeed, 1873.

Buck, Rev. Charles. *A Theological Dictionary.* Philadelphia: William W. Woodward, 1825.

Bullinger, E. W. *The Apocalypse or The Day Of The Lord.* London: Eyre & Spottiswoode, 1909.

Butterfield, Herbert. *Christianity And History.* New York: Charles Scribners Sons, 1949.

Coates, C. A. *An Outline Of The Revelation.* London: Stow Hill Bible Depot And Publishing Office, 1985.

Dean, I. R. *The Coming Kingdom – The Goal Of Prophecy*. Philadelphia: Philadelphia School Of The Bible, 1928.

De Haan, M. R. *The Days Of Noah*. Grand Rapids: Zondervan Publishing House, 1963.

Dewart, Edward, Hartley. *Jesus The Messiah*. Toronto: William Briggs, 1891.

Edersheim, Rev. Alfred. *The Life And Times Of Jesus The Messiah*. New York: Longmans, Green, & Co. 1896.

Feinberg, Charles. *PreMillennialism Or Amillennialism?* Grand Rapids: Zondervan Publishing House, 1936.

Goldstein, Rabbi Morris. *Jesus In The Jewish Tradition*. New York: The Macmillan Company, 1950.

Graham, Dr. Billy. *Angels*. Waco: Word Books, 1975.

Gundry, Robert, H. *The Church And The Tribulation*. Grand Rapids: Zondervan Publishing House, 1977.

Haldeman, I. M. *The Coming Of Christ*. New York: Charles C. Cook, 1906.

Hunt, Dave. *Whatever Happened To Heaven*. Eugene: Harvest House Publishers, 1988.

Hovery, Alvah. *Biblical Eschatology*. Philadelphia: American Baptist Publication Society, 1888.

Ironside, H. A. *Lectures On The Book of Revelation*. New York: Loizeaux Brothers, 1930.

Keith, Rev. Alexander. *The Signs Of The Times*. Edinburgh: William White & Co., 1832.

Kellogg, Samuel, H. *The Jews Or Prediction And Fulfilment*. New York: Anson D. F. Randolph & Company, 1883.

Kett, Henry. *History – The Interpreter Of Prophecy*. London: Trinity College, 1800.

Krailsheimer, A., J. *Pascal: Pensees*. London: Penguin Books, 1966.

LaHaye, Tim. *The Beginning Of The End*. Wheaton: Tyndale House Publishers. 1976.

Larkin, Rev. Clarence. *Rightly Dividing The Word*. Philadelphia: Erwin W. Moyer Co. 1943.

Lewis, C. S. *A Case For Christianity*. Grand Rapids: Baker Book House, 1977.

Litch, Josiah. *Messiahs Throne And Millennial Glory*. Philadelphia: Joshua V. Himes, 1855.

Litt, Charles, R. H. *Studies In The Apocalypse*. Edinburgh: T. & T. Clark, 1913.

Lockyer, Herbert. *All The Messianic Prophecies Of The Bible*. Grand Rapids: Zondervan Publishing House, 1960.

Ludwigson, R. *A Survey Of Bible Prophecy*. Grand Rapids: Zondervan Publishing House, 1975.

Luibheid, Colm. *The Essential Eusebius*. Toronto: The New American Library Of Canada, 1966.

Milner, Rev. Isaac. *The History Of The Church Of Christ*. Cambridge: John Burges, 1800.

Newton, Bishop Thomas. *Dissertations On The Prophecies.* London: R & R Gilbert, 1817.

Pentecost, Dwight, J. *Things To Come*. Grand Rapids: Zondervan Publishing House, 1958.

Peters, George. *The Theocratic Kingdom*. Grand Rapids: Kregel Publications, 1957.

Potts, Rev. J. H. *The Golden Dawn*. Philadelphia: P. W. Ziegler & Co., 1884.

Pusey, Rev. E. B. *The Minor Prophets*. New York: Funk & Wagnalls, 1885.

Rossetti, Christina. *The Face Of The Deep*. London: Society For Promoting Christian Knowledge, 1895.

Scherman, Rabbi Nosson. *Ezekiel: A New Translation With A Commentary Anthologized From Talmudic, Midrashic And Rabbinic Sources*. Brooklyn: Mesorah Publications, Ltd. 1969.

Seiss, J. A. *The Apocalypse*, Grand Rapids: Zondervan Publishing House, 1960.

Smith, Chuck. *The Tribulation & The Church*. Costa Mesa: The Word For Today, 1980.

Taylor, Rev. G. F. *The Second Coming Of Jesus*. Franklin Springs: The Publishing House, 1950.

Thompson, Rev. J. L. *That Glorious Future*. London: Morgan and Scott, 1887.

Thompson, Robert, N. *Liberation – The First To Be Freed*. Vancouver: Battleline Books, 1987.

Torrey, R. A. *Get Ready For Forever*. Springdale: Whitaker House, 1985.

Tristram, Rev. H. B. *The Seven Golden Candlesticks*. London: The Religious Tract Society, 1872.

Trotter, W. *Plain Papers On Prophetic And Other Subjects*. London: G. Morrish, 1869.

West, Gilbert. *Observations On The History And Evidences Of Jesus Christ*. London: R. Dodsley, 1747.

Zlotowitz, Rabbi Meir. *Genesis – A New Translation With A Commentary Anthologized From Talmudic, Midrashic And Rabbinic Sources*. New York: Mesorah Publications, Ltd. 1980.